AF361378

TRANSGRESSION AND THE AESTHETICS OF EVIL

TRANSGRESSION AND THE AESTHETICS OF EVIL

Taran Kang

UNIVERSITY OF TORONTO PRESS
Toronto Buffalo London

ISBN 978-1-4875-2907-9 (cloth)   ISBN 978-1-4875-2909-3 (EPUB)
                                   ISBN 978-1-4875-2908-6 (PDF)

Library and Archives Canada Cataloguing in Publication

Title: Transgression and the aesthetics of evil / Taran Kang.
Names: Kang, Taran, author.
Description: Includes bibliographical references and index.
Identifiers: Canadiana (print) 20210227346 | Canadiana (ebook) 20210227443 |
    ISBN 9781487529079 (cloth) | ISBN 9781487529093 (EPUB) |
    ISBN 9781487529086 (PDF)
Subjects: LCSH: European literature – 18th century – History and criticism. |
    LCSH: European literature – 19th century – History and criticism. | LCSH: Good
    and evil in literature. | LCSH: Aesthetics, European – 18th century. |
    LCSH: Aesthetics, European – 19th century.
Classification: LCC PN56.E75 K36 2022 | DDC 809/.93353–dc23

This book has been published with the assistance of a Yale-NUS College Subvention Grant.

University of Toronto Press acknowledges the financial assistance to its publishing program of the Canada Council for the Arts and the Ontario Arts Council, an agency of the Government of Ontario.

ONTARIO ARTS COUNCIL
CONSEIL DES ARTS DE L'ONTARIO
an Ontario government agency
un organisme du gouvernement de l'Ontario

For Claudine

Contents

Acknowledgments

This book has benefited greatly from the generosity of others. First and foremost, I want to thank my teachers from years past, to whom I owe an ongoing debt. I thank Dominick LaCapra, both for his kindness and for his many insights, from which I continue to learn. I am profoundly grateful to Isabel V. Hull, who has been incisive in her criticism and unfailing in her support. This book owes much to Michael P. Steinberg; it was during his thought-provoking seminar on Hannah Arendt many years ago that some of the ideas developed here began to emerge. Diana Reese provided a further impetus to these ideas through her imaginative reconceptualizations of important themes in Enlightenment and post-Enlightenment philosophy and literature. And I express my abiding gratitude to Dennis Sweeney for his guidance at a time when my scholarly interests were first taking form.

While the shortcomings of this work are my own, its merits owe much to the thoughtful comments of those who kindly gave their time in reading through large portions of the manuscript. My sincere thanks to Pedro Erber, Franz Hofer, and Peter Staudenmaier for their helpful promptings and astute criticisms; this book has profited from their comments and suggestions. I am grateful for vibrant intellectual exchanges with colleagues and acknowledge the support of friends through the years. I give thanks to Madeleine Casad, Scott Cook, Angeles Espinaco-Virseda, Sean Franzel, Daena Funahashi, Peter Gilgen, Kate Horning, Chris Kai-Jones, Emma Kuby, Ada Kuskowski, Nomi Lazar, Cathay Liu, Katrina Nousek, Anna Parkinson, Rajeev Patke, Jessica Ratcliff, Arina Rotaru, Mira Seo, Naoko Shimazu, Nico Silins, Christina Tarnopolsky, Robert Travers, and Emma Willoughby.

It was while I was a visiting scholar at Cornell University in 2014 that the plan for this project first crystallized; I thank the Cornell Department of History for hosting me. I am also grateful for the extensive holdings and the helpful staff at Cornell University's Olin Library. My home institution, Yale-NUS College, provided two semesters of leave, which gave me the precious gift of time to complete my book. At the University of Toronto Press, I had the good fortune to work with Mark Thompson and a very fine editorial team who helped guide this book to publication.

Finally, I give heartfelt thanks to my family. This work was made possible by the love of my mother, my father, my sister Veenu, and my wife Claudine.

TRANSGRESSION AND THE AESTHETICS OF EVIL

Introduction

The concluding canto of the *Inferno* portrays the devil in a state of abjection. Imprisoned in a wall of ice, he struggles in vain to free himself. The violent beating of his wings whips up algid winds that sweep through the ninth circle of hell and scourge his fellow sinners. At hell's very centre, the worst of all malefactors – Judas, Brutus, and Cassius – suffer an interminable mastication, crushed between the teeth of the devil's three mouths. Dante, who positions himself in the text as the spectator of their afflictions, presents us with a tormentor no less wretched than those whom he torments; the tears streaming from his eyes, mingled with bloody slaver, suggest not sadistic gratification but agony and despair. In the poet's arresting image of the arch-transgressor, the depicted pains and degradation that follow from the embrace of evil serve as an admonition. Lucifer's ugliness calls to mind the semblance of beauty he once possessed before it was lost on account of his perfidy, and this recollection warns us against the self-inflicted disfigurement that the pursuit of vice entails. Evil is represented here in such a fashion that we learn to shun it just as we are urged to turn towards the good.

From the perspective of moral didacticism, the portrayal of evil ought to edify, and the praiseworthiness of this portrayal, whether it assumes the form of a work of art or a historical narrative, can be determined, at least in part, according to the extent to which it fulfils a moral function. The adoption of this standpoint does not necessitate a heavy-handed preachiness, but it does call for some form of instruction, howsoever direct or oblique, conducive to our moral betterment. It also calls for checks against potentially corruptive depictions that incite moral confusion or that make wickedness alluring. Before Théophile Gautier, to whom Baudelaire dedicated

The Flowers of Evil, advocated *l'art pour l'art*, this didactic impulse was already subjected to criticism; in the nineteenth century, however, the calls for an autonomous art, unconstrained by the strictures of popular morality, became increasingly insistent. If the moral is subordinate to the aesthetic in a true work of art, then the appropriate representation of evil, at least within the confines of artistic production, is not the one that makes its audience more moral, but the one that arouses aesthetic pleasure or that displays consummate artistry. Within this framework, even the beautification of wickedness may find a justification so long as it is accomplished in a manner that satisfies the relevant aesthetic criteria.

Against both the moralization of art and the aestheticizing of evil, one might recommend that we simply show evil as it is – neither more nor less. But this matter-of-fact proposal, whether in the spirit of the Rankean *"wie es eigentlich gewesen"* or the Tacitean *"sine ira et studio,"* itself invites questions about the nature of "showing" and the manner in which it ought to be pursued. Should reprehensible acts – or what we take to be such – be reported with a commitment to factual objectivity and the omission of moral judgment, or should their description be interwoven with condemnation? Even if such an omission were warranted or salutary in some contexts, does that mean that the intrusion of an evaluative component is necessarily tantamount to distortion? Hannah Arendt insists that an account of the atrocities of the death camps that deliberately refrains from expressing moral judgment fails to make sense of the phenomena that it seeks to depict.[1] And if moral judgments are permissible or even obligatory in historical and journalistic representations of evil, are aesthetic ones more to be feared on account of their tendency to distort?

The imperative "do not aestheticize evil" aims to safeguard the border between the moral and the aesthetic; it is an admonition not to confuse literary and filmic representations that portray evil as fascinating with actual instances of it.[2] In surveying representations of violent criminality in literary fiction and the mass media, we might well wonder, though, what would remain of them if evil were de-aestheticized.[3] Once evil is deprived of its aesthetic aspect, once it has ceased to be viewed as glamorous or grotesque, as disgusting or sublime, it has lost important characteristics that distinguish it from the merely unethical. For those who believe that the category of evil impedes our understanding of human motivations and actions and who think that the word itself should be purged from the philosophical lexicon, the reduction of evil to the unethical may represent a move in the right direction.[4] But for those who wish to hold on to the category, the question must be asked: in de-aestheticizing evil, do we achieve moral clarity or do we misrepresent the actual appearance of evil in the world?

It is important, in grappling with this question, to give thought to both the conceptualization of evil and the perception of it. The perception of evil, its *aisthesis*, occurs at the intersection of the realms of the moral and the aesthetic. In my investigation of this borderland, evil is examined as an aesthetic phenomenon, not only in the broad sense as an object of perception, but also in the narrower sense as something that has historically been entangled with matters of taste and aesthetic judgment. The ways in which our notions and assessments of the morally bad are bound to aesthetic responses cannot be passed over if we seek to make sense of them. It might be countered that the task of philosophy is to purge ethics of this contamination, to free it from aesthetic judgments, rooted in cultural prejudice, and embodied aesthetic experience, a product of our physiological organization. But whether or not this leads to conceptual clarity or to a denaturing of morality, the pursuit of such a procedure neglects to consider the historical conditions under which moral positions arise, inclusive of the lived practices integral to their formation. An appreciation of the role played by the cultivation of aesthetic dispositions, which tend to resist easy conversion into the language of concepts, allows us to overcome the reduction of morality to abstractions and ties it back to the sensuous, to culturally mediated perceptions and processed artistic forms. It is not only that morality is aesthetically coded, translated into the realm of representation, but that these codings are themselves constitutive of morality. The educative role played by the sublime and the disgusting has not been lost on the more astute moralists of all ages. While methodical moral arguments usually leave us cold and seldom convince even those whose job it is to take them seriously, inculcated feelings of admiration and aversion – whether directed towards objects or behaviours or human beings – leave an impress behind even when we free ourselves from the moral principles that supposedly ground them. Those who attempt to beautify what is felt to be bad or who aim to remove our sense of disgust towards things that we have been taught to recognize as evil are thus quite rightly regarded as disturbing the existing moral order – a point whose concession depends on neither sympathy nor antipathy to the order in question. It is in these moments of disruption that the potency of the aesthetic is often most evident.

In the modern era, it is no accident that a transformation in moral sensibility occurs in conjunction with a revolution in aesthetics. What I label as a transformation has long been recognized as such by a number of scholars – although the precise features deemed distinctive of it, its principal causes, and its temporal parameters remain matters of intense dispute. There persists nonetheless a vague sense of some sort of shift that separates the modern, howsoever defined, from that which precedes it, and this shift is often held to bring forth or to be accompanied by new forms of subjectivity.[5] I want to highlight what I take to be a particularly relevant development, but my purpose in framing what follows with reference to it is not intended to recast how we think of the modern age so much as it is meant to facilitate a rethinking of the relations between the moral and the aesthetic. During the eighteenth and nineteenth centuries, transgression, once allocated the central place in the constitution of evil, undergoes a startling revaluation. The word "transgression" continues in this period and beyond to be used in a pejorative sense, often with reference to infractions of the law, but this lexical fact should not mislead us. The challenging of inherited standards, the critique of tradition, and the testing of the bounds of authority point to an intensifying transgressiveness, in which the limits placed on human freedom are questioned, oppugned, and sometimes effaced. It would be a mistake, however, to conceive of this tendency as a movement of negation; rather, in a spirit of self-affirmation, new ideals are proclaimed in contravention of the old ones that inhibit their realization. In the Augustinian tradition, pride is considered the worst of the vices, the one that lies, temporally and spiritually, at the root of transgression; the self that, in its will to assert itself, forgets its utter dependence on God cuts itself off from its own source of being and becomes alienated from all that is good and holy. The erosion of this tradition opens the way to reformulations of selfhood and reassessments of the good in increasingly subjective terms. The Luciferian spirit of transgression, condemned to and bounded in the inferno of the medieval imagination, begins to break free from its former constraints. What was denounced from the pulpit in no uncertain terms comes to bear, during the Enlightenment and its wake, a more morally ambiguous aspect. Gradually unmoored from sin, with its negative connotations of wickedness and unnaturalness, transgression acquires positive associations with self-expression and liberation. This shift in perspective, evident in the English Romantics' qualified rehabilitation of Satan and in Goethe's imagining of the redemption of Faust, must be understood as part of a broader change in European moral sensibilities.

How are we to account for this transition? Should it be explained in relation to developments within the sphere of politics, as the corollary of political revolutions with their promise of liberation from the shackles of despotism? Perhaps it derives from the emergence of a new economic system, a budding capitalist ethos in which the drive for profit becomes disconnected from any final purpose or discernable limit? Is it due to the rise of the scientific temper, which with its spirit of *plus ultra* recognizes no bounds to the field of human enquiry and no end to the quest for knowledge? Or maybe it is the result of a loss of religious faith, an erosion in the status of what were taken to be divinely sanctioned commandments once the belief in the source of those commandments falls prey to scepticism?

None of these developments should be discounted in understanding this shift in moral sensibility, an occurrence that resists monocausal explanations. And while any adequate account cannot dispense with the role of religion, the argument that this shift was simply a consequence of a declining belief in the Christian God neglects to consider the temporal priority of the slackening of belief in the devil. Although the two processes, the spread of scepticism towards God and the spread of scepticism towards the devil, were mutually reinforcing, the latter preceded rather than followed the former. It was not so much that the notion of sin collapsed with the advent of atheism as that it already had its meaning altered once Satan ceased to be viewed as an actual living character within a larger cosmic drama. Among intellectuals who prided themselves on being enlightened, the belief in the existence of the devil came to be seen as a superstition, to which only the uneducated and childish subscribed; shortly thereafter, skeptics deployed the same arguments to undermine the notion of a personal God. Did the devil perhaps fake his own death in the knowledge that God would lose his *raison d'être* following the demise of his infernal rival? In any case, the sequence of events suggests that this alteration in moral sensibility cannot be adequately understood merely as a fallout from "the death of God."

In addition to the domains of politics, economics, science, and religion, there remains yet another in light of which transformations in the modern understanding of transgression need to be understood. Although the domain of art might appear less consequential in its impact on the emergence of our contemporary moral sensibility, a consideration of the historical relationship between the aesthetic and the moral discloses aspects of this sensibility's hidden grounds. The late eighteenth-century cult of the artistic genius and the concurrent celebration of the sublime inform literary depictions of the devil and attendant reformulations of the problem of evil in both the Enlightenment and Romanticism. In addition to the language of liberation, this nascent aesthetic discourse drew upon the language of greatness, in which the transgression of inherited standards became closely associated with the figure of the genius and his realization of masterpieces. The will to break with classical artistic precedents, at work in the productions of the man of genius – who fashions his own rules in opposition to the prevailing rules of tradition – finds an analogue in the will to break with time-honoured moral precedents. More than a century before Nietzsche's Zarathustra called for the breaking of old tables of value and the creation of new ones in their stead, the questioning of long-standing aesthetic standards and the defence of originality in matters of poetic composition had already served to erode faith in the adherence to established rules and procedures. My argument, however, is not that these developments in the realm of art and aesthetics were the cause of a revolution in morality. The movement between these two realms proves far too fluid, too rich in interactions, interpenetrations, and intertwinements, to permit the determination of one as having a definite causal priority over the other. The point, rather, is that the status of transgression cannot be disentangled from this larger cultural constellation, at once moral, in its identifications of transgression with evil and good, and aesthetic, in its associations of it with the disgusting and the sublime. What is at stake here is not the mechanics of causation, but the character of a conjunction. It is in thinking through the different forms that transgression has assumed in modern aesthetics that the way is opened to a rethinking of the representation and representability of evil.

Some of the most striking instances of transgression in the modern period involve the active subversion of traditional gender roles, the undermining of sexual taboos, and the contestation of naturalized notions of masculinity and femininity. This is a large and important body of issues about which much important scholarship has been produced and to which the present study does not do justice. At the same time, the tendency to emphasize the liberatory potential of transgression, exhibited in the challenging of repressive patriarchal structures and disciplinary regimes, risks obscuring its connections to domination. In my own analysis, rather than treating sexuality as a privileged discursive site in the articulation of transgressive visions, I foreground the role of self-assertion; in this framework, the contravention of prohibitions and the refusal of socially assigned gender roles have less to do with sexuality as such than with a transgressive mode of comportment that finds expression in multiple domains. But a recognition of the role of self-assertion should not lead us to expect a uniformity in its expressive forms. It would be a gross understatement to say that transgressiveness in aesthetic matters has not been invariably accompanied by a radical questioning of norms regulating the behaviour of the sexes.[6] In fact, an adherence to or a reinscription of sexist hierarchies has been a feature of certain art movements with their explicit embrace of an ideal of manliness – as is apparent, for example, in the founding manifesto of Futurism. The breaching of convention and the disruption of external constraints are more than compatible with the introduction of new forms of exclusion as well as the intensification of existing ones.

Subversive acts may provoke the demonization of the transgressors, but in those instances where such acts successfully undermine respect for long-standing strictures, they can also play a part in altering verdicts about what constitutes evil. The portrayal of evil, as it appears in various discourses and cultural artifacts, should be understood not simply as the shadow of an agathological tradition, an after-image as it were of some original figuration of the good. According to Nietzsche, the dominant movement in Western morals for the last two millennia – the so-called "slave revolt in morals" – owes more to its conception of evil than to its conception of the good; the latter exists, in parasitic fashion, only by virtue of feeding off the former. Even if we remain sceptical of this inflation of the category of evil – and the narrative that undergirds it – in the role that it has played in the formation of Occidental culture, it is necessary to overcome the prejudice that what we designate as immoral derives from the moral, as if the latter were a more originary category than the former. Although the prefix of the former term suggests that it is posterior to the latter, this should not be taken as evidence that, speaking historically and psychologically, our identification of the good is anterior to our recognition of the bad; at times this may be the case, but it is not necessarily so. A consideration of the responses that evil excites – from terror to disdain, from intoxication to despair, from temptation to revulsion – deepens our understanding of the aesthetic modalities of evil and the nature of our perception of it.

Hans Jonas asserts that "the perception of the *malum* is infinitely easier to us than the perception of the *bonum*; it is more direct, more compelling, less given to differences of opinion or taste, and, most of all, obtruding itself without our looking for it."[7] If this were true, it would seem quite sensible for philosophers, who have traditionally placed a premium on certainty, to begin their moral reflections with a meditation on the aforesaid *malum.* Would it not be more prudent to construct a moral edifice on the sturdy rock of the bad, which we perceive with such ease and immediacy, than to build it on the shifting sands of the good, about which we disagree so profoundly? And yet, in the quest for unshakeable foundations, the attempt to ground an ethics on the concept of the bad is largely alien to the Western philosophical tradition. Perhaps the closest approximation we find to such an attempt, one which lies outside of the Occident, appears in Buddhism, which begins with the fact of suffering, the *malum* as such, before identifying the virtues and the procedures that facilitate liberation from it.

In *Leviathan*, Hobbes treats "violent death" and the fear it arouses as the worst of evils, and his theory of politics can be understood, in part, as a program on how to go about eliminating or at least minimizing the frequency of this *summum malum.*[8] The need, or imperative, to ensure the avoidance of violent death serves to legitimate civil society under a strong sovereign, which with all of its faults still remains preferable to the state of nature, where acts of killing occur much more often than in the commonwealth. With Hobbes, the *summum malum* refers to the greatest misfortune that could befall us. But the word *malum* contains an ambiguity; it can denote both natural and moral evils, the sufferings we endure as well as the wrongs we commit. The presence of such an ambiguity already gives us reason to pause and to consider more carefully what Jonas's claim entails. In the passage quoted above, the term *malum*, while somewhat nebulous, is primarily a reference to the occurrence of a misfortune. Jonas's particular concern is with the extinction of our species, and he argues that while it might be difficult to agree upon where humankind ought to be heading – the good to be pursued – we can nonetheless agree upon the undesirability of this catastrophic event. Richard Bernstein explicitly aligns himself with Jonas's position that we perceive the bad more easily than the good, but he goes further and applies this specifically to our perception of moral evils.[9] But is it the case that we do, in fact, perceive this kind of evil with greater ease than we perceive its goodly counterpart? And if we perceive it with such immediacy, does that result in a greater consensus about evil than about the good?

I am sceptical of the claim that our perception of moral evil is not heavily mediated, but I also think that Jonas's formulation, with its emphasis on the perception of the *malum*, offers a point of orientation for investigating a series of pressing questions that, while not altogether neglected in current scholarship, are seldom put forward as forcefully as they might be. In the business of philosophy, the accepted currency is the concept, and those things that are not or cannot be converted into it are often deemed to be of negligible value – or at least of negligible discursive value. The problem of evil tends to be treated then, not surprisingly, as a conceptual one. This is a problem with which the present work too is occupied, but there remains a potential danger in it insofar as it blocks the way to other enquiries, which are all too easily subordinated to it or even occluded by it. I have here two, in particular, in mind: How do we perceive evil? And how do we represent evil? With both of these questions, we find ourselves transported to the realm of the aesthetic, broadly construed. Giving thought to how evil appears to us, how we react to it, and how we represent it to ourselves (and others) invites further questions about the adequacy of our perceptions, reactions, and representations.

A consideration of these issues that does not lapse into arguments about timeless abstractions requires some recognition of the historical transformations at work in our understanding of evil. Susan Neiman's work, which reframes the history of modern philosophy by placing the problem of evil at its centre, provides a welcome corrective to standard approaches that accord primacy to matters of metaphysics and epistemology with little consideration of their moral implications, and this reorientation informs my own enquiry.[10] But much of the most thought-provoking and historically attentive philosophical work on evil, including Neiman's own, tends to let matters of aesthetics fall by the wayside. This neglect can itself be understood, at least in part, as the result of an enduring Kantian legacy.

Even in allowing for some kind of relation between the beautiful and the good, whether in the form of symbolic representation or in the manner of a preparatory exercise – by means of which the disinterested contemplation of the beautiful facilitates the overcoming of immediate self-interest that the performance of moral duty demands – Kant also decouples them, treating them in relation to different faculties. This breach between the *kalon* and the *agathon*, which in Plato are bound together, opens the way to a more precise differentiation of the beautiful and the good; unfortunately, it has also contributed to a conviction that aesthetic and moral issues can be treated in isolation without reference to one another, a conviction that has inhibited a consideration of their entanglements, conceptual as well as historical. Against this bifurcation, with its attendant anxieties about the muddying of moral waters, a historical examination has the potential to uncover the ways in which these seemingly autonomous realms are connected and, on occasion, even mutually constitutive. In its investigations of the grotesque, the disgusting, and the sublime, the present study draws on scholarship dealing with foundational categories and fundamental problems in the history of aesthetics.[11] More specifically, it foregrounds the ways in which aesthetic appeals in modern philosophy and literature have been tied to a valorization of transgression.[12] Since transformations in appraisals of transgression are not confined to a particular sphere of valuation, an examination of the vicissitudes of transgression allows us to grasp more concretely the dynamic between the aesthetic and the moral. These appraisals need to be understood as both reflecting and informing alterations in representations of evil. In the act of representing evil, we not only add flesh and blood to a pre-existing skeleton of moral concepts; there are times when, through this act of representation, we alter the marrow of the concepts themselves.

Before engaging with questions pertaining directly to the representation of evil, I first want to examine an issue whose connection to it might not appear immediately obvious, but which is nonetheless central to it – or, at least, central to the reading I put on offer here. A proper engagement with the representation of evil cannot neglect to consider the status of the representer, by which I mean the maker of representations conceived as a kind of creator. Of particular relevance to my enquiry are new figurations of genius in the Enlightenment and Romanticism, with their criss-crossing associations and dissociations of evil and transgression. Tarrying with the idea of genius not only allows us to see how the formulation of a fundamental aesthetic category was made possible by the adventures of the moral imagination; it also helps us to uncover how different kinds of evil were – and are – situated in incompatible moral hierarchies.

Chapter 1 thus begins with a consideration of the figure of the "evil genius." How does it happen that genius and evil are linked together through this figure? To answer this question, I go back to a period when theorizations of genius enabled this association. Emphasizing the significance of an emergent revaluation of transgression, this chapter explicates how it is that what was once conceived as the essence of evil comes to be valorized and celebrated. More specifically, it identifies the ways in which the undermining of the Augustinian view of evil – on multiple fronts – is tied to an alteration in understandings and assessments of transgression. The first part of the chapter examines the status of originality in eighteenth-century discourse on genius. The second part investigates the intensification of a celebratory attitude towards transgression as manifested in reflections on the relationship between the poet and the devil. I here interpret Romantic mobilizations of Satan not as a peculiarity of a few wayward poets, but as literary expressions of an ongoing transformation in notions of good and evil. Engaging with the writings of Edward Young, Goethe, Blake, and Shelley, this chapter excavates the moral implications of issues pertaining to the nature of genius during this time and locates them in relation to a wider shift in moral sensibility.

In pursuing the intersections between aesthetics and morality, chapter 2 explores two dominant aesthetic modes in which evil has been represented, namely the grotesque and the disgusting. Although the treatment of evil as something ugly has long-standing precedents and might seem to offer little substantive variation over time, theorizations of ugliness have their own history and their own historically situated moral investments. Instead of privileging the act of beautification, which tends to be foregrounded in treatments of the aestheticizing of evil, I call attention to reinscriptions of ugliness with their attendant paradoxes and dialectical reversals. Reading poetic and novelistic representations of evil with reference to Hegel's notion of the grotesque and Karl Rosenkranz's notion of the disgusting elucidates the relationship between emergent conceptualizations of aesthetic categories in the nineteenth century and these categories' literary instantiations. With a focus on the writings of William

Beckford, Sade, and Baudelaire, this chapter points to an intensifying transgressiveness in modern literature, in which traditional symbols of evil are turned on their head. Even in equating evil and ugliness, these three authors' symbolizations of immorality are meant to draw out evil's power and seductiveness, and they serve, at times, to themselves seduce. The equivocations of the portrayal of evil in this emergent literature of transgression reveal the imbrications of subversions of morality and modes of figural representation.

Among all the major aesthetic categories, the sublime has the greatest affinity with greatness, and it is for this reason that characterizations of evil as sublime tend to be met with indignation and outrage. Whereas chapter 2 concentrates on self-consciously transgressive writers, chapter 3 revolves around Edmund Burke and Hannah Arendt, two figures who were committed to the preservation of limits and aimed to stem the dangerous tide of excess. Examining Arendt's depiction of totalitarianism in light of Burke's theory of the sublime, I challenge the dominant view that Arendt de-aestheticizes evil and identify the aesthetic aspects of her representation of what she calls "radical evil." But prior to this reading, I first draw out the tensions between the aesthetic and the moral in Burke's own work and position it in opposition to Kant's. In my analysis, I question attempts to shield the sublime from contamination with evil by removing it from the realm of the phenomenal. This chapter concludes by arguing that the outrage evoked by the sublime's false attribution evinces its enduring moral import.

Picking up on the previous chapter's reflections on the ambivalences of the sublime, chapter 4 considers the moral status of spectators beholding scenes of suffering and acts of transgression, fictional as well as actual. Should we feel culpable if we find "aesthetic pleasure" in watching such scenes and acts? In considering this question, the first half of the chapter is devoted to theorizations of tragic drama in Schopenhauer and Nietzsche. I here examine how Schopenhauer's discussion of tragedy is aligned with his moral philosophy in its approbation of the denial of the will. I then go on to read Nietzsche as both drawing upon Schopenhauer's insights and actively subverting them in his reinterpretation of Greek tragedy as an artistic celebration of acts of transgression; this vindication of transgression, which contains the seed of his later abolition of the category of evil, is part and parcel of a larger attempt to aestheticize existence and to overcome its moralization. Against Nietzsche's absorption of the moral into the aesthetic, with the concomitant blurring between them, it might seem that the appropriate action would be to call for a more stringent separation, thereby ensuring the integrity of both. This procedure carries its own dangers, however, as the second half of the chapter demonstrates through an examination of Thomas De Quincey's writings on murder, where homicide is treated as a "fine art." Against the standard interpretation of De Quincey as engaging in a satirization of the aestheticizing of crime, I read him instead as providing a justification for it.

In my readings and juxtapositions of the aforementioned authors, I seek to rethink their texts' moral and aesthetic elements. One of the purposes of this exercise is to call into question the feasibility and desirability of insulating the moral from the aesthetic. Yet my decision to focus on writings from the eighteenth and nineteenth centuries might seem to discount the period most relevant to some of the issues here discussed. To pass by the radical interventions of artists and art movements in the last century, including Futurism, Dadaism, and Surrealism – not to speak of more recent developments – means to omit some of transgression's most self-conscious aesthetic articulations. It is worth noting, however, that in the manifestos of the avant-garde, the language of evil has receded into the background or has vanished altogether; living in an age when the rehabilitation of Satan had become such a commonplace as to be seen as a kind of Romantic cliché, Marinetti, Tzara, and Breton seize upon other disorienting inversions and subversions in voicing their challenges to the existing order. I want to go back to an earlier moment, though, in which I see the inception of certain tendencies that then become radicalized later on, a moment wherein the moral implications of aesthetic interventions, most evident in the recasting of the meaning of evil, point to a development that remains, in its reverberations, very much with us. And the works I have chosen to focus on – which straddle the fields of literature, philosophy, political theory, and history – show how this development was not confined to a particular scholarly discipline or discursive domain, but was part of a wider transformation. The obvious exception to this periodization is the inclusion of Hannah Arendt, whose writings on politics I situate in relation to eighteenth-century aesthetic discourse. I include Arendt not only because of her importance to modern theorizations of evil but also on account of the tendency to read her as an exemplary de-aestheticizer of evil, a reading that I wish to contest, thereby challenging some of the received wisdom about what it means to aestheticize evil.

Analysing points of connection between evil and aesthetics, the present study positions transgression as the crucial mediating term. Transgression has long-standing associations with evil, and these continue to inform our thinking and acting, sometimes most powerfully, to the present day. Yet the dominant attitude towards it in recent humanistic scholarship has been favourable to the point of idealization. Not surprisingly, the identification of transgression with liberation, play, self-expression, and the annulment of oppressive strictures on thought and action has tended to obscure its darker and more troubling dimensions.[13] We should take care not to forget that where liberal values undergird norms of behaviour, the disregard for convention and the pleasure of violating taboos can easily devolve into authoritarianism. In assimilating transgression to a progressive political project, we too often elide its destructive and nihilistic aspects. No doubt, modern advances in the field of humanistic studies are themselves indebted to the spirit of transgression insofar as practitioners of the humanities consciously disregard constraints and prohibitions that would impede free and unfettered enquiry. This very same spirit calls on us, however, not to embrace the sources of these advances in the fashion of complacent beneficiaries, but to investigate their moral ambiguities.

Chapter One

Genius and the Spirit of Transgression

"If I knew anything about history I would show you that evil has always come here below through some man of genius."[1] In Diderot's dialogue, this placing of genius at the origin of evil is tied both to the frightful potency of men of genius, their ability to alter the face of the earth, and to their indifference to accommodating themselves to social and familial roles. Torn between admiration and loathing, Rameau's nephew declares that "men of genius are pernicious" – "they don't know what it means to be citizens, fathers, mothers, brothers, relations, friends."[2] This denunciation might be read less as an account of the nature of genius and more as an involuntary confession of the speaker, who elsewhere admits that his jealousy of genius, personified in the figure of his uncle Rameau, stems from a dissatisfaction with his own mediocrity. But in calling attention to the difficulty that the genius experiences in normal human relationships, the young Rameau points to a reality that Diderot himself acknowledged. Whether this difficulty derives from the vices and the unsociability of men of genius or from the failure of society to integrate its most gifted members, it suggests that the genius represents something novel and original that disrupts the ordinary, everyday workings of things. And this external disruptiveness mirrors an internal disturbance. In his *Elements of Physiology*, Diderot claims that genius is always accompanied by "some sort of disorder in the machine."[3]

The attribution of a certain psychic imbalance to genius persists in contemporary popular culture. It is frequently accompanied by the idea that geniuses are inclined to disregard the normal conventions of society, both its rules of etiquette and its rules of moral conduct. Although the alignment of creativity, eccentricity, and derangement emerges out of a particular aesthetic discourse, it is the figure of the mad scientist, rather than that of the mad artist, that is most often evoked by the term "evil genius" today. Sometimes the designation "evil genius" is altogether bereft of moral import and denotes merely a high degree of cunning – when it is applied, say, to an especially wily football coach. But the term is also used to refer to individuals who really are seen as being evil in a more substantive sense, such as charismatic cult leaders or even mass murderers.[4] Later on, we will explore the opposition that characterizations of evil acts as sublime tend to call forth. Should characterizations of evil persons as geniuses be seen as similarly suspect or offensive? Arendt observes that "society is always prone to accept a person offhand for what he pretends to be, so that a crackpot posing as a genius always has a certain chance to be believed."[5] After noting the readiness with which modern society allows itself to be seduced by self-assured fanatics, she points outs that "to believe that Hitler's successes were based on his 'powers of fascination' is altogether erroneous; with those qualities alone he would have never advanced beyond the role of a prominent figure in the salons."[6] It would be more accurate to say not that the leaders of totalitarian movements are endowed with an irrational potency, but that those who follow them fail to exercise the reason they have. In accounting for the triumphs of these leaders, Arendt reads them in light of a breakdown in traditional institutions and forms of social organization. Her intervention can itself be read as a reaction against a particular aesthetic construct, namely that of the "daemonic," with its imputation of extraordinary, almost supernatural powers of fascination to select individuals.

In what follows, I want not to consider current depictions of the figure of the evil genius, but to go back to a period in which theorizations of genius made this association with evil possible and plausible. My interest is not in tracing a direct line of descent, but in foregrounding an association that will not go away. What we have in this emergent discourse on genius, as I read it, is a series of admissions and disavowals. There is a recognition of some sort of affinity between genius and evil, but also a disclaiming of it. And this denial must be understood less as a mechanism of repression, a refusal to acknowledge the disturbing ethical implications of an emergent aesthetic paradigm, than as a recasting of evil – sometimes, a highly self-conscious one – wherein evil is disassociated from transgression. The disassociation is not, to be sure, entirely successful since evil in the form of transgression continues to obtrude and refuses to be exorcised from moral discourse and sentiment.

In making sense of this development, we need to recognize the significance of the rehabilitation and mobilization of the devil in Romanticism – an appropriative act that is too often dismissed as an instance of literary posturing without substantial ethical content or broader cultural relevance. Rehabilitation here indicates not a wholesale embrace but a vindication of one defining aspect of the devil's persona, which opens the way to sympathy and partial approbation. The reassessment of the moral status of the arch-transgressor is one expression, albeit among the most provocative and telling, of a reassessment of the moral status of transgression as such; its significance lies not in its influence but in its symbolization of a wider transformation in moral sensibilities. In extricating evil from transgression and aligning it with the act of tormenting, Romantic poets gave voice to a change in moral sentiments that was already well underway. The choice of the devil as a symbol of liberation and opposition to the forces of repression was apposite in making evident the degree of deviation from a venerable moral framework subjected to dismantling; yet it also evoked unease among those who, while sharing the moral sentiments of the rehabilitators, were nonetheless troubled at the invocation of a figure traditionally meant to personify evil. The corollary of the celebration of the transgressive Lucifer was the condemnation of the tormentor God who punishes the upstart angel for his impious self-assertion. With the emergent moral ethos that made this revaluation possible, the infliction of suffering on others is taken to be the locus of evil while self-expression is presented as a social good and a fundamental individual right – sometimes even a God-given one.

Our judgments about how evil ought to be represented cannot be divorced from our understandings of what actually constitutes evil, and this necessitates a closer look at the antagonism between competing moral outlooks. In thinking through this antagonism, I draw attention to a series of anti-Augustinian moments that I take to be critical in reconfiguring evaluations and depictions of evil. To assume that we all know what evil is and then to examine the aesthetics of evil in light of this assumption is dubious on two counts; first, it fails to take account of the existence of moral dissensus; and second, it means reducing the aesthetic to a detachable supplement. Rather, we must pay heed to the traffic between the aesthetic and the moral and not take either one as given or as having an intrinsic priority over the other. At times the boundaries between the two are not easy to determine. The problem of the nature of genius was a central concern in eighteenth-century aesthetic discourse, but theorizations of genius were also invested with an existential significance and participated in a reconceptualization of the self that makes it dubious to treat them in isolation from matters of moral interest. While the invocation of genius – often seen as a vestige of Romanticism – has gone out of fashion in today's scholarly circles, the eighteenth-century cult of genius, far from being the last gasp of a vanishing aristocratic culture, was formative for the modern ideals of individuality, originality, and self-expression. In the form of the poetic genius, the Luciferian spirit of transgression dissolved the fetters of tradition, boldly asserted its right to reverential acknowledgment, and opened the way to a revaluation of values. On account of its successes, it also opened up a box of moral dilemmas pertaining to the proper representation of the evil-doer and the intersections between evil and greatness.

Rule-Breakers

Lucifer refuses to remain in the station that has been allotted to him. He prefers the pursuit of his own desire to the obedient performance of his God-given duty. Milton's Satan proclaims to the rebel angels, on the eve of the first battle waged in heaven, that "Our puissance is our own, our own right hand / Shall teach us highest deeds" (V.864–5).[7] Through the most extreme form of self-assertion, which entails a denial of his creaturely status and his dependence on God, the devil seeks to establish a space for himself free from subjection to external authority. He is the first individualist.

In Augustine's exposition of the devil's fall, disobedience born of pride not only operates as one vice among many, but is located as the single vice at the heart of the devil's origin and nature. For Augustine, the truth of the devil's origin and the truth of his nature go hand in hand; the former discloses the latter. Since the story of the inception of evil is also the story of its extremity, it functions as an admonition to be on guard against that vice that takes us furthest away from the good. In one of his most intriguing works of biblical exegesis, *On the Literal Meaning of Genesis*, Augustine describes "obedience" as "the one and only virtue for every creature that is a rational agent under the authority of God"; conversely, "the first and greatest vice [of a rational agent], puffing it up to its own downfall, is the wish to assert its own authority, the name of this vice being disobedience."[8] The decision to disobey God leads to the ruin of both Adam and Satan; but while Adam after a momentary albeit catastrophic lapse subsequently repents, Satan shows no such remorse and stubbornly persists in his defiance. The details surrounding the devil's fall remain obscure, but Augustine is confident about its cause and the sequence of the relevant events – "So then scripture does not say when it was that pride cast the devil down so that he distorted the goodness of his natural being by a twisted will; reason nonetheless declares unambiguously that this happened first and that as a result of this pride he became jealous of the man."[9] Notwithstanding the fact that the devil bears full responsibility for his sin and self-incurred punishment, in attributing the act of casting down to "pride" (*superbia*) rather than to the devil himself, Augustine calls attention to the transgressor's shameful state of defeat. The image of the devil being laid low and suffering a distortion in his nature conveys the degradation and disfigurement that follow from turning away from the good. The disfigurement pertains to the devil's essence, his "twisted will" (*prava voluntate*), but in later pictorial representations it finds an analogue in his outward deformity – the sign, symptom, and consequence of insubordination. Although Satan seeks to exalt himself, it is by virtue of the desire for pre-eminence that he brings about his own downfall. Since Augustine denies the positivity of evil, he finds the notion of pure evil to be necessarily incoherent; insofar as it is even permissible to assert that evil exists, it does so only as a privation – or at most a perversion – of the good. In conceiving of evil in terms of a deficiency, Augustine denies any trace of sublimity to the transgressor and the act of transgression. The overstepping of limits is not a proof of excess of strength but demonstrates a lack, the incapacity to resist temptation and the failure to properly use the freedom that God has granted us.

From the early Church Fathers to the modern day, the figure of the devil as transgressor has been a staple of traditional representations. Its most epic realization in literature occurs in the seventeenth century, in a work that presents itself as both poetry and theodicy. *Paradise Lost* has often been read as staging Satan's moral decay, dramatizing a movement from bad to worse in which residual angelic remnants in the devil are extirpated. But Milton's narrative is less a story of Satan's degeneration than a story of his unveiling, in which the true nature of his prideful disobedience is stripped of its outward lustre and reveals itself to be both morally and aesthetically repugnant.[10] The unveiling is evident in the narrator's sustained undercutting of Satan's posturing through a series of commentarial deflations as well as in the epic's larger narrative arc. He who began as the bearer of light and an exemplar of celestial pulchritude is deprived of his radiance in the fall from heaven into the lake of fire, a disfiguration that inhibits recognition among his fellow fallen angels and that excites lamentation with the realization of what has been lost. Even then he maintains some semblance of his original grandeur, but in assuming the posture of a cormorant and a toad and in transforming himself into a serpent, he unwittingly shows his proximity to the beastly and the base. In the final scene in hell, he and his fellow devils are transformed into hideous snakes, an alteration that serves both as a degrading punishment and a revelation of the nature of the fallen; while the false form that Satan assumes to seduce Eve is a disguise, it also shows us, ironically, his hidden essence. After allowing Satan to engage in his duplicitous game of metamorphoses, God finally brings into alignment, howsoever temporarily, appearance and reality. The epic unmasks the deceiver and shows that the ostensible hero who has the power to charm both Eve and the poem's readers was, all along, a venomous and degraded creature, frightful to behold to the unclouded eye. While the beautiful and the good ultimately belong together, they do not always appear in conjunction in the world, and the devil seeks to exploit the resulting incongruity. In reminding us that if evil were manifestly repellent, it could never be a source of temptation, Milton exposes the insidiousness of evil – and not just evil in its venial manifestations, but in its most extreme form.

The difficulty we have in perceiving evil, especially in ourselves, is due to our knack for self-deception, our penchant to convince ourselves that the things we like are good on account of our liking them. But this difficulty is also to be attributed to evil's affinity for forms that are not proper to it, its assumption of an appearance that conceals its reality and thereby draws us towards it. Milton's description of Eve's susceptibility to the enticements of the serpent – and the baleful outcome that follows from it – serves as a warning to the reader to remain vigilant in the face of temptation; vigilance demands fortification of the will as well as learning to detect evil in unsuspected places. In his reading of *Paradise Lost*, which argues for the orthodoxy of the epic and notes its agreement with Augustinian theology on the essential doctrinal points, C.S. Lewis attributes misreadings of Milton to a failure to recognize – or take seriously – the poet's moral and theological commitments. He interprets Satan as a figure of "absurdity," whose abortive strivings, contradictory assertions, and incoherent logic are intended to elicit our ridicule and contempt.[11] But if Milton seeks to unmask the devil as a wretched self-deceiver, the exalted language he places in his mouth and the audacious exploits he attributes to him also seem calculated to excite awe. Milton offers both extended monologues, in which Satan speaks in his own voice, and a narrative commentary on Satan's utterances, and the latter invariably subverts the former, revealing how cleverly vice can disguise itself in the garb of heroism and virtue. Yet these deflationary insertions have not been sufficiently persuasive to forestall readings of Satan as a kind of tragic hero.[12] The poet has devised a deceiver with such formidable powers of deception that we have come to mistake diabolical evil for laudable resistance. Diabolical evil denotes both the most extreme form of evil and the particular type of evil that the devil instantiates. What happens, though, when these two things no longer hold together, when the devil, even if marred by certain flaws, is represented as standing not for extreme evil, but for a cause worthy of our respect and sympathy? The argument that such a division already occurs in *Paradise Lost* is dubious, but this division does, in fact, appear in late eighteenth- and early nineteenth-century Romantic poets, among whom were some of Milton's most fervent admirers. This fissure opened up the space for a critique of prior conceptions of evil and for a vindication of what was hitherto denigrated as sin. The recasting of Satan as a sublime resistor effects a stunning inversion of the Augustinian stance, according to which evil is something necessarily contemptible, a form of moral defect as well as ontological deficiency.

With the valorization of transgression, the language of deficiency comes to be supplanted by the language of potency. But what does it mean to say that transgression as such is valorized when what constitutes transgression varies depending upon the cultural system and, more specifically, the system of rules and commandments in which it occurs? Insofar as a particular morality can be reframed or retranslated, sometimes not without grave distortion, into the language of rules, all manner of actions can be redefined as transgressions of various sorts. Every crime, for example, can be read as an act of transgression, one that infringes the legal code; that does not mean, though, that to cast doubt on the synonymy of evil and transgression is tantamount to an endorsement of criminality. The question remains, on what grounds is it wrong to commit certain criminal acts? Is it because they result in others being harmed or because they are wrong as such, simply by virtue of the fact that it is unethical to break the law, regardless of whether or not any suffering is entailed? The act of inflicting suffering on others is not as straightforward as it sometimes appears, and judgments about whether an act amounts to torment is subject to disagreement depending upon the vantage point of the judge and spectator; nonetheless, it seems to be less ambiguous than the act of transgressing, more easily recognizable as such, and less dependent – at least comparatively – for its meaning on a wider interpretive context. But if transgression appears, at once, as something so abstract and as something so contextually specific, bound to a particular system of rules and commandments, we might well question how helpful it is to speak of transgression or transgressiveness without consideration of what institution, code, or power is being transgressed against. This misgiving is not unjustified; nonetheless, the consecration of obedience as a virtue and the condemnation of disobedience as a vice, indeed as the worst of all vices in Augustine and his spiritual kin, suggest that the locating of evil in transgression possesses a certain unity of sentiment and even conceptual coherence, notwithstanding the obvious fact that what counts as a transgression in one context may be seen as a fulfilment of duty in another. Kierkegaard, in a preface to *The Book on Adler*, written on the cusp of the Revolutions of 1848, writes that "the misfortune of our age – in the political as well as in the religious sphere, and in all things – is disobedience, unwillingness to obey."[13] Such a sentiment is not unusual for conservatives and traditionalists of various stripes who cannot abide disrespect for rules, the denigration of authority, and the profanation of the sacred. Yet in the wake of the horrors perpetrated by the totalitarian regimes of the last century, whose dutiful servants were only too willing to follow orders, one might very well counter that it is a surfeit of obedience that constitutes the greater misfortune of our age. Be that as it may, it is significant that Kierkegaard does not simply commend obedience to a particular religious or secular institution, but that obedience as such is pronounced praiseworthy – especially where the spectre of disobedience is raised up as the perilous alternative.[14] Where disobedience is envisioned as the principal danger to the spiritual, moral, and social order, an oversensitivity to suffering – an excess of compassion – may itself be seen as a potential threat to the order of things insofar as it leads individuals to place the happiness of their fellows above the dictates of the law – understood as the law of country, the law of God, or the moral law that every rational being bears within itself.

The notion that there are laws before which we should submit simply on account of their being laws continues to exercise a hold on us; it is at work whenever a man, upon learning that one of his fellows is to endure a draconian punishment for a trivial offence, shrugs his shoulders and says matter-of-factly, "Well, that's the law." This "legalism" finds countless thoughtless adherents and a number of thinking ones. It has also called forth opposition under the banners of self-expression and liberty. In *On Liberty*, Mill contrasts the ideal of individuality, which he espouses, with the Calvinist interpretation of human nature, according to which "the one great offence of man is self-will." For the Calvinist, "all the good of which humanity is capable, is comprised in obedience. You have no choice; thus you must do, and no otherwise: 'whatever is not a duty, is a sin.'"[15] Mill's repudiation of strict compliance with social norms and his vindication of self-expression finds its foil in this opposing "theory of life," which, far from being the preserve of a religious minority, finds an audience among "many who do not consider themselves Calvinists."[16] In asserting that eccentricity should be prized for its own sake, even if it has nothing else to recommend it, insofar as it serves to disrupt the forces of conformity and "the despotism of custom," Mill goes beyond providing an argument for the legitimacy of freedom of expression and comes to advocate, in stark contrast to the preachers of obedience, the deliberate transgression of customs and conventions.[17] Notwithstanding his own push for the extension of the franchise, Mill feared the homogenizing effects of modern institutions and the spread of mass mediocrity. Seeking an antidote to their ill effects, he discovers a requisite remedy in the practice of individuals' developing their powers to the utmost. The cultivation of our faculties is not only an inalienable right, but an exercise that proves conducive to one of the most beneficial social effects of freedom of expression, one that mitigates democracy's levelling tendency – the flourishing of men and women of genius. The uninhibited genius who refuses to be bound by the dictates of convention is a rarity, but she is also an exemplification of the ideal of originality that Mill hopes will inspire and be embraced by the many.

Before being taken up into the discourse of politics, the problem of originality was formulated as an issue of artistic practice in the eighteenth century; to say that this problem proved to have moral implications would be to understate that it was implicated in moral matters from the outset. When art is loosened from craftsmanship and becomes tied to the expression of the unique personality of the artist, then the authority of traditional guidelines is placed in doubt. Nietzsche writes, in *Human, All Too Human*, that "'Egoistic' and 'unegoistic' is not the fundamental antithesis which has led men to make the distinction between 'in accordance with custom' and 'in defiance of custom,' between good and evil, but adherence to a tradition, a law, and severance from it."[18] In this framework, "being evil" means deviating from tradition rather than being egoistic or causing harm to others; the latter is deemed immoral only to the extent that established custom happens to prohibit certain forms of harming. What then becomes of the category of evil in an era that is inclined to show less and less respect for tradition and that feels less compelled to adhere to its directives? Respect for tradition in the modern age suffers denigration for a range of reasons, some at cross-purposes with one another; tradition is objected to because it stifles our desires and denies us pleasure; because it prevents us from realizing our authentic selves; because it impedes the emergence of greatness; because it seems an unhelpful source of guidance in a rapidly changing world; because subservience to authority, whether past or present, is itself seen as something morally dubious. The results of the erosion of tradition are liberatory as well as oppressive in their introduction of new forms of empowerment and new structures of domination. But whatever its inconsistencies and incoherences, the challenge to received codes of conduct brings about an axiological reconfiguration.

Few eighteenth-century works were more explicit in undermining reliance on tradition in the realm of art than Edward Young's *Conjectures on Original Composition*, published in 1759, one century before the appearance of *On Liberty*. At the time of its publication, Young was in his declining years, but his *Night Thoughts*, completed a decade and a half earlier, continued to inspire young poets seeking to plumb the depths of the human soul and find new modes of lyrical articulation. In opposition to those who called for the imitation of classical models, Young asserted, in his *Conjectures*, that "all eminence, and distinction, lies out of the beaten road; excursion, and deviation, are necessary to find it; and the more remote your path from the highway, the more reputable; if, like poor *Gulliver* (of whom anon) you fall not into a ditch, in your way to glory."[19] This valorization of deviation comes with an acknowledgment of the dangers it entails, the falls that it sometimes occasions, but the element of risk at play in wandering from "the beaten road" lends the practice of original composition an aura of the heroic, which it would never possess if it were merely an exercise in imitation. With reference to the ancients, Young explains that "too great awe for them lays genius under restraint, and denies it that free scope, that full elbow-room, which is requisite for striking its most masterly strokes."[20] The genius, like a swordsman, requires some form of schooling in his art, but more important still is that freedom of movement that allows him to showcase his gifts. Young not only likens genius to a swordsman and a force of nature, but also to one who wields supernatural powers. While "*good understanding*" is compared to an architect, genius is equated with a magician conjuring forth worlds "by means invisible."[21] Are there then any uses to rules of art, which should regulate such magical acts of creation? Young answers that "rules, like crutches, are a needful aid to the lame, tho' an impediment to the strong."[22] This assessment stands opposed to the advice given in the *Ars Poetica*, in which Horace claims that the attainment of poetic excellence requires careful adherence to rules of composition, which he enumerates in some detail. From fellow poets and literary critics, the aspiring lyrist can glean the standards according to which his verses ought to be conceived, composed, and polished; he comes to know "what is appropriate for him and what is not, where the right path leads and where the wrong."[23] Such a procedure does not entail slavish copying, but it does necessitate a dependency on traditional exemplars in learning what we ought to emulate and what we ought to avoid.[24]

Notwithstanding its deviations from tradition, genius for Young is not necessarily disruptive; it also has the potential to bring forth order and can even "set us right." He writes that "with regard to the moral world, *conscience*, with regard to the intellectual, *genius*, is that god within. Genius can set us right in Composition, without the rules of the learned; as conscience sets us right in life, without the laws of the land: *This*, singly, can make us good, as men: *that*, singly, as writers, can, sometimes, make us great."[25] Young does not press the parallel further than this and perhaps with good reason; while conscience tends to restrain us from committing wrongs, genius as he describes it does not inhibit or moderate, but intensifies activity. And unlike conscience, which invites us to consciously reflect upon and pass judgment on the motives of our actions, genius is not an organ of judgment but is itself an inscrutable power that lies hidden deep within us. Urging us to look inwards, he writes:

> Therefore dive deep into thy bosom; learn the depth, extent, bias, and full fort of thy mind; contract full intimacy with the stranger within thee; excite and cherish every spark of intellectual light and heat, however smothered under former negligence, or scattered through the dull, dark mass of common thoughts; and collecting them into a body, let thy genius rise (if a genius thou hast) as the sun from chaos; and if I should then say, like an *Indian, Worship it,* (though too bold) yet should I say little more than my second rule enjoins, (*viz.*) *Reverence thyself.*[26]

In a work that eschews the following of rules, Young nonetheless puts forward two complementary imperatives that are meant to guide us in our poetic pursuits – "know thyself" and "reverence thyself."

It is instructive to consider the relationship between these two imperatives and those of Augustine in the *Confessions.* Augustine also urges us to know ourselves, but the self-knowledge that results from this undertaking leads not to self-reverence; even in acknowledging the presence of laudable attributes within himself, Augustine interprets these as gifts from God and thus not things that properly belong to him, in which he might take pride. Reflecting on his youthful indiscretions, he explains that "my sin consisted in this, that I sought pleasure, sublimity, and truth not in God but in his creatures, in myself and other created beings."[27] Through the act of confession, Augustine seeks to become cognizant of the sinfulness of his life, to realize more fully his utter dependence on God, and to reform himself in alignment with God's will. The *Confessions* has subsequently been hailed for its novelty in showing us – in a fashion hitherto unknown to antiquity – the rich interior life of a single individual. Yet rather than delighting in his idiosyncrasies and the uniqueness of his enterprise, Augustine warned of the dangers of venturing on untrodden pathways; it is in the imitation of Christ, in following the unparalleled exemplar of the life of the saviour – and inevitably failing to follow it – that our proper vocation lies.[28] The failure of this imitation reveals to us the truth of our nature, our inability to merit salvation through our own works, and our need for divine grace; the injunction to "know thyself" here serves an ancillary role in contributing to the higher commandment to worship the Lord.

The contrast between Augustine and Young, as presented here, might seem to be beside the point since they appear to be talking about two distinct spheres of human life, the religious and the artistic. Augustine is offering a sustained meditation on his spiritual condition whereas Young is presenting scattered observations on poetic composition. The transgression of moral and religious precepts is one thing, and the transgression of inherited rules of artistic production is another, and these should not be conflated. It is certainly possible, moreover, to advocate transgression in the realm of art and yet to denounce it in matters pertaining to morals and religion. We should not forget that Young himself was a royal chaplain who delivered sermons vindicating providence and the truth of the Christian faith. The point, however, is that Young, not unlike Augustine, is engaged in an attempted re-examination of our spiritual life, which leads him to reconceive our comportment to the depths of our own interiority. His advice, unlike Horace's or Longinus's, does not occur at the level of concrete instructions with reference to literary practice, but takes the form of an existential injunction. It is in the hallowed encounter with ourselves that we awaken the slumbering forces within and, realizing our hidden native strength, break the bonds of external constraint. The decision to invoke the example of the non-European heathen, before quickly offering a partial disavowal, indicates an awareness of a departure from the long-standing Christian tradition that enjoins humility. Even after he moderates his initial imperative encouraging self-worship, Young's call to self-reverence retains a degree of self-regard for our uniquely personal gifts sufficient to render it suspect among those who see in pride the primordial sin. What is being advocated is a mode of comportment that allows us to properly esteem our creative powers, a first step towards their realization. Knowing oneself is not an exercise in knowledge accumulation or even a kind of becoming-acquainted-with so much as it is an act of transformation, a mobilization of "the stranger within." In speaking to the aspiring poet, Young writes "if a genius thou hast," suggesting that it is not the common property of all or, at the very least, is not evenly distributed among men, but he also maintains that "genius is not so very rare as you imagine."[29] His message is not reserved for an elite coterie of recognized artists, but speaks to the many whose latent talents have yet to be actualized.

Young writes, "I shall not enter into the curious enquiry of what is, or is not, strictly speaking, *Original*, content with what all must allow, that some compositions are more so than others; and the more they are so, I say, the better."[30] While the parameters of originality are not carefully delineated in Young's reflections, the repeated references to "imitation" as its virtual antonym indicate its strong associations with deviation from prior models. Yet the appeal to originality in Young's day was equivocal since it could refer to two distinct, indeed potentially oppositional things. On the one hand, to be original meant to be new or to express something novel; on the other hand, to be original connoted a return to nature or even to God. Even Young's deployment of the term, which is obviously more closely aligned to the former usage than to the latter, betrays some uncertainty here, as is evident in the characterization of genius as having "a *vegetable* nature," which implies inherent powers of growth rather than a penchant for artifice.[31] Attempts to synthesize the two meanings of originality, at work in Romanticism, further complicate the concept. In the writings of Rousseau, the primitivist idealization of the state of nature is coupled with a celebration of individuality, especially as it occurs in the figure of "the solitary walker," who appears as an eccentric to his modern contemporaries on account of his refusal to conform to the expectations of society. Rousseau maintains that "an animal cannot deviate from the rule that is prescribed to it, even when it would be advantageous to do so, while man deviates from it, often to his own detriment."[32] It is by virtue of this capacity to deviate, which is inseparable from human beings' freedom and "perfectibility," that Rousseau locates the *differentia specifica* of our species.[33] This notion appears in conjunction with the imperative "*Learn whom God has ordered you to be, and in what part of human affairs you have been placed.*"[34] It should not be forgotten, however, that the man who penned this imperative was the same one who boasted at the beginning of the *Confessions* that nature had broken the mould when it came to fashion him.[35]

While Young's pronouncements on originality may seem tepid or innocuous in their moral implications, his image of the genius as a rule-breaker contains *in nuce* the idea that enabled associations between genius and evil to be made. In quick succession, we see a series of increasingly radical accounts of genius that flirt with its dangerous and disruptive aspects or even enunciate them outright. Young's heathen

Indian holds the stage for but a moment before being whisked away. Later theorizations of genius introduce the figure of Prometheus as a mythic prototype on account of his creative powers and his transgression of divine interdictions. Already with Shaftesbury, we see a connection drawn between Prometheus and the poetic, but it is one wherein unruliness is disparaged and divorced from artistry. In his *Characteristics of Men, Manners, Opinions, Times*, published in 1711, Shaftesbury speaks of the true poet as "a second Maker, a just Prometheus under Jove."[36] The modifier "just" leads us to imagine that the original Prometheus was unjust, an impression reinforced by the subsequent reference to "our modern Prometheuses" as "mountebanks."[37] Shaftesbury writes, "the moral artist who can thus imitate the Creator and is thus knowing in the inward form and structure of his fellow creature, will hardly, I presume, be found unknowing in *himself*, or at a loss in those numbers which make the harmony of a mind. For knavery is mere dissonance and disproportion."[38] The equating of the good with the harmonious and the equating of wrongdoing with a lack of proportion highlight the aesthetic dimensions of moral conduct and the moral inflections of the poetic. The poet deserving of the name is not a fashioner of pretty verses but one whose inner concord grants him the ability to "describe both men and manners and give to an action its just body and proportions."[39] Shaftesbury's meditations on the importance of harmony found a welcome reception in diverse quarters in the eighteenth century, but rather than "the moral artist," of whom he speaks so highly, it is the "unjust Prometheus" who comes to be apotheosized in the subsequent discourse on genius. In him, a new generation of artists, who felt their creative endeavours hampered by the weighty demands of tradition, discovered their symbol of resistance. Breaching the ramparts of heaven like the thief of fire before him, the genius defies those prohibitions that impede his quest for the heights. In their revaluation of transgression, later invocations of Satan perform the same function as do allusions to Prometheus, though often with a deeper self-consciousness and awareness of what is at stake. With each of these successive articulations, the acknowledgment of something morally suspect in the figure of the genius becomes more acute, the resonances with evil more apparent. But we can also see a countermovement at work in these representations, a push in the opposite direction whereby traditional moral positions and judgments themselves become objects of suspicion. The mention of Satan is an admission of an affinity between genius and evil, but the rehabilitation of transgression that accompanies it also serves to undo the force of the admission. In its ambiguities, the likening of the genius to the devil strangely parallels those much more frequent comparisons of the genius to God in the eighteenth century, which may be read both as a sacralization of the human creator and as a sacrilegious encroachment on divine prerogative. The rule-breaker, no longer acknowledging rules by which he is bound, reimagines himself to be a rule-maker – an act of self-election that may itself be interpreted as the extremity of rule-breaking.

In Goethe's "On German Architecture," first published as an anonymous pamphlet in 1772 before being incorporated into *On German Customs and Art* (a manifesto of sorts for the Sturm und Drang), sacralization and sacrilege constitute the structuring opposition in terms of which genius is represented and conceived. Imagining the people milling about at the foot of the Strasbourg Cathedral as ants, the young poet envisions Erwin von Steinbach, the man who planned the monument's construction, as the creator on high – "you are like the Great Architect who piled up mountains into the clouds."[40] Comparisons of Steinbach to God sit uneasily – and intentionally so – next to identifications of him with those who infringe the Lord's commandments. Speaking of the "few [who] have been blessed with a mind capable of conceiving a Babel-like vision," Goethe overturns the narrative of Genesis, in which the builders of the great tower are punished for their audacity and scattered to the ends of the earth.[41] The heterodoxy of his eulogy is enshrined in a series of deliberately provocative allusions to scripture. In Psalm 139, the psalmist writes, "If I take the wings of the morning, and dwell in the uttermost parts of the sea; Even there shall thy hand lead me, and thy right hand shall hold me." Joyous in the knowledge that the Lord will always be with him, the psalmist recognizes his relationship of dependency and takes comfort in it. Goethe adopts the expression "the wings of morning" (*die Flügel der Morgenröte*), but deploys it in order to undercut the humility animating the psalm. In his encomium to the man of genius, Goethe proclaims that "he does not want to be borne up and carried off on wings not his own, though they be the wings of morning."[42] The genius disavows the power that allows him to take flight if he cannot call it his own. He does not deign to soar, like Icarus, on borrowed wings.

The genius participates in the divine, but unlike the figure of the rhapsode described in Plato's *Ion*, the architect does not submit to an external entity taking possession of him and working through him. Even when Goethe claims that "Genius came to our aid and inspired Erwin von Steinbach," as if genius were something coming from the outside, the applicability of the term to the man himself suggests its inseparability from him; it originates within.[43] Goethe draws together elements of a Platonic interpretation of the poet, who experiences spontaneous inspiration originating in the divine, and a more modern understanding of subjectivity, which emphasizes the autonomy and self-directedness of the subject. Moments of contact with the divine are themselves the product of an activation of inner powers. Goethe's essay concludes with an apostrophe to the innate artist – "Hail to thee child who art born with an eye for proportion, ready to practice your talent on all nature's forms."[44] Privy to the riches of the surrounding world, familiar to all but perceived by only a few, the eye of the artist discerns – in a manner reminiscent of Shaftesbury – the harmonies of nature and hones its vision in the act of discernment. After this child is "sated with earthly beauty and worthy to rest in the arms of the goddess," Goethe expresses his hope that "then, more than Prometheus, may he bring down the bliss of the gods upon our earth."[45]

Goethe's gaze, as described in the essay, is directed upwards; inviting us to participate in a vision of the soaring structure, he casts his sights on the heavens. We as readers, borne aloft by the image of the Strasbourg Cathedral and Goethe's own expansive rhetoric, are meant to join in the author's feeling of elevation. But the concluding reference to Prometheus effects a reversal of this ascendant movement; after a series of exercises in upwards striving, Goethe concludes with an expression of hope for a turn downwards, in which "the bliss of the gods" who dwell above is brought to earth. These two movements capture the twin activities of genius, his wandering in higher worlds and his communication of these worlds to his fellow human beings through works of artistic creation. The ascent into the heavens, exemplified in the figures of the builders of the Tower of Babel, must be followed by a descent to earth, in which the genius disseminates the gifts obtained to those residing down below; the archetype of this latter movement is Prometheus. In Goethe's choice of literary and mythological referents, both of these movements are cast as moments of transgression. Goethe describes the prophesied artist as being in need of "heavenly beauty," whom he characterizes as a "mediator" (*Mittlerin*), a role that implies a reconciliation between heaven and earth; however, his decision to invoke Prometheus suggests a more appropriative relationship than the trope of mediation allows, one in which the beautiful is actively possessed.[46] The anticipatory conclusion draws our thoughts to Prometheus's theft of fire from the gods, an act of beneficence towards humankind and an act of transgression against Zeus, for which the transgressor was chained to a mountain in the Caucasus. The danger of Prometheus's gift, from the perspective of Olympus, was that in depriving the gods of one of their unique prerogatives it threatened to place human beings on an equal footing with them. The climax of Goethe's essay participates in this hope of equality, not for the sake of despoiling or impoverishing the gods, but simply to enrich humankind, so that it might share in their bliss.

The desire to be like God also sets in motion Eve's transgression against the Lord's interdiction and the resulting fall of man. "And the serpent said unto the woman, Ye shall not surely die: For God doth know that in the day ye eat thereof, then your eyes shall be opened, and ye shall be as gods, knowing good and evil" (Genesis 3:4). These are the same words that Goethe's Mephistopheles inscribes, in Latin translation, in the book of an eager young student seeking his advancement in the world – "*Eritis sicut Deus, scientes bonum et malum*" (2,048).[47] It is necessary, in identifying the moral ambivalences of the attempt to "be like God," to distinguish between two opposing modes of the *imitatio dei*. The first type, which finds its paradigm in the imitation of Christ, is an exercise in obedience, wherein the faithful humble themselves just as the Lord humbled himself in taking on the form of a servant in the likeness of man. The second type of imitation does not content itself with faithfully following in the steps of Jesus, but bears the aspect of a rivalry. In this case, the imitator arrogates powers and prerogatives to himself that uniquely belong to God; such an overstepping of limits finds its exemplar in the figure of Lucifer, who instead of modelling himself on God's goodness aspires to occupy his position in the cosmic hierarchy. Taken to its extreme, the desire to emulate culminates in a quest to dethrone and to vanquish.

gift to fashion but also the power to break free from social and spiritual constraints. And the extremity of this breaking is more evident in Lucifer than in Prometheus; the former does not rest content with violating a particular prohibition but balks at any external imposition placed upon him. The incorporation of this transgressive dimension into the image of genius, already present in Young's advocacy of deviation, becomes radicalized in the wake of the French Revolution. To it, we owe our associations of genius with the free-loving bohemian and the political incendiary, the absinthe drinker and the opium addict, the restless nomad and the reckless adventurer. In these figurations, creative activity becomes intertwined with destructiveness and self-destructiveness. Before gifting us with celestial visions, the poet must first burn through a world of stifling conventions; he bathes in the light of heaven, but his torch draws its flame from the infernal fire.

The Poet and the Devil

The eighteenth-century cult of genius has been read as "reactive" to the extent that it arose in response to an emergent democratic and egalitarian ethos; according to this reading, its adherents were motivated to carve out a place for greatness in an age of eroding distinctions of rank and declining faith in transcendence.[54] Without gainsaying the elitist dimension of modern invocations of genius, to characterize them as reactive runs the risk of occluding the degree to which they participated in a reconceptualization of the self and its expressive possibilities that was consonant with the democratizing tendencies of the age. Rather than reading the cult of genius as being antagonistic to the new spirit of egalitarianism, we might with equal justification see the former as paradoxically aligned with the latter insofar as both worked together to undermine a respect for established authorities and rules of tradition. If it were otherwise, we would expect the advocates of genius to be preponderately antidemocratic in sentiment; but a remarkable range of political allegiances may be found in the ranks of its enthusiasts, among whom must be counted radical visionaries, such as Blake, whose appeals to genius are inextricable from their revolutionary commitments.

Blake asserts in *The Marriage of Heaven and Hell* that "the road of excess leads to the palace of wisdom."[55] In a subversion of the Aristotelian precept that locates virtue as the mean between two extremes and in contravention of the Christian commendation of renunciation, according to which overindulgence is a sin, Blake offers us a hymn to extremity. The pushing of limits and the overturning of convention function as unifying threads holding together a text that in its ingenious mixing of styles, genres, and modes of address resists literary classification. The extent to which Blake's own voice ought to be identified with "the voice of the Devil" in the text has generated a considerable amount of disagreement among scholars intent on disentangling the satirical strand in the work from Blake "talking straight."[56] But whatever the idiosyncrasies of *The Marriage of Heaven and Hell*, it shows its affinities with Blake's other writings in its attempt to rehabilitate those vital forces that moralists have tended to condemn as evil.[57] Written in a time of revolutionary upheaval, it encodes a political radicalism in the language of religious prophecy, a procedure that becomes still more pronounced in *America, A Prophecy*, published shortly after it in 1793, where Blake mobilizes a complex and idiosyncratic mythology in his commentary on contemporary political realities and makes use of the devil's voice, once again, to enunciate the overthrow of oppressive constraints.[58] Unlike *America*, however, the revolutionary import of *The Marriage of Heaven and Hell* is to be found less in its articulation of a political program, which comes through most forcefully in the concluding "Song of Liberty," than in its theorization of the poet and the poetic. The "diabolical" energies that are valorized in this work are intimately related to Blake's conception of genius, which, in its mingling of the poetic and the prophetic, is simultaneously aesthetic and religious.

In the first "Memorable Fancy" in *The Marriage of Heaven and Hell*, Blake writes, "As I was walking among the fires of Hell, delighted with the enjoyments of Genius; which to Angels look like torment and insanity. I collected some of their Proverbs: thinking that as the sayings used in a nation, mark its character, so the Proverbs of Hell, shew the nature of Infernal wisdom better than any description of buildings or garments."[59] The image of the author strolling through the inferno and gathering together the sayings of its inhabitants is so startling that it easily leads us to overlook the significance of the reference to genius. The first thing to note about Blake's use of the term is its connection to joys that are misconstrued; "the enjoyments of Genius" not only have the appearance of "insanity" in the eyes of the angels – in itself not altogether surprising given the long-standing association between genius and madness – but they even bear the aspect of "torment." Among the three "Errors" that the voice of the Devil attributes to "All Bibles and sacred codes," the third is that "God will torment Man in Eternity for following his Energies."[60] But the angels, described in the aforementioned passage, are not simply labouring under the false belief that the pleasures of the moment, the result of following one's energies, lead to damnation; they cannot even recognize these momentary pleasures as such. Since we are told that "Energy is Eternal Delight," how does it come about that the angels perceive its joyous manifestations as a kind of suffering?[61] Blake does not proffer an explanation of the causes of this failure of angelic vision; it seems, however, that the restlessness, the movement, and the expansiveness of genius are painful to these who find their solace in rest, stillness, and the peace that comes from dwelling in fixed horizons. The limitation of the angels follows almost necessarily from their nature since they themselves are represented in *The Marriage of Heaven and Hell* as agents of restraint and impediment. The act of restraining can be a mark of power, the capacity to contain a rival force; but it is associated here less with potency than with the weakness of the opposition – "Those who restrain desire, do so because theirs is weak enough to be restrained; and the restrainer or reason usurps its place & governs the unwilling."[62] The genius, in alignment with the diabolical, appears as that which proves too strong to be restrained.

In the subsequent and most infamous section of the text, the "Proverbs of Hell," there are two further references to genius – "When thou seest an Eagle, thou seest a portion of Genius. lift up thy head!" and "Improvement makes strait roads, but the crooked roads without Improvement, are roads of Genius."[63] The concluding imperative of the first of these two proverbs is a call to acknowledge the heights to which genius soars, a recognition that serves as an occasion to raise ourselves up. The prior assertion that "No bird soars too high. if he soars with his own wings" locates exaltation in the independence that enables its attainment.[64] This epigram, which resonates with Goethe's pronouncement that the man of genius "does not want to be borne up and carried off on wings not his own," situates genius in opposition to renunciation and limitation, which are the proper elements of the angels. The second proverb that makes an explicit reference to genius, in the association it draws between genius and "crooked roads," equates improvement with the making of straight ones. Whereas the son of David laments that "*That which is* crooked cannot be made straight" (Ecclesiastes 1:15), the devilish proverb makes the crooked the mark of a higher pathway and turns the act of straightening into a fall into mediocrity. Taken in conjunction with the earlier proverb that "The tygers of wrath are wiser than the horses of instruction," it exhibits a suspicion of all those rules that serve to guide us on preordained paths.[65] These rules, or "instructions," encompass guidelines of poetic composition as well as moral codes of behaviour, and the refusal to acquiesce to them occurs simultaneously at the level of artistic activity and at the level of moral conduct.

The two proverbs in which genius is named accord with Young's *Conjectures* in their advocacy of deviation and self-exaltation.[66] However, Blake's work expresses a deeper awareness of the morally disruptive implications of their avowal; it candidly admits their diabolical character, as configured in a long-standing religious tradition that situates transgression at the heart of evil. The text does not justify transgression by freeing it of its associations with evil but presupposes their intimate relationship. Commentators have made much, quite rightly, of the playfulness of *The Marriage of Heaven and Hell*, evident in its polyphony and its mischievous irony.[67] But to reduce the transgressiveness of the text to a matter of play fails to appreciate the extent to which Blake's poetic intervention takes the orthodox definition of evil seriously even as it overturns the orthodox evaluative hierarchy. The force of the destabilizing of established moral categories relies on their being acknowledged before being undone. The stylistic innovations of the work are mirrored in the heterodox pronouncements pertaining to morality and religion. Blake does not balk at the moral consequences of identifying genius and originality; since poetry is akin to life in its generative power, it cannot be cordoned off from life's most vital concerns. Such a separation would be possible only if poetry were a craft, a matter of mechanical practice. Against a mimetic theory of art, Blake sees art as an outflowing of the artist, a making manifest of the personality. This "expressivist" turn emphasizes self-realization rather than the attainment of some objective ideal of beauty.[68] The laudations to energy in *The Marriage of Heaven and Hell* are not reducible to a valorization of creative power, something admittedly indispensable to the poet; it is, more specifically, energy's centrifugal tendency that aligns it with genius. If "Reason is the bound or outward circumference of Energy," as the voice of the Devil tells us, the danger of unresisted rationality is that it will lead to an ever-contracting circle that stifles the development and emergence of the human person.[69] "The cistern contains: the fountain overflows."[70] The waters, trapped in the cistern, attain visibility in the act of gushing forth. With its propensity for expansion, its surging and flowing outwards, energy makes possible the process of poetic expression, which too is an act of overflow.[71]

Today, the designation "evil genius" often means little more than superior intellect coupled with wicked intentions; the combination of intelligence and malice remains incidental since there is no sense of a special intimacy between them. But in Blake's reflections on evil and genius, the two are joined together by their "Energy." There can be no genius without the power to break through barriers, and this capacity for overcoming distinguishes both the poet and the devil. Contra Augustine, Blake rebuts – though with a vision rather than through argumentation – the characterization of evil as a privation of the good. Although transgression, for Augustine, means crossing a line that we should not cross, it is on his reading more a falling short than an exceeding. The primal "fall" of our ancestors in the garden is typical and prototypical; it is not a moment of overcoming, but a lapse, one that we repeat every day in succumbing to sin. Does evil partake of potency or does it betray deficiency? This, in a nutshell, is the contention between Blake and Augustine. One might object that what Blake dubs as evil is not actually so, even in his own eyes, and so the disagreement between the poet and the theologian is less real than apparent. This objection misses the mark, however, since that which Blake calls by the name of evil – whatever valuational inversion might be attached to it or howsoever ironically he employs the term – would be recognized as such by Augustine. The point warrants emphasizing lest we think that when Blake and Augustine speak of evil, they do not share the same referent. For both, transgression is the locus of evil, but their accounts of the nature of transgression are antithetical. The relevant point of difference, at least in this instance, is to be found not so much in their rival moral evaluations as in their rival readings of the character of what they both designate as "evil." If we reformulate the alternatives as equations – evil = potency vs. evil = deficiency – then an easy dismissal is ready at hand, namely that the equated terms in the two formulae are not actually equivalent; there is no intrinsic connection between evil and strength or evil and weakness, not to speak of an identity relationship. Yet this straight-forward resolution does not take us very far. Even if there are not intrinsic connections, are there contingent conjunctions? Are there such things as "potent evil" and "deficient evil"? And if so, how does the difference be-tween these manifestations of evil inform the manner in which they ought to be represented? The problem of evil is entangled with the problem of power, as both Blake and Augustine recognize; although the one per-ceives potency where the other discerns deficiency, there is a shared sense that getting the power status of evil right is key to properly representing it. And as we will see going forward, whether or not we imagine evil – or a particular instance of evil – as potent or deficient bears on the aes-thetic mode of representation adequate to it.

In the most oft-cited line of *The Marriage of Heaven and Hell*, Blake declares that "the reason Milton wrote in fetters when he wrote of Angels & God, and at liberty when of Devils & Hell, is because he was a true Poet, and of the Devils party without knowing it."[72] This interpretation might be construed as meaning that Milton's unconscious partiality for the Sa-tanic cause was the source of his gift for presenting it so compellingly; this is surely right, as far as it goes, yet the alignment of the "true Poet" and "the Devils party" pertains not only to Milton.[73] True poets, regard-less of the idiosyncrasies that distinguish them, have an innate propin-quity with Hell. Whereas the principle of evil liberates from restraints, to write under the influence of the angels is necessarily to write "in fetters." And what applies to writing is true *a fortiori* for living. Blake writes:

Once I saw a Devil in a flame of fire. who arose before an Angel that sat on a cloud. and the Devil uttered these words.

The worship of God is. Honouring his gifts in other men each according to his genius. and loving the greatest men best, those who envy or calumniate great men hate God, for there is no other God.

The Angel hearing this became almost blue but mastering himself he grew yellow, & at last white-pink & smiling, and then replied,

Thou idolater, is not God One? & is not He visible in Jesus Christ? and has not Jesus Christ given his sanction to the law of ten commandments and are not all other men fools, sinners, & nothings?

The Devil answer'd; bray a fool in a morter with wheat. yet shall not his folly be beaten out of him: if Jesus Christ is the greatest man, you ought to love him in the greatest degree; now hear how he has given his sanction to the law of ten commandments: did he not mock at the sabbath, and so mock the sabbaths God? murder those who were murderd because of him? turn away the law from the woman taken in adultery? steal the labor of others to support him? bear false witness when he omitted making a defence before Pilate? covet when he pray'd for his disciples, and when he bid them shake off the dust of their feet against such as refused to lodge them? I tell you, no virtue can exist without breaking these ten commandments: Jesus was all virtue, and acted from impulse: not from rules.

When he had so spoken: I beheld the Angel who stretched out his arms embracing the flame of fire & he was consumed and arose as Elijah.[74]

In response to the angel's invocation of Jesus Christ, before whom all else are "fools, sinners, & nothings," the devil identifies Jesus himself as the consummate transgressor. This subversive interpretation of scripture exemplifies what it means to understand the Bible "in its infernal or diabolical sense."[75] The "virtue" attributed to Jesus refers not to angelic goodness or to the spirit of obedience; in keeping with the etymology of the word, it connotes rather the strength of man. Its connection with impulse, sister to the spontaneity and originality ascribed to genius, places virtue in the realm of energy, which is also the source of evil.

The transformation of the indignant angel, regenerated through fire and reborn as the prophet Elijah, whom the text turns into an advocate of diabolical wisdom, suggests the absorption of the good into the evil and its raising to a higher power. In the clash of contraries, the parochialism of the angels yields to the expansive vision of the devil, and angelic prosaicism gives way to the infernally poetic. At the outset of *The Marriage of Heaven and Hell*, we are told:

> Without Contraries is no progression. Attraction and Repulsion, Reason and Energy, Love and Hate, are necessary to Human existence.
> From these contraries spring what the religious call Good & Evil. Good is the passive that obeys Reason. Evil is the active springing from Energy.
> Good is Heaven. Evil is Hell.[76]

In stating that "the religious" designate these contraries "Good & Evil," Blake distances himself from the aptness of these designations, yet this does not constitute a disavowal of them, as if the truth lay in the inversion of their conventional naming. And notwithstanding the claims made in the name of one of the two contraries, the title of the work suggests not the triumph of hell but the joining of two oppositional principles. Such a union indicates the necessity of both rather than the subordination of one to the other. At the same time, the idea that the denizens of hell have access to aspects of the truth, howsoever partial, to which the angels are not privy is insupportable to the heavenly party. In his introduction to *The Great Divorce*, a title that already makes clear its opposition to the reconciliation of Blake's contraries, C.S. Lewis condemns the belief that good and evil can be reconciled as a "disastrous error."[77] Opposing the notion that progress derives from the union of two warring principles, Lewis counters that "evil can be undone, but it cannot 'develop' into good."[78] The centrality of this conviction to Lewis's vision of the afterlife is evident in both the title of the work and its opening epigraph, a quotation from George MacDonald, who avers that "there is no heaven with a little of hell in it – no plan to retain this or that of the devil in our hearts or our pockets. Out Satan must go, every hair and feather."[79] For Blake, however, the uprooting of the devil strikes at one of the roots of life, a principal source of its nourishment and flourishing. Without this impulse, the truths of poetic genius would lapse into the derivative and disfiguring platitudes of the priests and philosophers. Against the repressive forces of heaven, Blake champions an expansive vision of life, in which internal divisions and ruptures within the self and the world are healed and integrated into a higher unity.

A similar integration appears in Goethe's later works, both poetic and scientific.[80] In his *Theory of Colours*, published in 1810, Goethe maintains against Newton – who was also a target of Blake's ire – that it is through the mixture of light and darkness that colours are generated; colours themselves are conceived "as consisting entirely of semilight or semishadow."[81] For Goethe, darkness functions not simply as an absence of light, but opposes and interacts with it. He identifies "polarity" as a principle operative throughout nature, and he envisions one of the aims and contributions of his work to be the uncovering of its workings in the field of chromatics.[82] Although Goethe sometimes characterizes colours as weakened forms of light, which brings to mind some sort of dilution, he couples the principle of polarity with the process of "intensification" (*Steigerung*), which connotes the climbing to new heights through the interpenetration of opposites.[83] These reflections on light and darkness are carried over into Goethe's musings on good and evil, where those forces associated with evil are presented as not merely inimical to life, but as part of it, a source of its variety and colourfulness. Mephistopheles, when first speaking to Faust, introduces himself as "the Spirit of Eternal Negation" (1,338), but he also confesses, not without a touch of embarrassment, that he unintentionally brings about the good.

In his youth, Goethe drew out the associations between genius and the figure of Prometheus. In his later years, he gives increasing thought to what he names the "daemonic." Like the term "genius," which originally referred to a tutelary spirit before it came to be employed to describe human beings with extraordinary intellectual capacities, Goethe's "daemon" participates in the realms of the human and the divine, mediating between the two. The semantic complexities of Goethe's idea of the daemonic have defeated all those scholars audacious enough to seek out a single, unifying principle at its foundation.[84] It operates in so many different registers that its essence quickly dissolves into its manifold appearances. Goethe's own pronouncements about what it is – which are as rich in evocation as they are puzzling in their paradoxicality – and what it is not – which are reminiscent of negative theology in their refusal of predication of the ineffable – gesture to its straddling diverse domains, none of which are properly home to it. In *Poetry and Truth*, he recounts his own struggle in trying to make sense of it – "It was not divine, for it seemed irrational; not human, for it had no intelligence; not diabolical, for it was beneficent; and not angelic, for it often betrayed malice."[85] In justifying his use of the term, Goethe appeals to its usage among the ancients and sidelines its post-classical, Christian associations with the diabolical; the degradation of the tutelary daemon of the pagan Greeks into the evil demon of medieval theology finds a reversal in Goethe's demonology, in which the daemonic is reinvested with affirmative powers.[86] The daemonic appears as something propitious in spurring men on to greatness – although it may subsequently abandon them to ruin in an hour of need.

After noting that "the daemonic element can manifest itself in anything corporeal or incorporeal," Goethe proclaims that it is "at its most fearful when it emerges predominantly in some individual."[87] Among political figures, Napoleon was especially close to Goethe's thoughts when he was reflecting upon the appearance of the daemonic in his own times and considering its role in shaping human history. But there also existed in his mind an intimate relationship between the daemonic and the great artists.

Shakespeare, Raphael, and Mozart are all linked to the daemonic, three figures who, for Goethe, stood atop the summit of their respective arts – poetry, painting, and music respectively.[88] In Goethe's cryptic remarks about the daemonic, he draws attention to the modalities of the concept rather than a denominator common to all of them. At times, the daemonic brings to mind an independence that overcomes all impediments, whereby the will of the individual becomes effortlessly actualized; at others, it points to a lack of rational self-governance, as when an artist or statesman seems to act at the behest of an unconscious or foreign power.[89] In the latter sense, it serves as a reminder of our proximity to and our dependence upon forces that we do not adequately understand. Goethe remarks, in his autobiography, that the daemonic appears to shun the possible and to delight in the realization of the seemingly impossible – "everything that limits us seemed penetrable by it"; transcending those barriers that otherwise look to be insuperable, it calls forth the extraordinary.[90]

In Goethe's employment of the language of the daemonic, the concept continues to have transgressive resonances even as it is distanced from Christian readings of it as something evil. In a conversation with Johann Peter Eckermann, in which the younger man asked him if Mephistopheles displayed characteristics of the daemonic, Goethe explicitly denied the applicability of this designation to him since the daemonic is "a thoroughly positive force" (*eine durchaus positive Tatkraft*) and Mephistopheles is "too much a negative being" (*ein viel zu negatives Wesen*).[91] After posing this question, Eckermann did not proceed to enquire about the relationship between the daemonic and Faust, a character who shows himself, in his passion and restlessness, to be closer to the daemonic than is his demonic companion. As for Goethe's characterization of Mephistopheles as "negative," it seems to be consonant with long-standing Christian conceptions of the devil until we recall what a peculiar devil he actually is, a fact obscured by the influence that Goethe's portrayal of him has had on subsequent representations of the prince of darkness. His negativity resides less in the negation of limits, at work in the strivings of Faust and Milton's Satan, than in a corrosive and deflationary spirit of irony. Notwithstanding his self-proclaimed status as an embodiment of "sin" and "destruction" (1,344), he appears more good-humoured, more playful, and even – at least to some readers – more likeable than the soul whom he seeks to seduce. In the preface to *The Screwtape Letters*, Lewis writes that, among all the literary representations of the devil, "the really pernicious image is Goethe's Mephistopheles. It is Faust, not he, who really exhibits the ruthless, sleepless, unsmiling concentration upon self which is the mark of Hell. The humorous, civilized, sensible, adaptable Mephistopheles has helped to strengthen the illusion that evil is liberating."[92]

The image of the devil as a debonair and even amiable fellow, whom one would not be averse to sitting down with for a drink, has become familiar enough to us, through its various fictional reworkings, as to be no longer troubling. We have been disarmed by Mephistophelean irony. With Goethe, the devil transitions from being an object of irony to being an agent of it, and this "ironic reversal" marks a pivotal moment in the modern aestheticizing of evil. The Augustinian devil is an ironic figure who unwittingly degrades himself in seeking exaltation; after his initial lapse, he persists, to his own ruin, in his defiance. How can a creature be so daft as to imagine that victory can be attained in a struggle against the omnipotent creator? Lewis expresses reservations about Milton's attribution of a certain allure to Satan, yet he ultimately remains untroubled by the sublime posturing of Milton's Satan since he sees it as implicated in this stupidity, which renders the devil ridiculous. Yet Goethe's Mephistopheles, who has fewer pretensions to sublimity, proves intolerable to Lewis as a representative of evil. There are moments, it must be conceded, when Mephistopheles himself is subjected to irony, most notably in the conclusion of the drama, where he loses Faust's soul due to his distraction at the sight of the bottoms of the fair-faced angels. But he is also infused with an ironic consciousness, a self-awareness permeated with negativity, to which he subjects himself and everything around him. For Hegel, it is not irony's power to negate, but the fact that it negates indiscriminately, annihilating without distinction the unsubstantial and the "inherently excellent and solid" that makes it objectionable.[93] Yet the danger of "ironic evil" lies not only in its targeting of the "solid" good, but in its turning on itself, negating that which according to Hegel deserves to be negated. Since evil in its ironic form dissolves itself, it deprives us of the power and the opportunity to deny it; we must first reconstitute it, struggling against its self-targeting forces of dissolution, before it can then be denied. Irony destabilizes the category of evil, instills in us an uncertainty as to its distinguishing marks, calls into question its parameters and even its existence; and when evil does appear in a recognizable form, irony has the power to make it seem comical, thereby misleading us into thinking that it is really not to be taken so seriously. Explaining why he has given up his old horns and cloven hooves, Mephistopheles observes, "Refinement's making everybody slick, and so the devil too has been affected" (2,495–6).

Lewis's claim that the attractiveness of Mephistopheles derives from the presence of characteristics that are not properly diabolical occurs in conjunction with the judgment that the truly devilish impulse is exhibited in the figure of his human quarry.[94] In conformity with the tradition that identifies pride as the epitome of evil, he deems the transgressive protagonist, supposedly the more morally ambiguous character, to betray the more Satanic disposition.[95] Faust is the real devil. And yet he is ultimately saved. The portrayal of Mephistopheles as a charming trickster and the dénouement of the drama, in which the consummate egoist is whisked off to heaven, constitute a twofold subversion of the moral and religious position that Lewis seeks to uphold. Faust's longing to exhaust the mundane world, his refusal to content himself with his current station, and his pledge to dissipation lead not to perdition, as in previous accounts of the legend, but to salvation. What warrants the intervention of the angels to save this man? In the extent and depth of his immoral conduct, Goethe's Faust proves to be not inferior to Marlowe's Faustus, who suffers a brutal death, torn to pieces by the devils coming to drag his soul down to hell. What is redeemed in *Faust*, however, is not simply the individual, but the spirit of transgression that animates him. The Lord's pronouncement in the "Prologue in Heaven," acknowledging the inseparability of erring and striving, functions as an exculpation of Faust's deeds that he, in his omniscience, already sees in advance. Although his acts of errancy are themselves not commended, the spirit that gives rise to them, and of which they are the corollary, is vindicated. The triumph of the transgressor is assured at the outset of the play, not because he will cease to transgress, but because a life of restless activity remains worthy of approbation – a sentiment echoed in the proclamation of the angels in the concluding act that "for him whose striving never ceases / we can provide redemption" (11,936). But striving to what end? The aim is made subordinate to the activity. The comic-comedic finale of the "tragedy" does not mean, obviously, that Goethe offers a wholesale endorsement of his hero. For Goethe himself, the education of the spirit was an exercise in self-discipline and self-fashioning, one that necessitated limits and horizons; it is this ethic of self-imposed limits that lies at the core of his vaunted "Olympianism." Yet these limits, be it noted, come not from the outside, in the form of external commandments, but are grounded in the agent's own activities and ideals. In his *Essays in Criticism*, published more than three decades after Goethe's death, Matthew Arnold underscored the subversiveness of this orientation, which moves "from within outwards"; he writes:

> Goethe's profound, imperturbable naturalism is absolutely fatal to all routine thinking; he puts the standard, once for all, inside every man instead of outside him; when he is told, such a thing must be so, there is immense authority and custom in favour of its being so, it has been held to be so for a thousand years, he answers with Olympian politeness, "But *is* it so? is it so to *me*?" Nothing could be more really subversive of the foundations on which the old European order rested; and it may be remarked that no persons are so radically detached from this order, no persons so thoroughly modern, as those who have felt Goethe's influence most deeply.[96]

Goethe's vision of self-realization, the actualization of powers within, stands opposed to an ethic of obedience that condemns – sometimes to damnation – those who fail to adhere to commandments originating from without. His reservations about Faust are not ethical, at least not in a narrowly deontological sense, but existential. Faust's mode of comportment risks a dispersal of vital forces that Goethe recognized as imperilling his own ideal of equilibrium. But his transgressiveness is also an expression of these same forces. The movement "from within outwards," like the centrifugal tendency of energy in Blake's *The Marriage of Heaven and Hell*, liberates the self from inhibiting constraints.

The various reworkings of the Faust legend in the early nineteenth century testify to the attraction its hero exercised on the contemporary, Romantic imagination. Byron alone created an entire literary landscape populated with figures akin to Faust, sharing his world-weary discontent, his disregard for conventional morality, and his readiness to commune with dangerous forces. Among all his literary contemporaries, Goethe identified Byron most strongly with the daemonic.[97] A poet who showed a marked sensitivity for the depths and complexities of the Faustian soul, Byron lived the life of the transgressive artist – stories about which the

media of the day did much to popularize – and brought to life characters fashioned in his own defiant image. In his depiction of "the Satanic
school," Robert Southey asserted that its productions were "characterized
by a Satanic spirit of pride and audacious impiety, which still betrays the
wretched feeling of hopelessness wherewith it is allied."[98] Southey took
Byron to be the leader of the school, but it was actually his younger associ-
ate Shelley who was the more intransigent critic of hallowed pieties. In his
polemics against Christianity, he showed himself to be more belligerent
than Byron, less compromising, and less disposed to take refuge in irony.
He also went further in his vindication of Satan. In *A Defence of Poetry*,
Shelley proclaims:

> Nothing can exceed the energy and magnificence of the character of Satan in
> *Paradise Lost*. It is a mistake to suppose that he could ever have been intended
> for the popular personification of evil. Implacable hate, patient cunning and a
> sleepless refinement of device to inflict the extremest anguish on an enemy –
> these things are evil; and, although venial in a slave are not to be forgiven in a
> tyrant; although redeemed by much that ennobles his defeat in one subdued,
> are marked by all that dishonors his conquest in the victor. Milton's Devil as a
> moral being is as far superior to his God as one who perseveres in some purpose
> which he has conceived to be excellent in spite of adversity and torture is to one
> who in the cold security of undoubted triumph inflicts the most horrible re-
> venge upon his enemy, not from any mistaken notion of inducing him to repent
> of a perseverance in enmity but with the alleged design of exasperating him to
> deserve new torments.[99]

Whereas Blake suggested that Milton was of the devil's party without
knowing it, Shelley perceives the presence of a much more conscious par-
tisanship. But like Blake, what Shelley finds admirable in Milton's Satan
is his "energy," a vigour and tenacity in the face of daunting impediments
and obstacles. This celebration of defiance, with which we are by now well
familiar, is coupled, more interestingly, with an indictment of the creator.
For Shelley, the capacity to enter most intimately into the thoughts and
feelings of others is a distinguishing mark of both moral virtue and poetic
sensibility; conversely, what is inexcusable is precisely the refusal to sympathize and to commiserate; it is in this context that we need to understand his rejection of the Judaeo-Christian God. In his "Essay on the Devil

and Devils," Shelley expresses his indignation at the injustice of this malevolent deity, who seems to have given his creatures free will only "that he might excuse himself to his own conscience for tormenting and annoying these unfortunate spirits when they provoked him by turning out worse than he expected."[100] While it is difficult to find a human analogue to God's "very disinterested love of tormenting," Shelley discerns its closest approximation in the activities of "a troop of idle dirty boys" torturing animals.[101] To the extent to which the devil himself also engages in the tormenting of others, Shelley expresses a similar repugnance. But even here, he maintains that "the Devil has a better excuse, for, as he was entirely made by God, he can have no tendency or disposition the seeds of which were not originally planted by his creator."[102] Going still further in his exculpation of the devil, he proposes a rather curious account of his origins, in which after his fall from heaven, the devil still maintained his "benevolent and amiable disposition"; God, exasperated at the devil's heroic resolve in the face of the hellish torments to which he was subjected and seeing how vain any further infliction of suffering would be, employed his powers to bring about "an enduring and a terrible vengeance," namely by turning the devil's "good into evil."[103] Henceforth, the devil was compelled, "in spite of his better nature," to commit acts of wickedness; even as he continues to be "tortured with compassion and affection for those whom he betrays and ruins," he finds himself constrained to assume the role of tormentor.[104] Here, the devil appears as "the chief and the original victim" whereas God plays the role not only of tormentor, but even of corruptor.[105] The proud refusal to submit wholly to God, the will to transgress – what Southey calls the "spirit of pride and audacious impiety" – is the last remaining remnant of the devil's angelic goodness, the vestige of his virtue, not the fruition of his vice.[106]

Where transgression is decoupled from evil, evil is not thereby abolished; rather, it is displaced. In his reflections on human wickedness, Schopenhauer states that "no animal ever torments another for the sake of tormenting: but man does so, and it is this which constitutes the *diabolical* nature which is far worse than the merely bestial."[107] With Shelley, the rehabilitation of the transgressive Satan goes hand-in-hand with the demonizing of the tormentor God. It is not in disobedience but in the infliction of suffering that evil is to be located. In *The Marriage of Heaven and Hell*, suffering is not a significant structuring category; Blake's angels are instruments of restraint, not agents of torment. Offering a kind of im-manent critique, Blake operates within an existent moral and religious paradigm and subverts it by turning it inside out. Shelley, whose ethics is informed by the principles of British utilitarianism, takes up a stance external to the Christian tradition and seeks to batter it down from the outside. His diatribe against the cruelty of the deity offers a further blow, though from a different angle, to the Augustinian account of evil with which Blake's vision was also at odds. While his attack was shocking to his contemporaries on account of its irreligiosity, the moral sentiment that animated it, the intolerance of causing pain to others, was already on the ascendant. Although the sentiment finds clear conceptual expression in a strand of eighteenth-century consequentialism, it was not and is not con-fined to a particular philosophical school of thought. Indeed, even those philosophers committed to deontological ethics have increasingly turned towards discovering or providing moral grounds for not causing pain to others.[108]

Augustine enjoins us, as Christ teaches us, to love our neighbours, but that commandment does not entail a repudiation of retribution. The idea that the sufferings of Satan and the other fallen angels – in addition to those of innumerable damned human souls – should ulti-mately slacken and be alleviated strikes Augustine as inimical to divine justice. He thus contradicts, in *The City of God*, those misguided "com-passionate Christians," such as Origen, who entertain the possibility that damnation, instead of being eternal, might be only a temporary state.[109] Although the problem of theodicy has sometimes been pre-sented as a problem of reconciling the existence of God with the ex-istence of suffering in the world, this interpretation unduly inflates the importance of suffering as such without giving due consideration to the more important question of the identity of the sufferers. As Augustine explains, "what matters is the nature of the sufferer, not the nature of the sufferings."[110] The dilemma, with which we are confronted in the Book of Job, is not "why is there suffering?" – the question that guides and grounds the Buddhist tradition of moral philosophy – but, rather, "why does the good, God-fearing man suffer?" The fact that Job's afflic-tions are initially presented as the work of Satan, and only indirectly as the work of God, indicates an uncertainty about where ultimate respon-sibility for the misfortunes of the just and the pious resides. But even as later theologians struggled to account for the presence of suffering in this world, they simultaneously attributed to God the creation of hell, a world of eternal torment that surpasses, in both intensity and duration, anything to be found in the terrestrial sphere. Instead of being an objection to God's existence, this realm of suffering bolstered faith since it guaranteed that those who committed wrongs would be held accountable for their transgressions and rightly punished. On this view, while the presence of suffering in our world is not a mark against omnibenevolence, the absence of suffering in the world to come would indicate a deficiency in divine justice. The upholding of justice is equivalent to the upholding of a penal system of severe retribution.

Charles Taylor argues that "the hegemony of this juridical-penal model plays an important role in the later rise of unbelief, both in repelling people from the faith, and in modifying it in the direction of Deism."[111] Taylor's insight applies not only to changing religious convictions, but to a shift in moral value judgments about good and evil; when and where "this juridical-penal model" begins to offend moral sensibilities, the theological system that undergirds it falls into disrepute and becomes an object of scepticism. In Shelley's dialogue "A Refutation of Deism," the character Eusebes claims that "it is among men of genius and science that atheism alone is found."[112] The genius sees through the prejudices of the vulgar and subjects to critical scrutiny what others thoughtlessly accept without investigation. But this critical impetus is a support rather than the source of unbelief. Ultimately, what lies behind Shelley's brand of atheism is not a materialist ontology or a scepticist epistemology, but a moral vision, one grounded in sensitivity to suffering.

Shelley writes, in *A Defence of Poetry*, that "the great secret of morals is love," and that "a man, to be greatly good, must imagine intensely and comprehensively; he must put himself in the place of another and of many others; the pains and pleasures of his species must become his own."[113] For Shelley, the quality that makes a man "greatly good" is the same that makes him a great poet. The power of the imagination enables the movement out of ourselves towards another, a movement indispensable to poet and philanthropist alike. He even compares poetry to a form of "exercise" whereby the imaginative faculty strengthens itself and thus becomes more able to flex its moral muscle in realizing one of the chief ends of man, namely the love of others.[114] Against the contractive forces of prejudice and tyranny, the exercising of the imagination enables "the circumference of society" to expand; it ensures the furtherance of liberty and social solidarity alike.[115] It is important to note, in this context, that "Shelley's account of the imagination was originally developed as part of his moral philosophy, rather than of his aesthetics."[116] Through a repositioning of the role of the imagination, he seeks to articulate a defence of altruism and to rebut the motivational theory that all acts are the result of self-interest.[117] Even as he cleaves to the utilitarian ethic, he resists its prosaicism and its attempts to ground morality in individual advantage. Shelley's attribution of a heightened imaginative capacity to the poet, with an accompanying sensitivity to others' sorrows and joys, transforms a particular disposition and mode of comportment into a fundament of the literary spirit. His intolerance towards cruelty is not incidental to his reconceptualization of poetic genius, a moral supplement as it were to a finished aesthetic theory; rather, this reconceptualization emerges out of a specifically moral standpoint. The cruel individual remains locked up in himself, incapable of feeling his way into the soul of another, and this incapacity for self-transcendence marks him as the antipode of the poet, a figure who merits our veneration because he lifts us up to behold the beautiful and the good. An implacable enemy of injustice and prejudice, the poet stands opposed to both the pitiless man and the pitiless God. The punitive deity who torments the devil, and whose withered powers of empathy render him unable to commiserate with his suffering creatures, is – in addition to being a tyrannical despot – a figure of poetic deficiency.

Notwithstanding the moral failings of Satan, in their antagonism to the forces of repression there is a decided convergence between the poet and the rebel angel. But Shelley does not draw out, by virtue of this convergence, the poet's affinity for evil. The invocation of the wicked muse and the self-conscious delight in dreaming of doing evil, found in later decadent poets such as Baudelaire, finds no analogue here. On the contrary, we are told that "the greatest poets have been men of the most spotless virtue."[118] This alignment of the poet and the morally good may be read as a return to and reformulation of Shaftesbury's ideal of "the moral artist," whose inner harmony finds outward expression in his literary compositions. Yet the attempt to shield poetic genius from contamination with immorality foundered on the very success of the image of the genius as a rule-breaker. The associations between genius and transgression ensured that genius would continue to have resonances with evil so long as transgression was not disentangled from evil. Whether the genius assumed the role of a poet or a statesman, a composer or a general, he was henceforth seen as a figure who did not yield to the dictates of convention but pursued a course of action in accordance with his own impulses or rules of his own making. Even when the results were beneficial, bringing forth artistic masterpieces or contributing to national glory, the disregard for accepted mores was nonetheless recognized as potentially dangerous and disruptive to the social order. The energy that Blake and Shelley so admired in Milton's Satan and that Goethe saw as a hallmark of the daemonic has the power to liberate, but it can also bring about the destruction and subjection of those unfortunate enough to be in the path of its overwhelming bearer. In Balzac's *Père Goriot*, the criminal Vautrin – who is himself something of an evil genius – declares that "people bow their heads to a genius, they hate him, they try to drag him down, because he only takes, he doesn't give, but as long as he keeps going, people yield, they have no choice – in a word, if you can't bury him in the mud, you fall on your knees, you adore him."[119]

Even though we might balk at characterizations of criminals as evil geniuses, the discourse that enabled such comparisons has lost its power to unsettle. These theorizations of genius – let us confess it – are not terribly offensive or distressing to us. And this fact is itself worth pondering. According to Augustine, transgression stems from a moment of weakness; it is a falling away from the good due to our inability to remain upright. According to Blake, it is a manifestation of energy, an expression of the power to break through the fetters, whether social or spiritual, that bind us and keep us in a state of submission. The linking of transgression and potency, with which the discourse on genius – from Young to Goethe to the Romantics and beyond – is shot through, often occurs in the context of an appeal to the ideals of self-expression and liberty. But the rehabilitation of transgression remains partial insofar as the category cannot be wholly purged of its associations with things destructive and reprehensible; indeed, morally problematic aspects are occasionally foregrounded in drawing attention to the dangerous character of genius and the daemonic. The question then arises: if transgressive acts of liberation are expressions of potency, does the same apply to transgressive acts of wickedness? And if such acts do partake of potency, does that mean that they participate in a kind of greatness? We are much more at risk of falling into the trap of seeing evil in the guise of greatness than are those faithfully following in the footsteps of the Augustinian tradition, which demonstrates greater resistance to the "sublimification" of evil acts and evil-doers. This observation is meant not as a recommendation to re-adopt the standpoint of Augustine so as to obviate this danger, but to bring home the fact that the aestheticizing of evil, at least as it occurs in our contemporary context, is bound to a particular historical transformation in our image and evaluation of transgression. A meditation on the problem of evil's aesthetic status must not overlook the historical conditions that have made this problem a problem at all.

Chapter Two

Symbols of the Morally Bad

For those eighteenth-century literary critics who insisted on the necessity of normative rules in the practice of poetic composition, one of the dangers of unschooled genius was that it was liable to lapse into the grotesque. The fastidious advocates of French Neoclassicism perceived such a lapse in Shakespeare, whose garrulity and indifference to the classical unities they took to be evidence of his barbarism.[1] If unruliness and unfettered energy were characteristic of genius, then a lack of equipoise and a proclivity for the hyperbolic in works of genius would hardly be surprising – assuming that the transgressive character of the artist corresponded, in some fashion, to the transgressive character of his art. But it was also argued that by virtue of a certain psychic imbalance, the genius was privy to the darker recesses of the soul and thus the most able to provide an account of the dark side of human nature. Byron, whom Lady Caroline Lamb famously described as "mad, bad, and dangerous to know," came to exemplify the instantiation of this particular type of genius; his ability to lay bare the spiritual turmoil of his fictional heroes derived from the fact that they themselves were closely allied to his own psychological state, indeed were even semi-autobiographical.

In seeking out faithful representations of evil, are upright moralists more to be trusted or troubled souls who have an intimate relationship with that whereof they speak? Perhaps "the bad" have access to the relevant content, but are they in possession of the requisite judgment? Should we listen to the musings of "evil geniuses" for answers? The question of who is most well equipped to portray evil is tied to the yet more difficult question of how it ought to be portrayed. In the *Critique of the Power of*

Judgment, Kant notes that the beautiful and the good are often not found in conjunction with one another in actuality, but he insists that the beautiful still possesses a symbolic moral status. After identifying the beautiful as "the symbol of the morally good," he observes that "we often designate beautiful objects of nature or of art with names that seem to be grounded in a moral judging"; while the beautiful and the good should not be conflated, Kant finds merit in this transposition of attributes insofar as "taste as it were makes possible the transition from sensible charm to the habitual moral interest without too violent a leap."[2] If the beautiful is the symbol of the morally good, what then is the symbol of the morally bad? Ugliness has been seized upon as a likely candidate. And as with the disjunction between the beautiful and the good, the failure of ugliness and evil to go hand in hand in the phenomenal world should be expected; indeed, the gulf separating aesthetic appearance and moral reality has proved to be a particularly fruitful topic of literary exposition. In *The Picture of Dorian Gray,* Wilde shows this incongruity in the figure of the novel's protagonist, whose hideously disfigured soul lies concealed beneath an agelessly beautiful exterior. At the same time, our conviction that these two ought to align with one another has exercised such a hold on the imagination that even those who fancy themselves to be sober and scientific truth-seekers have fallen prey to it. Whereas Wilde exposes appearance's lack of correspondence to reality, leading social theorists and alienists of his day, inspired by the emergent field of anthropometrics, were intent on uncovering the telltale signs of moral depravity that would allow the discerning scientific expert to identify depraved types at a single glance. The long-standing prejudice that the interior moral state of the evil-doer finds a correspondence with his exterior form was given a veneer of scientific respectability with the flourishing of nineteenth-century physiognomy, phrenology, and criminology. One need only recall Lombroso's depiction of "the born criminal" as an ugly physical specimen marked by asymmetry of features and the exhibition of regressive, even proto-human bodily traits.[3] In Bram Stoker's *Dracula,* we are told that "the Count is a criminal and of criminal type. Nordau and Lombroso would so classify him."[4]

We should be wary of confusing symbols with the things they symbolize. Yet to say that evil should not be confounded with its symbol or symbols does not mean that the aesthetic modes from which these symbols are derived are necessarily inadequate to representations of it. Aesthetic depictions of evil may be highly worked over, a result of deliberate and self-conscious artistic refashioning, but they can also elucidate the experience of evil, the responses that the morally bad excites and that abstract treatments are sometimes inclined to gloss over or to dismiss in their subordination of percepts to concepts. And lest we imagine that this amounts to little more than a story of an individual's personal impressions, it should be added that inspecting evil in light of different aesthetic categories facilitates an apprehension of its characteristics, thereby enriching our conceptualizations. In *The Origins of Totalitarianism*, Arendt points to "the grotesque haphazardness with which concentration-camp victims were chosen in the perfected terror state."[5] The haphazardness of this process of selection occurs in conjunction with an elaborate system of classification, a hierarchy of categories designating the victims; she remarks that "the gruesome and grotesque part of it was that the inmates identified themselves with these categories, as though they represented a last authentic remnant of their juridical person."[6] Arendt's references to the "grotesque" character of the camps are meant to draw out the senselessness of a process of dehumanization, to show the inadequacy of attempts to interpret this process with reference to "common sense" or some sort of utilitarian logic. Moreover, the portrayal of the atrocity of the camps in terms of an aesthetic of the grotesque captures evil's connections to distortion, its active deformation of human beings that itself stems from a twisted ideology and political system. In the next chapter, I explore the tensions internal to Arendt's representation of what she calls "radical evil." For the moment, I simply want to note that aesthetic treatments of evil as ugly, whether historical or fictional, should not be dismissed out of hand as if they were nothing more than expressions of subjective valuation or instances of a confusion of symbol and symbolized. This defence should be taken not as an endorsement of the aestheticizing of evil, but as a call to attentiveness in reflecting on evil's aesthetic modalities. The term "aestheticize" itself must be employed with caution since its suffix suggests a kind of making, which might lead us to imagine that aestheticizing is inevitably an act of invention and, by extension, an act of misrepresentation. When I use the term, it is with the inventive dimension very much in mind. Ultimately, however, "the aesthetics of evil" is a more helpful terminological constellation than "the aestheticizing of evil" since it does not decide, in advance, in favour of either discovery or invention but leaves open the possibility that there might be something present in evil that is already aesthetic waiting to be discovered.

Going forward, I want to give thought to two particular aesthetic categories – two distinct forms or species of ugliness – as they relate to evil, namely the grotesque and the disgusting. Rather than treating these categories abstractly, divorcing them from their historical articulations and then assessing the extent to which evil happens to or fails to align with them, it is more instructive to note the specific reappropriations and redeployments to which they have been subjected in the representation of evil. These need to be understood as intertwined with an intensifying transgressiveness in the modern period, some of the anti-Augustinian features of which were discussed in the previous chapter. Given the historical character of such an approach, it seems only apt to consider these developments with reference to the Hegelian philosophy, whose treatment of aesthetics distinguishes itself by its preoccupation with historical transformations and by its opposition to "abstraction." This engagement is further justified by the fact that it belonged to Karl Rosenkranz to first subject the ugly to a sustained philosophical interrogation. In the mid-nineteenth century, we see the emergence of a discourse on art and literary criticism that makes room for the ugly and takes it seriously as an object of aesthetic analysis and criticism, and Rosenkranz's neo-Hegelian *Aesthetics of Ugliness*, published in 1853, marks a watershed in this respect. The work begins with the claim that "if the idea of beauty is to be considered, an investigation of ugliness is inseparable from it. The concept of ugliness, of negative beauty, thus is a part of aesthetics."[7] Rosenkranz not only expands the scope of aesthetics through the addition of a category that was, prior to his work, marginal to it; by virtue of this inclusion, he initiates a reconceptualization of the field of enquiry. To speak in a quasi-Hegelian idiom, which was Rosenkranz's own, the quantitative enrichment of the concept eventuates in its qualitative transformation.

More than a century and a half after Rosenkranz's intervention, many today still treat the term "aestheticize" as if it were synonymous with the term "beautify"; it is this synonymy that often underlies warnings that we should not aestheticize evil. The treatment of evil as grotesque and disgusting seems to offer, no doubt, a much less morally offensive and politically dangerous alternative than does its beautification. And yet the most radical and innovative authors of the post-Enlightenment literature of transgression did not shy away from the more aesthetically displeasing aspects of evil. Their symbolizations of immorality are simultaneously conventional, drawing upon a long-standing tradition that equates evil and ugliness, and revolutionary, turning these aspects into marks of evil's power and seductiveness. A look at the transgressive writings of Beckford, Sade, and Baudelaire illuminates how their appropriations of the ugly disrupt and disable traditional moralistic uses of it. None of these authors was averse to the outlandish, and so their treatments of evil might strike us, at times, as bizarre and disconnected from the world with which we are familiar. In subsequent chapters, I devote attention to the aesthetic status of evil in works describing actual events, but prior to this focus on representations of historical phenomena, an engagement with fantastical narratives allows us to see the untethered imagination at work, the resulting images of which have spawned, in turn, a host of literary and filmic offspring. There are moments in which the three aforementioned writers present evil as something beautiful, and this manner of portraying it has proved resilient. Sartre writes, with reference to the semi-autobiographical writings of Jean Genet, that "the Beautiful and Evil are one and the same thing."[8] That does not mean, though, that ugliness is out of the picture; Sartre himself refers to the power of Genet's writings to induce vomiting or, to be more precise, to induce the feeling of wanting to vomit so as to be rid of what one has read. While the act of beautification is usually granted the central role in treatments of the aestheticizing of evil, it occupies a subordinate place in my analysis. Compared to beautification, the reinscription of ugliness involves, with its paradoxes and dialectical reversals, a more counter-intuitive operation and a more interesting one. A destabilizing procedure through which the symbols of the morally bad acquire new meanings and resonances, such a subversion does not stop at elevating evil by linking it to beauty, but goes further in embracing evil's ugliness.

Grotesque Subversions

The grotesque has not always been a welcome guest in the house of philosophy. Among those who prize the rigour of the concept, such a figure of distortion tends to be met with a haughty reserve. In his lectures on the philosophy of fine art, delivered at the University of Berlin in the 1820s,

Hegel uses the label "grotesque" in a derogatory sense; it not only serves as a descriptive term but also expresses discomfort and even distaste. Since Hegel neglects to provide a sustained exposition of the grotesque in the lectures, to glean his meaning it is necessary to examine his employment of the designation with reference to works of art and to the aesthetic sensibilities of different peoples and eras. Although some scholars have taken the grotesque to be pre-eminently modern and Western, Hegel finds the most striking instances of it in the Orient, particularly in the "fantastic symbolism" of ancient India.[9] Marred by distortion and excess, Indian art, according to Hegel, indiscriminately mixes domains that ought to be conceptually distinguished and separated. In its hybridity – a term that Hegel himself does not employ, but which encapsulates a principal characteristic of the grotesque as he conceives it – the grotesque mingles the sacred and the profane to the detriment of both. Inverting the proper order of things, it raises the lowest to the highest and degrades the highest to the lowest. Its affinity with excess derives from a tendency to pursue the representation of objects to an extreme, losing itself in a chaotic proliferation. The longing for infinity, translated into the realm of the sensuous, manifests itself in the production of disfigured plastic and poetic forms – "to reach universality, the individual figures are wildly tugged apart from one another into the colossal and grotesque."[10] The impossibility of capturing infinity in the mode of sensuous representation, which is necessarily bounded and finite, condemns Indian art, which wrongheadedly undertakes this task, to "a monstrous extravagance."[11] Taking no pains to conceal his aversion to the results of this procedure, Hegel explains that in Indian art "there is the most extravagant exaggeration of size, alike in the spatial figure and in temporal immeasurability, as well as the multiplication of one and the same characteristic."[12] After noting that "Indian art in its excess" attains to the level of neither the sublime nor the properly symbolic, he also denies the appellation of the beautiful to it – notwithstanding certain superficial charms present in Indian poetry.[13] He concludes this damning assessment with the assertion that "Indian art does not go beyond the grotesque intermixture of the natural and the human, so that neither side gets it right, and both are reciprocally vitiated."[14]

Hegel's unsympathetic verdict derives, in part, from his revulsion towards the plastic forms of Indian sculpture and from his impatience with the apparent absurdity of Indian poetic compositions, yet it cannot be reduced to a matter of aesthetic appreciation – or a lack thereof. Unfavourable aesthetic judgments are interwoven in the lectures with critical assessments of the Indian people's religion and morality, and this moving between seemingly distinct levels constitutes one of the contributions of Hegel's aesthetics. According to Hegel, the artwork of a people does not stand in isolation from its morality, its political constitution, and its religion; all of these must be understood in relation to one another since they are all expressions of the spirit of the nation. He affirms that "truth in art, like truth in general, requires the harmony of inner and outer, of concept and result."[15] The deficiencies of Indian art stem from a too fertile imagination, but beyond that, they manifest the failings of Indian civilization as a whole in its inability to bring inner and outer into harmony; this inability is evident in the people's conception of God, their political institutions, and their moral precepts. In trying to make sense of India's "fantastic symbolism," Hegel thus devotes much less attention to individual works of Indian art and literature than to the religious consciousness of its people. He argues that through its naturalization of the spirit, Indian religion obscures the difference between the free domain of the spirit and the realm of nature, which lacks the power of self-determination. This confusion gives rise to a frightful inversion, wherein human beings, the bearers of spirit, degrade themselves before nature and, in acts of theriolatry, even prostrate themselves before animals and images of gods depicted in the likeness of animals. The attendant failure to attain ethical life, due to the lack of recognition of spirit's autonomy, leads the people of India to produce artworks in which the distinctions between spirit and nature are occluded. On the basis of the travel reports of the British, whose accuracy he blithely accepts, Hegel declares that, among the Hindus, "cheating, stealing, robbing, murdering" are habitual; indeed, "deceit and cunning" are their defining character traits.[16] For Hegel, the primitive aesthetic of Indian culture mirrors the primitive morality of the people; the grotesque corresponds to their inner moral turpitude since it is, in fact, an externalization of it.

This association of the grotesque with the Orient traded on long-standing racist tropes and prejudices, to which Hegel gave a philosophical imprimatur.[17] Against the Oriental aesthetic, the art of ancient Greece, with its harmonization of interior and exterior, was held up as the antithetical exemplar. Following in the footsteps of Winckelmann, and in keeping with the philhellenism of the day, Hegel discovers in the sculpted human form of Greek statuary the plastic ideal brought to perfection. After this age of classical art, the age of romantic art – a rubric Hegel uses to include European art from the medieval period to his own time – shows a dissolution of classical equipoise. In Hegel's historical schema, nineteenth-century Europe stands for a higher stage of development than fifth-century Greece since the former has more fully realized the task of the spirit; in its religious consciousness and its political organization, the modern age achieves a degree and a kind of human freedom unknown to antiquity. Yet the triumph of freedom, with its accompanying loosening of conventional strictures on art, results in aesthetic losses as much as aesthetic gains. Greek art shows the perfect coincidence of spirit and form, a harmonization unattained in the Orient; but contemporary European art and literature also lack this ideal unity, not because of a spiritual deficiency, as was the case with India, but because the spirit has now outstripped any form that would be adequate to it. Hegel explains that "art in Greece has become the supreme expression of the Absolute, and Greek religion is the religion of art itself, while the later romantic art, although it is art, yet points already to a higher form of consciousness than art can provide."[18] As a result of this development, the modern age offers a surprising moment of convergence with a superseded stage of history. Romantic art, it turns out, has a curious affinity with the grotesque. But whereas Hegel confounds Indian art and the grotesque, he declines to make such a reductive equivalence in regard to art in the modern West. And when he does characterize contemporary works as such, his impatience with them is evident; Hegel notes that "in most recent times what has especially become the fashion is the inner unstable distraction which runs through all the most repugnant dissonances and has produced a temper of atrocity and a grotesqueness of irony."[19] He singles out E.T.A. Hoffmann as an author with a predilection for this form of irony. The presence of irony differentiates the modern European from the ancient Indian grotesque; in the former case, distortion and excess are embraced with deliberate intent and a marked, sometimes even advertised self-consciousness. Hegel's pronouncement about the artistic tendency of "recent times" immediately follows his assertion that evil, on account of its inherent repugnance, does not lend itself well to artistic representation. He judges the devil in particular as being "aesthetically impracticable" since what he represents stands opposed to the affirmation of the spirit that art ought to take as its object.[20] Hegel's pronouncement is all the more striking given the fact that, during his lifetime, the devil was becoming an increasingly popular literary character.

This period also witnessed a mushrooming of literature devoted to the Orient, a narrative setting that, in keeping with Hegel's own associations, proved particularly fruitful for the depiction of the grotesque. With this literature, the Orient retains the repellent characteristics Hegel attributes to it even as it functions as a site of fantasy, one in which the transgressive desires of Western writers and readers can be played out without the danger of being too closely implicated in them.[21] These desires can always be disavowed and – bolstered with the evidence of travel reports and other ethnographic data – ascribed to the decadent people described in the narrative. The attribution of unrestrained eroticism to the peoples of the East expresses not so much a fear of the moral depravity of the other – though it certainly does function as a mechanism of cultural differentiation – as it indicates a projective fantasy of breaking free from the social conventions and sexual constraints that are normally binding. The exotic foreign locale, in which impermissible desires are staged, serves as a sort of testing ground for the transgressive imagination, whereby native European traditions and prohibitions are called into question and subverted. The grotesque acquires a different function in the modern European context than it has in Indian art, at least as Hegel characterizes it. In the latter case, the grotesque, reflecting the religious and spiritual condition of the culture in which it appears – a culture locked in a stage of historical development superseded long ago – remains passive and ultimately static; in the former, the grotesque possesses a corrosive potency that, deployed to subversive ends, actively undermines the existing order of things.

The bringing together of evil and the grotesque finds various Orientalist expressions in the eighteenth century, among which William Beckford's *Vathek*, first published in 1786, distinguishes itself by virtue of the boldness of its imaginative vision. In its reworking of the Faust legend, transposed to ninth-century Persia, Beckford's novella takes the world of Scheherazade as a stage on which to dramatize the headlong descent into evil. Like his Germanic cousin, the caliph Vathek longs for the infinite, but unlike the protagonist of the original Faust chapbook and Marlowe's tragedy, his pleasure-seeking attains such excess as to appear comical. The caliph, tasked with the defence of the Islamic faith, shows little inclination to fulfil his duties in his assigned role as

Mahomet's vicegerent on earth. He occupies his time, instead, with the attempted satisfaction of his many appetites, a vain endeavour since they prove quite insatiable. In his impatient desire to know the arcane secrets of nature and to augment his power thereby, he enters into a pact with "the Giaour," a strange visitant to Samarah, the capital city of Vathek's kingdom. Renouncing Mahomet as the Giaour demands, Vathek undertakes a journey with an enormous entourage to a subterranean palace, where he hopes to attain the superhuman powers promised to him. The wilful embrace of evil, hastened by his mother Carathis, a godless Greek well versed in the dark arts, and his love-interest Nouronihar, culminates in the trio's damnation in the aforementioned palace, which turns out to be not the hoped-for reward for their abjuration of the faith, but the site of eternal punishment.

In its portrayal of excess, *Vathek* moves back and forth between the ridiculous and the horrific. The protagonist's sacrifice of the fifty most beautiful youths of Samarah to the blood-thirsty Giaour constitutes his most extreme act of butchery. Even here, however, the descriptive mode leaves the reader unsure as to what response the author means to evoke. Many of the crimes of Vathek and Carathis are so beyond the pale as to lapse into farce, and this constitutes one aspect of their grotesque character. Moreover, the presentation of their atrocities in a detached voice seems intended to make it permissible for readers to be amused at their perpetration. In its skilful employment of this device, *Vathek* draws together the irony that Hegel saw as characteristic of the grotesque in modern literature with the wild excess he discerned in the art of the Orient.

Vathek suffers from an insatiable appetite for food and drink as well as an unquenchable thirst for knowledge. Both his gluttony and his zeal for science stem from the same impulse, which animates all of his actions, namely an intemperate will to transgress all limits. Ultimately, it is the desire to know the forbidden that leads to his doom – "for, of all men, he was the most curious."[22] Standing atop the pinnacle of a tower modelled on the Tower of Babel, he learns from the configuration of the planets that a foreigner will soon visit Samarah and initiate "the most marvellous adventures."[23] The "extraordinary personage, from a country altogether unknown" turns out to be the Giaour with whom Vathek will make an unholy pact.[24] The villain, who later informs Vathek that he is "an Indian; but, from a region of India, which is wholly unknown," is described as "a man so abominably hideous that the very guards, who arrested him, were forced to shut their eyes."[25] With his protuberant belly, bulging eyes, oversized mouth, and exaggerated facial expressions, the Giaour typifies the Rabelaisian grotesque body as Mikhail Bakhtin characterizes it. When he visits the palace, his obnoxious pronouncements, boorish behaviour, and boundless appetite for food and drink prove too much for the patience of the caliph, who unseats him with a swift kick to the backside. What follows from this assault is a scene of cartoonish absurdity, in which the members of the court take turns kicking at the Giaour, who curls up into a ball that passes from one assailant to the next; soon, the whole city participates in this endeavour, seized with a fury to kick the rolling foreigner as he bounces through the streets. The narrator explains the transformation of the community, in which all are overtaken with an irrepressible urge, as due to a mysterious possession by an "invisible power."[26] When the frenzy passes, Vathek expresses regret for having maltreated his guest, who was his best hope for attaining his fantastic desires, and holds a nightly vigil in hope of the Indian's return.

Here as elsewhere, the wicked are shown to behave in a manner both buffoonish and bizarre. To be sure, the good do not fare much better. Yet the prevalence of the ridiculous in the text, sparing neither the pious nor the depraved, does not preclude a particular intimacy between evil and the grotesque. If transgression, understood as a refusal to adhere to the rules or to recognize one's place in the order of things, is constitutive of evil, then the representation of evil in the mode of the grotesque may capture an important aspect of it. In the *Inferno*, Dante describes Lucifer as a figure of degradation and impotence, notwithstanding his enormous size. The hirsute devil with his flapping bat-like wings, his six tearing eyes, and his blood-spattered mouths evokes repugnance. His three faces – one red, one yellow, and one black – are meant as a grotesque inversion of the Holy Trinity, and through this depiction Dante shows us, in good Augustinian fashion, evil's derivative nature and the debased condition of those who fall prey to it. The poet uses the grotesque in the service of a moral and aesthetic project that celebrates the good and the beautiful and that mocks evil for its distance from them. Likewise, in *The Screwtape Letters*, Lewis's portrayal of the demons in hell as both bureaucrats and ravenous monsters who devour one another seeks to deprive them of the sublimity the Romantics invested in the Satanic. In his intimations of the elder Screwtape gobbling up his neophyte nephew, Lewis draws upon the medieval grotesque with its depictions of demons as voracious eaters, as found in such works as *Tundale's Vision* and Bosch's *The Garden of Earthly Delights*.[27] Noting the close alignment between eating and the grotesque during the Middle Ages and the Renaissance, Bakhtin emphasizes the festive and celebratory dimensions of excessive indulgence in food and drink.[28] But while the grotesque may function as a celebration of the body and its powers, it can also serve as a reminder of the corruptibility of the flesh, the baseness of bodily appetites, and the perversions of the spirit. In opposition to the regenerative aspects of the carnivalesque, which Bakhtin valorizes, the grotesque in *Vathek* instantiates a state of corruption, wherein hunger leads not to replenished life but to destruction.

Representing evil as grotesque undermines it, bringing out its departure from the measure and harmony exhibited in the good. However, as Beckford's novella demonstrates, such a treatment can also be used to remake evil into something frivolous, where the divergence from right action elicits the laughter of indulgence. Here, what ought to be condemned in deadly earnest becomes a matter of amusement, an object of play. And where sin ceases to be taken seriously, then it has already lost its hold on our conscience. The mixture of the playful and the sinister in the grotesque makes it a particularly unstable category, one that readily lends itself to subversive ends.[29] Transgression, with its affinity for excess and its crossing of limits, finds its sensuous analogue in an aesthetic that freely plays with the contours of form and delights in their exaggeration. In the case of *Vathek*, its stylistic extravagances and zest for the hyperbolic are due not only to the influence of fanciful Oriental tales on its author and his conscious attempt to reproduce the mannerisms of the *Arabian Nights*; they are also expressions of his "rebellious, non-submissive nature."[30]

In medieval morality plays, the representation of the devil and the personified vices as figures of ridicule was intended to expose the debased status of evil. In Beckford's work, the representation of the wilful caliph as ridiculous makes us ask ourselves whether the precepts he violates really warrant being taken so seriously. In the penultimate paragraph of *Vathek*, the narrator declares:

> Such was, and such should be, the punishment of unrestrained passions and atrocious deeds! Such shall be, the chastisement of that blind curiosity, which

would transgress those bounds the wisdom of the Creator has prescribed to human knowledge; and such the dreadful disappointment of that restless ambition, which, aiming at discoveries reserved for beings of a supernatural order, perceives not, through its infatuated pride, that the condition of man upon earth is to be – humble and ignorant.[31]

The "atrocious deeds" remain unspecified, and the concluding indictment makes no mention of lives lost. Instead of cataloguing Vathek's most violent crimes, such as his murder of the youths of Samarah, the summative moral of the story singles out the desire for knowledge as the source of downfall. But the recommendation of ignorance, so antithetical to the spirit of the Enlightenment, rings more than a little hollow. It makes it seem as if the alternative were between contented ignorance and a Satanic bargain. Such a judgment is not alien to the Augustinian tradition, with its suspicion of curiosity and its denunciation of pride, but in the mouth of the tale's narrator, it seems dubious at best. Our sense of the implausibility of the pious finale is only augmented by the last sentence of the work, in which we are told that "the despised Gulchenrouz passed whole ages in undisturbed tranquility, and in the pure happiness of childhood."[32] Given Beckford's own erotic predilections, the youth Gulchenrouz might serve as a viable love object, but are we really to take this timorous Ganymede as an exemplar worthy of emulation? The misalignment between the moralistic conclusion and the narrative preceding it, with its almost palpable delight in the pursuit of the extreme, has itself something of the ironic grotesque.[33]

The irony of the narrative undoes anything solid that we as readers might hold onto and use to orient ourselves. Hegel observes that irony, in addition to occupying itself with the frivolous, "likes to delight especially in villains"; the source of this inclination to the villainous rests, in part, on irony's likeness to evil, as Hegel conceives it, insofar as both are devoid of positive content and participate in an indiscriminate negation.[34] Even in Hegel's contemptuous dismissal of the ironic consciousness, there remains a danger in it since it threatens to release the negative from its careful confinement in his own integrative system, one wherein it finds its proper place and function. Disparaging "this art of annihilating everything everywhere," which betrays "the aspect of inner inartistic lack of restraint," his characterization of irony's unleashing of the negative as it occurs in recent works of European literature strangely parallels his account of Indian art, with its reduction of difference to identity and its pursuit of the empty infinite.[35] The flight from finitude exhibited in the Indian grotesque mirrors modern irony's negation of all finite forms. These two tendencies lend themselves, paradoxically, to a synthesis of sorts, albeit one rent with internal fissures. With its joining of the hyperbolic and the ironic, Beckford's *Vathek* moves exuberantly in two opposing directions; combining outward expansion and inward negation, evil flippantly transgresses moral strictures and then, more flippantly still, dissolves itself as if it were nothing to be taken seriously. In its more ludic varieties, the operation can be so successful that, at the end of it, we as readers are not sure whether what we have been reading about even warrants being designated as evil. And perhaps it does not – but there lies the rub. Prankish treatments of evil can help to free us from the complacencies of convention, leading us to the realization that what we thought of as morally bad was merely a matter of moral prejudice to be overcome or discarded, but they can also disorient and cause us to lose our moral bearings. In its more egregious forms, irony may be mobilized to belittle the sufferings of victims, to reduce the infliction of lasting harm to a joke or a matter of sport in which we are licensed to find amusement.

The comic surfaces briefly in Beckford's descriptions of acts of torment, but it is more pronounced in the depiction of acts of transgression. Vathek longs to know the secrets of the superlunary realm, but this is coupled with all too earth-bound desires, in whose thrall he often finds himself. In a moment of melancholy at the beginning of the novella, he briefly loses his interest in food so that "of the three hundred dishes that were daily placed before him, he could taste of no more than thirty-two."[36] Shortly thereafter, his desire for food yields to an unquenchable thirst; as he crawls on the ground, his receiving mouth, likened to a funnel, takes in draughts of cold water without pause in a manner reminiscent of Gargantua. Whereas Carathis, "being chastity in the abstract," shows a fixity of purpose in her "chaste" pursuit of forbidden wisdom, Vathek lacks this attentiveness and readily falls prey to the charms of the objects laid before him.[37] In those moments when one appetite fails him, it is because another, stronger one has dislodged it. Excess here appears as the product of impotence, as the incapacity to resist external stimuli, and the end result is quite fittingly an image of the transgressor laid low. But the narrative also shows Vathek and Carathis as initiators of destruction, powerful agents who fearlessly pursue the forbidden and who run roughshod over those in their way. Meanwhile, the pious and well-meaning characters are uniformly ineffectual, weaklings or dupes who allow themselves to be trampled, sometimes quite literally. The grotesque, figured as an aesthetic of excess, can indicate both deficiency and potency, both an inability to remain within the contours of proper form and an energy that outstrips the form that confines it; form means, in this context, established rules of good taste as well as the disciplining rules of moral conduct. On account of its labile power status, the grotesque proves more indeterminate than the sublime; there are moments in which, in its transgressing of limits, it even gropes at the sublime before tumbling into the ridiculous. And this tumble can itself be a source of pleasure.

In *Vathek*, the transgressive imagination functions as a liberating force, sweeping us along in a narrative that revels in the violation of moral conventions and readerly expectations; this holds even where the transgressive protagonists themselves appear as objects of mockery. The affirmation of the grotesque, the delight in evil's disfigured and disfiguring manifestations, releases us from the shackles of convention and allows us to find amusement not only at convention's expense but in the aesthetic that enables this release. Those critics who have discerned heroic qualities in Vathek and Carathis have been inclined to read their ludicrousness as extrinsic rather than essential to their characters. Against this reading, the argument for the inseparability of the audacity and the absurdity of their ventures hits closer to the mark. But the mockery of the transgressors does not amount to a condemnation of transgression as such.[38] The parodic, in its power to desacralize, to make the holy appear ridiculous, constitutes one of evil's most effective tools of subversion. Luther suggests that "the best way to drive out the devil, if he will not yield to texts of Scripture, is to jeer and flout him, for he cannot bear scorn."[39] But even if such scorn from the devout wounds the devil, he himself makes, in turn, good use of jeering and flouting in his degradation of the holy. At times the devilish trickster does not spare himself in the act of parodic degradation; with a droll earthiness, he demeans the divine and brings the sacred down to his own level of profanity. The authors of the emergent transgressive literature of the eighteenth century pursue a similar undertaking. They do not need to exalt evil to make it inviting; when good and evil are reduced to the same plane, when they have both become objects of mockery, then good has already been laid low and evil has already emerged victorious.

It is noteworthy, however, that there remains a pivotal character in *Vathek* who does not suffer the indignity of the narrator's lampoons. Whereas the transgressor, Vathek, and the corruptor, the Giaour, are depicted in the mode of the grotesque, Beckford portrays Eblis, the ruler of hell's torments, more earnestly. Sitting upon his throne of fire in the subterranean palace, Eblis, with his cold delight in the sufferings of the damned, has nothing laughable about him. In medieval iconography, the devil, combining characteristics of the cloven-hooved goat and the winged angel, appears as a kind of malformation that does not properly belong to the realm of either the animalistic or the angelic. Beckford consciously departs from this tradition of the diabolical grotesque in his portrait of Eblis, who, assuming the aspect of a majestic young man, is neither a parodic caricature nor a monstrous hybrid. And while the field of transgression bears the marks of the burlesque, all traces of the comic vanish in the place of torment, over which Eblis presides. Should the genuinely disturbing vision of subterranean punishment, which Borges characterized as "the first truly atrocious Hell in literature," be taken as evidence of the serious nature of Vathek's transgressions, so farcical in their appearance yet still worthy of punishment?[40] Or does it indicate that while the excesses of the sybarite are, in fact, merely comical, the subjection to intense suffering is no laughing matter?

It should not be forgotten at this point that Beckford's own life was hardly that of a humble self-denier. Indeed, his undertakings as a procurer of artworks and as a builder of an extravagantly palatial estate at Fonthill echo those of his damned protagonist.[41] A voluptuary who put little stock in the conventions of the time, Beckford led a hedonistic lifestyle, which, with its rumored sexual exploits, was sufficiently scandalous to thwart any political ambitions he might have had – his affluence and social status notwithstanding. But one need not look to biographical parallels outside the text. The caliph's pleasure palace corresponds to the writer's literary masterpiece. Beckford fashions a lush, colourful world, in which the reader is greeted with a profusion of flowers, fabrics, gemstones, and mouth-watering delicacies. An immersive aesthetic experience, in which sights, sounds, and smells are intermingled, these rich descriptions – almost psychedelic in their vibrancy – invite the reader to be absorbed into a world of sensuous delights. The master of the grotesque also possesses a keen eye for beauty and the temptations it arouses.

Ugliness has often been interpreted as a kind of privation or lack of beauty, but the grotesque partakes of excess. It can even temporarily align itself with the beautiful, driving it to such an extreme so as to make it unravel. An aesthetic mode well suited to the challenging of existing codes and standards, its ubiquity in Gothic literature must be understood in relation to its transgressive dimension. Gothic literature makes use of exotic and medieval settings, but some of its most popular exemplars – including *Frankenstein*, *Wuthering Heights*, *Strange Case of Dr. Jekyll and Mr. Hyde*, and *Dracula* – are staged in the contemporary Occident. Foregoing the insulations of geographical space and the passage of centuries, these works bring the monstrous home to Western modernity. In Matthew Lewis's *The Monk*, set in Madrid during the Inquisition, the scene of action skirts the worlds of the medieval and the modern, the magical and the rational; with a setting at once recognizably foreign and uncannily familiar, the narrative incites readers to delight in this world's alien otherness and to be offended when the resemblances strike too close to home. Coleridge, in his review of *The Monk*, observes that Lewis's novel degrades "by blending, with an irreverent negligence, all that is most awfully true in religion with all that is most ridiculously absurd in superstition."[42] This mixing of the high and the low was the same charge that Hegel levelled at Indian religion, but here it serves not to reflect the existing moral order, but to disrupt it. Sade was more well disposed to this aspect of *The Monk* than was Coleridge, yet he felt that Lewis's reliance on the supernatural risked "forfeiting the reader's credulity."[43] For Sade, one of the principal tasks of the novelist was to reveal "the nature of man," evident in those moments when human beings remove their public masks and retreat into the private realm.[44] Where the fantastic gains the upper hand, the novel's potential to provide psychological and philosophical insights into human nature is undermined, as is its potential to effect a change in the sentiments and morals of its readers.

Much of the potency of the grotesque in Sade's work is due to the realism with which scenes of excess are portrayed; free from the taint of the supernatural, whose presence might have the effect of placing its violence and debauchery at a remove, his fiction gives us a world turned upside down in the evaluations it proposes even as it aims to make plausible the incidents portrayed. His writings explicitly urge readers to adopt the principles espoused and to imitate the behaviours depicted; in *Philosophy in the Boudoir*, the recommendation that mothers place the work in the hands of their daughters expresses the wish that, through dissemination, the fictional will become factual. In his *Psychopathia Sexualis*, first published in 1886, Krafft-Ebing defines sadism as "the experience of sexual pleasurable sensations (including orgasm) produced by acts of cruelty, bodily punishment afflicted on one's own person or when witnessed in others, be they animals or human beings."[45] A pronounced cruelty distinguishes all of Sade's heroes, and they all find the act of harming and humiliating others to be a source of sexual arousal. Nonetheless, this aspect of their psychic constitution cannot be taken to stand for the whole personality of either these characters or their author. Such a metonymic reduction neglects to consider that cruelty functions only as one element among others in the psyche of Sadean protagonists and that it actually occupies a subordinate position in relation to another, still deeper impulse guiding their actions and structuring their thinking. The protagonists of Sade combine all the vices within themselves – unless, like Justine, they embody the virtues, for which they are relentlessly punished. In *Juliette*, the novel's eponymous heroine is simultaneously transgressor, corruptor, and tormentor. And no one would deny the malice that motivates her violent undertakings. But it is ultimately in transgression, rather than in cruelty, that she and Sade's other literary creations find their true *raison d'être*; there are moments when their exploits do not result in the immediate harm of any particular individual, but these actions invariably involve some contravention of an established rule or moral imperative, the violation of which produces immense satisfaction.

Sade shows a particular proclivity for profanation. His atheistic libertines are fixated on the deity whose existence they deny; in the climaxes of their most intense orgasmic pleasures, they augment their delights with blasphemous utterances execrating the divinity. God is never far from their thoughts since he embodies all the principles they are intent on violating. Not surprisingly, the convent is a favoured site of debauchery in Sade's works. Turning a house of God into a scene of depravity has a special allure for the depraved imagination, and the realization of this fantasy of contaminating the high with the low is experienced as a treasured victory for the libertine spirit. Copulating among the corpses of former abbesses and nuns of the convent, Juliette's preceptors take the Lord's name in vain as they engage in acts of sodomy. The affair in which Juliette is initiated into the arts of torture centres around the violation of a child entrusted to the care of the current abbess Madame Delbène, during which the young charge endures the most brutal sexual abuse at the hands of her merciless tormentors. These grotesque scenes, in which the holy and the innocent are explicitly sought out in order to be violated, are bizarre and more than a little over the top, but they are not farcical, even when they are meant to be amusing. Instead of the obliquity of the ironic grotesque at work in *Vathek*, Sade's work forthrightly announces the seriousness of its destructive intention.

The excess that Hegel sees in the grotesqueries of Indian art occurs through an exaggeration of size, an amplification of temporal duration, and a replication of external features. Commenting on the Indians' penchant for representing deities with numerous appendages, Hegel identifies senseless proliferation as integral to the grotesque in Indian art; he draws particular attention to "the multiplication of one and the same characteristic, the many heads, the mass of arms, etc., whereby attainment of the breadth and universality of meanings is pursued."[46] Hegel finds such a mode of presentation wearisome in its repetitiveness and futile in its quest to attain universality through multiplication. With Sade, excess also manifests itself in a tiresome redundancy, in which addition does not add anything qualitatively new. We seldom meet two individuals copulating alone with one another in his writings; instead his orgies depict a mass of shifting bodies. Here, the significant multiplication occurs not in relation to body parts – as in Indian sculpture – but in relation to actors and acts. The repetition of the same act, with minor positional variations, is one of the hallmarks of Sade's fiction. Excess means constant indulgence in sex as well as maximizing the number of partners. As Dolmancé explains, "every excess triggers pleasure, and the best thing a woman can do is to multiply those excesses beyond the very limits of possibility."[47] This longing for the impossible, the will to exhaust the infinite through finite means, instantiates Hegel's "bad infinity." It is both a source and a consequence of a philosophical inhumanism in which human beings are reduced to objects to be used and discarded.

Sade draws on the philosophy of contemporary atheistic materialists, but he pushes their ideas to such an extreme that they become monstrous parodies of the originals. According to d'Holbach, who seeks to naturalize and thereby justify our pleasure-seeking, it is not possible to be happy without being virtuous, and virtue – closely tied to utility – consists, in large part, in contributing to the happiness of others.[48] In jettisoning such scruples and purging philosophy of the language of virtue, Sade releases hedonism from its moral confines. On account of his appeals to nature and the pursuit of pleasure, he seems to participate in the Enlightenment project, but he actually holds fast to older associations linking pleasure and sin; even as he ridicules the theology that underwrites these associations, he echoes them in his insistence on our innate depravity. In regard to the role of nature in Sade, Simone de Beauvoir writes that "Sade, though rejecting the first part of the generally accepted credo: 'Nature is good; let us follow her,' paradoxically retained the second. Nature's example has an imperative value, even though her law be one of hate and destruction."[49] With this rejection, the conclusion that we ought to follow nature acquires a radically new meaning, one alien to the *philosophes.* What most inclined Sade to this "deduction" was not so much its perceived correctness as its unprecedented deviation from a venerated principle. His embrace of nature is, in actuality, an embrace of excess in disguise; where nature shows wastefulness and wantonness, he invokes it, but where it presents itself in less disruptive and destructive forms, he disregards it.[50] His heroes express disdain for bonds of affection between parents and offspring even though such ties are widespread in the animal kingdom; instances of cannibalism, however, while much less common are seized upon as revealing the essence of nature in its unconcealed harshness. It is for this reason that the same characters who reproach others for failing to follow nature cheerfully admit the pleasures of outraging it. Sade's predilection for sodomy stems not only from his experience that it was the most pleasurable form of intercourse, but from the sterility of the deed, its opposition to the reproductive end of the sexual act; the act of sodomy simultaneously serves nature, making use of the most pleasurable means nature has given us to attain orgasm, and outrages it, thwarting its productive aims.[51]

In *Rabelais and His World*, Bakhtin reads the grotesque in the time of the Renaissance as possessing a generative power subsequently lost with the rise of modernity. The grotesque body, unlike its Apollonian counterpart, expresses, with its amplified protuberances and enlarged orifices, an openness and boundless potency.[52] For Bakhtin, this corporeal symbol carries with it positive political and cultural resonances; the transgression of social and aesthetic norms embodied in the grotesque is aligned with generativity, liberation from oppression, human solidarity, inexhaustibility, and an affirmation of life's joyous bodily pleasures. Hegel, in a far less laudatory mood, also notes the primacy accorded to generation in Indian mythology, which he sees as part and parcel of its grotesque aesthetic.[53] But in Sade, excess has ceased to be productive of life and leads rather to its prevention and even annihilation. The sterility of the grotesque is unmistakable in Sade's *The 120 Days of Sodom*, where the protagonists' aversion to the sight of female genitalia indicates not only a penchant for proscribed sexual acts, but also a repugnance towards fecundity and generative desire. The grotesque, deprived of its carnivalesque utopianism, has here been enlisted in the service of a barren nihilism.

Within this framework, in which pleasure is cut off from the perpetuation of life, all those societal norms that lead to life's nurturing are dismissed as arbitrary conventions in conformity with neither nature nor reason. In reference to the tale of Nala and Damayanti, narrated in the *Mahabharata*, Hegel states that "the real conflict, on which the whole thing turns, is only for the ancient Indians an essential transgression of something sacrosanct. In our eyes it is nothing but an absurdity."[54] The apparent absurdity of the transgression, which consists of "making water and treading on the ground thus urine-infected," leads Hegel to distinguish between those peoples who devise arbitrary rules of conduct and those – namely modern Europeans – who have "a consciousness of the genuinely ethical and sacrosanct."[55] But what Hegel finds to be absurd in the story of Nala, Sade discerns at the heart of the "ethical substance" of contemporary Western society. All of its laws and commandments, which aim to deprive the strong of their prerogatives and to prevent them from obtaining pleasure at the expense of others, are no less ridiculous than the chimeras of barbarians and savages. In *Juliette*, the cataloguing of the practices of foreign and ancient peoples engaging in acts of debauchery shows that what modern Europeans take to be natural and common-sensical rules governing behaviour are merely a matter of historical and geographical accident.[56] Sade finds more wisdom in the wanton sexual practices of Orientals and non-European savages – or, rather, the practices ascribed to them – than in the moral codes of contemporary Europe.

During an act of incestuous intercourse, Madame de Saint-Ange exclaims, "Oh Lucifer! Lone and single god of my soul! Inspire me more! Offer my heart new deviations, and you will see me plunge into them!"[57] Deviance has here attained such extremity that rules are deliberately sought out in order to be transgressed. The Luciferian imagination labours to conceive of scenarios where as many norms as possible can be violated in the most irreverent fashion; it is an endeavour that animates the Marquis's fiction as well as his philosophy. Among the Romantic champions of Prometheus, who prided themselves on refusing reverence to rules sanctified by tradition and who subjected prohibitions hallowed by time to sceptical scrutiny, a sense of justice and humanity prevented the spirit of self-assertion from degenerating into a new despotism, no less despotic than the one it opposed. In the case of Shelley, his transgressiveness was tempered by his abhorrence of cruelty, and this humane sentiment was sufficient to lend his "Satanism" an aura of the angelic. But for Sade, compassion, no less than a puritanical prohibition against "unnatural" sexual acts, appears as yet another restraint on egoism, yet another line that must be crossed.

The attempts to rehabilitate Sade, to recast him as a liberationist and even humanitarian critic of society's repressive forces – a process already underway in the late nineteenth century, which intensifies in the interwar years – owe much to rethinkings of the nature of sexuality and sexual perversion, in which Sade came to be seen as forthrightly enunciating the fantasies of the everyman.[58] But these rehabilitative efforts, also at work in his literary canonization, not infrequently suffer from a paradox, the normalizing of a thinker whose significance is held to reside in his uncompromising transgressiveness.[59] Whether or not a full-throated philosophy of transgression, one that raises transgression to a principle of action, is even logically coherent remains a matter of dispute. Kant, for one, maintained that it was not.[60] In their pairing of Kant and Sade – a coupling calculated to disconcert that itself owes something to the latter's provocative spirit – Horkheimer and Adorno read Sade's oeuvre as "an intransigent critique of practical reason" that extends and consequently disrupts its Kantian antecedent.[61] Commenting on Juliette's scientific credo, they maintain that "she loves systems and logic. She wields the instrument of rational thought with consummate skill."[62] Yet her "love" for systems and logic is like her love for her human victims; if Juliette makes use of logic as a battering ram to break down the prejudices of bourgeois society or if she systematizes her own acts of vice in order to exhaust all possible permutations, it is with the knowledge and satisfaction that her use of these instruments is an abuse of them. It should be noted, in this context, that Sade's heroes, who cannot seem to decide whether they wish to adhere to nature or to outrage her – and who sometimes, when they are not able to resolve the contradiction between these alternatives, simply proclaim that in the act of outraging her they are best adhering to her – are not terribly vexed by instances of logical inconsistency. It is only when these inconsistencies threaten to inhibit the actors' wicked undertakings that they need to be addressed in order to be divested of their effect – and this can be accomplished with rhetoric, or with brute force, just as well as with reason. While this might constitute a reproach to any other philosophy, for one that does not take itself to be bound by rules there is a paradoxical coherence in a lack of consistency. A cavalier disregard for logic at the level of propositional utterance is consonant with a philosophy that refuses to remain in thrall to even the most seemingly universal rules governing our conduct, whether moral or cognitive. The recognition that there exists some sort of connection between logic and morals has not escaped the attention of the more astute philosophers of transgression; one need only recall Nietzsche's remark, "I am afraid we are not rid of God because we still have faith in grammar."[63] The wildness of Sade's philosophy, the extremity of its claims and the breathless motion of its ideas, makes the grotesque mode particularly well suited to its visible expression. In translating concept into image, the ethics of perversion and the logic of transgression find their correspondence in an aesthetics of distortion.

The Dialectic of Disgust

In the medieval period, the association of the devil with filth and excrement was a commonplace. Theological tracts, hagiographies, sermons, and popular tales drew upon this association in order to instruct readers and auditors about the nature of evil. The physiological necessity of excreting bodily waste was not only taken as a symbol of the corruption of the flesh, but was considered to be an actual result of the fall with all its baneful consequences; and the call of nature, with its attendant by-products contaminating the streets of the medieval town and city, was a constant reminder of sin and fallenness. No doubt, literary references to human and animal waste in the Middle Ages were often bawdy and made with the deliberate intent to amuse, but underwriting them was a moral cosmology that was deadly earnest. By reminding human beings of their inherent sinfulness and by teaching them to turn away from vice with the feeling of repugnance that it warranted, the portrayal of evil as disgusting served an eminently moral function. To separate the aesthetic aspect of medieval representations of evil from their moral content amounts, then, to a denaturing of both, in which the educative role of disgust is forgotten.[64]

Today, the connection between excrement and evil seems much less obvious to us than it did to the men and women of medieval Europe. Yet the vague sense that evil and the disgusting bear some sort of relationship to one another persists, although the points of intersection between them are seldom articulated with precision. At the least, when we decry certain evil acts and evil-doers as disgusting, this characterization does not elicit looks of incomprehension but is readily understood. Rosenkranz explains that "the disgusting is the sensibly hideous, which however, as we have recognized, in its unnatural extremes already hangs together with the practically hideous, with evil."[65] With its connection to processes of decay, the disgusting finds its proper home in the realm of the organic – "the disgusting as a product of nature, sweat, slime, dung, abscesses, and the like is something dead that the organism separates from itself and thus gives over to decay."[66] Such refuse lacks the form and coherence possessed by the organism who casts it off; as "a non-form originating in physical or moral decay," the disgusting, in its sensuous and practical manifestations, conflicts with the principles of freedom and reason.[67] In articulating the antagonism in these terms, Rosenkranz reveals his indebtedness to Hegel, but he also departs from the master in maintaining the suitability of evil as an object of aesthetic representation. After citing Hegel's remark that the devil is not a properly aesthetic character, Rosenkranz concedes that this holds insofar as it applies to "the devil alone, torn loose from the entire context of the world, as isolated object of art."[68] But in order to grasp "the purely affirmative idea" as it manifests itself in the world, it is necessary to take account of the role evil plays in its antagonism towards the good, and the figure of the devil, taken as the personification of evil, may serve to elucidate this enduring opposition.[69]

In addition to providing a metaphysical justification for representations of the devil in works of art, Rosenkranz also defends artistic portrayals of Satan – along with those of criminals, witches, and monsters – on aesthetic grounds. While it is true that "evil is aesthetically repulsive," "the representation of the bad" can nonetheless "be aesthetically interesting."[70] The disgusting itself has a place in art when it is subordinated to a higher principle that animates the whole. Rosenkranz observes that "one could say of decay that through the Christian religion it has nonetheless become a positive object of art, in that painting has attempted the *raising of Lazarus*, of which the text itself reported that he already stank."[71] In this instance, it is the victory over death that renders the scene aesthetically interesting and makes the portrayal of the decaying body suitable for the canvas. Elsewhere, however, the examples taken from painting and poetry indicate less the triumph of life than its ebbing and negation. Asserting that "our whole discussion of the repulsive culminates in the concept of evil and the diabolical," Rosenkranz gestures towards the intersections of the aesthetic and the moral; in this context, he refers to "the evil will" as "the ethically ugly" (*das ethisch Häßliche*) although the meaning of the latter term is not explicated.[72] But even as he insists on the "empirically objective reality" of evil, he adheres to the long-standing philosophical position, upheld by Augustine among others, that "its essence is the nothing of a non-essence."[73]

The disconnect between appearance and reality at work in evil, a nothing that nonetheless appears as a something, raises difficulties in determining the aesthetic most adequate to its representation. The falsely beautiful has been appealed to as an appropriate symbol of the morally bad since it captures the mendacity inherent in evil. Warning his fellow Christians that Satan is able to assume the form of "an angel of light" (2 Corinthians 11:14), Saint Paul calls attention to his aptitude for deception; but the fact that the devil's appearance is interpreted as a disguise, a form of dissemblance, suggests that the beautiful and the good ultimately belong together. Beneath his donned angelic garb, the devil conceals his true nature which, if we could see it for what it is, would cause us to recoil in horror. In a sense, it is only fitting that evil should appear to us in the guise of the beautiful since it is in the nature of evil to mislead and to present itself falsely; if it appeared to us in the form of the ugly, it would honestly show itself as it actually is. In the homilies of the moralists, the emphasis on the false charms of evil serves to ward off its enticements, its promises of bodily pleasure and material gain. The disclosure of the off-putting interior beneath the outward mask aims to cure the enraptured subject of unreflective desire. But what if this revelation, instead of dampening lust, excites it further? If the properly aesthetic experience of the beautiful, as

Kant defines it, entails pleasure free from arousal, the disgusting, in Sade's representation, titillates even as it repulses. In Mattheus van Helmont's *The Temptation of Saint Anthony*, the scantily attired woman tempting the saint betrays the marks of a thinly veiled diabolical ugliness, a representation that gives pictorial form to the conviction of the moralists that to know evil in its hideousness means to know to turn away from it. In the literature of transgression this moral truth is turned on its head so that what ought to be the surest safeguard against our lapse into temptation itself becomes a vehicle of seduction. Saint Anthony's fair-faced temptress, in letting slip her serpent's tale, would not dissuade Sade's heroes from desiring her; for them, the grotesque marriage of the beautiful and the monstrous proves doubly inviting.

Sade introduces *The 120 Days of Sodom* with the boast that it is "the most impure tale ever written since the world began," and the scenes that follow provide compelling evidence in favour of this seemingly hyperbolic claim.[74] Interrupting the main narrative are insertions of briefer tales told by four "storytellers," women who recount debauched exploits in order to inflame the lusts of their libertine auditors. All of the raconteurs are past their prime, although the first three are described as retaining traces of their former loveliness. However, the last of the four, Madame Desgranges, appears as "vice and lechery incarnate: tall, thin, 56 years of age, pale and emaciated, lifeless eyes, dead lips, she was the very image of crime at death's door" – "little more than a skeleton that could inspire nothing but disgust."[75] In addition to having "one breast missing and three fingers cut off," this limping cyclops is said to be an unrepentant perpetrator of unspeakable crimes.[76] Why does Sade choose to assign the role of narrator to a disfigured old hag, whose appearance seems calculated to excite revulsion? The decision to cast a markedly repulsive woman as the speaker of the erotic adventures that follow seems more in keeping with the practice of the moralist, intent on unmasking the allurements of sin and laying bare the ugliness that lies at their root, than with that of the promoter of vice. But notwithstanding the assertion that her appearance "could inspire nothing but disgust," this disgust, it turns out, proves to be a source of intense sexual arousal. In *Philosophy in the Boudoir*, Madame de Saint-Ange explains to the young Eugénie that "the foulest, the filthiest, the most forbidden things are always the most exciting."[77] And on the rare occasions when such things do not automatically excite, they should be indulged in until the desired stimulation results. Saint-Fond, in the same spirit, advises Juliette to "wallow in ordure and infamy; let all that is of the dirtiest and the most execrable, of the most shameful and the most criminal, of the most cynical and the most repulsive, of the most unnatural, illegal, irreligious, be for those very reasons that which dost please thee most."[78]

The wallowing in filth accompanies the language of cleansing as applied to moral doctrines and religious dogmas. Madame Delbène, on the occasion of her first seduction of the thirteen-year-old Juliette, proclaims, "I should like to cleanse her of all those infamous religious follies which spoil the whole of life's felicity."[79] Shortly thereafter, God is decried, in her discourses to her young ward, as an "infinitely disgusting phantom" and later as "this disgusting fruit of his [man's] delirious imagination."[80] Seeking to excite a feeling of loathing towards the idea of the deity, Sade simultaneously aims to undo our aversion to things that commonly arouse disgust; this is nowhere more apparent than in his characters' coprophilia. The delight in excrement distinguishes not a few of Sade's libertines. Not only are the victims of these characters' crimes forced against their will to imbibe bodily waste, an act meant to torment and humiliate them; Sade's perpetrators themselves indulge in the ingesting of feces as if it were a delicacy. Saint-Fond, who presents himself as a very proud man demanding the obeisance of others, tells Juliette of his inclination for this particular form of debauchery.[81] Whereas the medievals condemned the devil to filth as a way of degrading him, Sade has his haughtiest roués drop to their knees in pursuit of a taste of excrement. This posture, far from reducing their stature, exhibits the extent of their self-assertion, manifest in a startling freedom from the judgments of society and an utter lack of inhibition – the same qualities that distinguish the author who dares to write about such things. And just as Juliette exerts her power over her victims in subjecting them to her wildest fancies, Sade exercises his authority over his readers in a corresponding fashion. The eroticizing of excrement is intended to both horrify and seduce; where the latter is achieved, then a strong bulwark against the will to excess has been demolished. If such a seemingly natural revulsion as our disgust towards feces can be overcome by the potency of libidinal desire, then the more feeble resistances of conscience will be no impediment to the spirit of transgression.

Rosenkranz, to his credit, treats the disgusting as a category worthy of consideration from the standpoint of aesthetics. In spite of his own displeasure at having to occupy himself with repugnant matters, he patiently attends to forms and functions of disgust in art and literature. Yet he still treats it one-sidedly – a cardinal sin for a Hegelian. Any aesthetic pleasure taken in the beholding of disgusting objects is attributed to a pleasure in the artfulness of the artist's representation of them and in their subordination to a larger whole; the phenomenon itself remains intrinsically displeasing. This analysis neglects to consider the curious points of connection between disgust and desire that poets and novelists of the time were already excavating. Sade stands at the threshold of this emergent literature; ultimately, however, his vision is more striking for its audacity than for its insights into the nuances of human psychology. Baudelaire was less brutal and crudely pornographic in his portrayal of wickedness, yet he went further than the Marquis in bringing to light the psychic depths of human perversity.

The naturalization of evil, which he shares with Sade, undergirds his inquiries into the ambivalences of love and the paradoxes of desire.[82] A self-proclaimed Catholic who composed hymns to Satan, Baudelaire adopts the Romantic celebration of transgression, but simultaneously cleaves to the Augustinian standpoint, according to which transgression lies at the heart of evil. The tension that animates Baudelaire's poetry can partly be accounted for in terms of his resistance to diluting or sacrificing either of these positions in favour of some conciliatory synthesis. The celebration of transgression merges with a meditation, sometimes taking the form of a lamentation, on the state of corruption that gives rise to transgressive acts. In "To the Reader," the poem that introduces *The Flowers of Evil*, Baudelaire observes that "We offer lavishly our vows of faith / And turn back gladly to the path of filth."[83] The reversion to "the path of filth" (*le chemin bourbeux*), along with the delight it occasions, stems from a deep-rooted perversity within as well as the potency of an alien power without – "Satan Thrice-Great, who lulls our captive soul."[84] Baudelaire exclaims, in the following stanza,

> Truly the Devil pulls on all our strings!
> In most repugnant objects we find charms;
> Each day we're one step further into Hell,
> Content to move across the stinking pit.[85]

The contentedness of souls who walk down the infernal path owes something to delusion and self-deception, the failure to recognize how petty acts lead imperceptibly to perdition. Yet Baudelaire maintains that to achieve clarity in such matters, to recognize our wretched state and the peril in which we live, gives little hope of redemption. The Socratic identification of knowledge with virtue, the claim that none of us does what we truly know to be bad, finds its antipode in Baudelaire's vision of sinfulness, with its emphasis on our weakness of will, our instinctive attraction to evil, and our subjection to the machinations of the devil. The perplexing fact that we continue to advance through "the stinking pit" leading to damnation, even when we know the baleful outcome that awaits us, can be explained as a result of our enthralment to a corrupting power who "pulls on all our strings." The introduction of the devil, in this context, is not a gratuitous insertion, but an attempt to make sense of why it is that what we know to be wrong nonetheless exerts a hold on us. Without the intrusion of such a corrupting power, whether conceived as a diabolical spirit or an irrational propensity to wickedness, our self-destructive actions would remain inexplicable.[86]

If the tendency to delight in the sordid is natural to human beings, a spontaneous expression of innate depravity, then Baudelaire raises this thoughtless instinct to the level of conscious reflection. His poetry, which excels in discovering the "charms" of "repugnant objects," treats the base as worthy of aesthetic contemplation and artistic refashioning. In *Aesthetics of Ugliness*, published less than half a decade before *The Flowers of Evil*, Rosenkranz affirms that "all works of poetry which have taken as subject something simply ugly have been unable to achieve the slightest popularity."[87] Even as he seeks to justify the presence of the ugly in works of art, where it may serve an auxiliary role in giving sensual realization to the idea, he insists that "no one can take real pleasure in such works," among which he includes French "didactic poems concerning pornography and even syphilis."[88] With its fantastic juxtapositions and ironic distortions, Baudelaire's poetry partakes of the grotesque.[89] But it does not stop there; it goes further in its embrace of the disgusting, in its transposition of objects of revulsion into elegant alexandrines. His poem "A Carcass" narrates an encounter, during a summer morning constitutional, with a corpse lying on the side of a pathway. Overrun by "an army of maggots," the rotting cadaver emits a "stench" so nauseating that the narrator's female companion "nearly collapse[s] in a swoon."[90] Bringing to life the image of death and decay, the poet likens "la carcasse superbe" to a blooming flower.[91] With the strange music of the insects buzzing around it and the pulse of their monotonous movements, the decomposing body exerts an almost hypnotic power.

In the realm of the organic, the two objects most representative of the disgusting are excrement and decaying flesh; the former predominates in the novels of Sade, the latter in the poetry of Baudelaire. Human beings' physiological responses to them, rooted in evolutionary adaptation, acquire a range of figurations in the symbolic order, and these can be deployed to ends conservative as well as subversive. With Baudelaire, scenes of organic decomposition are used to draw attention to the ephemerality of beauty, the frailty of life, and the inevitability of death – all standard tropes in the lyric tradition; but they also function as sites of desire, in which the perversity of our attractions is brought to light. The worm feeding on the corpse may stand for regret, as when Baudelaire warns a wanton beauty that, in death, "like remorse the worm will gnaw your flesh."[92] More provocatively, the image of maggots dining on the dead connotes the pursuit of the beloved and the performance of the sexual act.[93] The work of putrefaction, the eating away at human flesh, not only becomes an object of aesthetic contemplation but also signifies the poet's hostile movement towards an object of desire. In his lyric "I love you as I love the night's high vault," Baudelaire writes, "I climb to the assault, attack the source, / A choir of wormlets pressing towards a corpse."[94] Piqued by the ruthlessness of the beloved, he cries out, in his apostrophe to her, "ô bête implacable et cruelle!"[95] The coldness of her beauty, drained of the warmth of life, makes her a fitting target for the wormlets in their corpse-loving quest.

Such moments of passionate longing are seldom unequivocal in their affective modalities; tenderness mingles with aggression and adoration with contempt. Not infrequently, the initial attraction to the beloved yields to antipathy and even revulsion; but since traces of the prior passion resist deletion, the power that the beloved continues to exercise becomes a source of humiliation. The instability of the object of desire, which simultaneously attracts and repulses, derives from the instability of the desiring subject, who moves from being enamoured with the object to being disgusted with his own desire for it. In "The Vampire," the poet likens his obsession not only to a form of drug addiction, but to a process of decomposition, where he assumes the role of a scavenger.

> As the drunkard is to the jug,
> As the gambler to the game,
> As to the vermin the corpse,
> – I damn you, out of my shame.[96]

On account of his "cowardice," the poet remains condemned to a state of "wretched slavery," all the more degrading since it is brought about through his own weakness and therefore deserved.[97] The representation of the adored yet despised woman as a corpse, a not uncommon trope in *The Flowers of Evil*, is coupled with the attribution of vampiric life to her. The two figures constituting the erotic dyad are characterized in parasitic terms – vermin feeding on a dead body and a vampire draining its living victim. Decay, in Baudelaire's portrayals of it, not only symbolizes desire; it also excites it. The comparison of the beloved to a cadaver and the lover to scavenging vermin operates on distinct, though interrelated, semantic levels. It functions as a meditation on the corruptibility of the flesh and a reminder of its subjection to decay; it points to the aggressiveness and destructiveness of desire, the eating away of the thing we love; it expresses a *ressentiment*, in which revenge is enacted upon a being whose hold the lover execrates; it appears as a therapeutic exercise, an attempt, howsoever futile, to shake the lover from a tormenting romantic obsession; it serves as a reminder of the sickness and debased condition of the lover, who is so wretched as to adore, in necrophilous fashion, a dead body. In this last instance, the disgust with the object is itself a consequence of self-disgust, a disgust with the desiring subject, which is then projected back onto the desired object as if it were the object in-itself that warranted such a reaction. This aggressive projection has little curative effect as it only serves to intensify the hated feeling of attraction, accelerating a downwards spiral into sadomasochism.[98]

In Baudelaire's love poetry, disgust does not stand opposed to desire; it has the seeds of desire within it. Because of human beings' innate depravity, those things that ought to be most repugnant to them, physically and morally, possess a captivating allure. In attempting to account for this paradoxical attraction, Baudelaire revolts against the two dominant views of human nature promulgated in the Enlightenment – that human beings are innately good and that they are neither good nor bad but exceedingly malleable – and aligns himself with the medieval doctrine of fallenness. However, in his embrace and radicalization of this doctrine, the disgusting loses the educative function it possessed in the Middle Ages; since our depravity runs so deep as to place us beyond redemption, the recognition of evil as disgusting fails to mitigate our desire and only stimulates it. What Rosenkranz one-sidedly takes to be a negation of the beautiful, Baudelaire reveals to be a power in its own right, with its own generative force and internal contradictions. The symbol of this generativity is not the blossoming and fructifying flower, which Hegel offers us at the outset of the *Phenomenology of Spirit*, but the decaying corpse that feeds multiplying maggots.[99]

Unlike its Hegelian variety, the dialectic here does not resolve itself in an integrative synthesis.[100] The closest that the movement, the shuttling back and forth between disgust and desire, comes to attaining reconciliation lies in the disturbing moment in which the two coincide – wherein the object is desired precisely because it is disgusting. But far from constituting a higher unity, this represents a nadir of sorts, a low point of abasement and self-debasement. In the process, wisdom is won, but it is the wisdom of despair. Schopenhauer claims that the imploring "lead me not into temptation," as given in the Lord's Prayer, means in actuality "let me not see who I am," since our behaviour during moments of temptation teaches us who we truly are, a lesson that is rarely to our liking.[101] In Baudelaire, such hardwon self-knowledge does not lead to moral betterment, but to a recognition of our wretchedness. If the poet warns us of the dangers of succumbing to temptation, he does so with the understanding that admonitions are ultimately impotent in the face of our insurmountable perversity.

Knowing the truth of our nature proves useless in overcoming it. Indeed, reflection not only shows itself to be sadly powerless; it may even bring about a lapse that impulse initially preserves us from. In his prose poem "The Temptations, or Eros, Plutos and Fame," Baudelaire describes a nocturnal visitation from three devils, who seek to entice him with their corrupting gifts. The second of these "Satans," as they are called, shows himself, with his "decayed teeth" and "immense belly," to be particularly repulsive, and the poet tells us how he "turned away in disgust" from the fiend.[102] The other two devils, especially the third, prove more seductive in appearance. But the poet perceives the hollowness of all their offers and dismisses them from his sight with a high-minded contempt. When he wakes from this strange reverie, however, all trace of his former "courageous self-denial" deserts him. He laments, "Ah! if only they would come again while I am awake, I would certainly not be so squeamish."[103] But notwithstanding his pathetic imploring and his promises to humble himself, they do not return. In this account, the dream, conventionally taken as the site of uninhibited desire, becomes the space in which moral scruples triumph over base wishes and animal appetites. Conversely, it is in waking that the poet becomes conscious of the missed opportunity, the pleasure glibly cast away before the intensity of desire is belatedly recognized. An object of contempt, and even disgust, transforms upon reflection into its opposite.

In Baudelaire's work, it is not always an external object that excites desire; the thought of committing an act of sin itself exercises an attraction. The aforementioned prose poem intimates that the excitation caused by the prospect of wrongdoing is not less seductive than the material goods the three Satans promise. In an essay on the life and writings of Edgar Allan Poe, written in 1852, Baudelaire quotes a passage from Poe's *The Black Cat*, in which the protagonist of the story asks, "who has not, a hundred times, found himself committing a vile or a stupid action, for no other reason than because he knows he should *not*? Have we not a perpetual inclination, in the teeth of our best judgment, to violate that which is *Law*, merely because we understand it to be such?"[104] In the notes appended to the 1857 version of this essay, Baudelaire singles out Poe for recognizing "the primordial perversity of man," which he calls "the great forgotten truth."[105] Mocking those who have faith in the original and ultimate goodness of human beings, he exclaims that "we are all born marked for evil!"[106]

In portraying the individual's enslavement to external objects and internal passions, Baudelaire offers us a vision of abject heteronomy. The excitation that an object causes in us is a mark of its power over us, especially when we are not able to withstand its attraction against our best efforts. Nietzsche identifies the inability to resist reacting to external stimuli as one of the hallmarks of "degeneration," and it is this same inability that Baudelaire attributes to himself in his lyrical self-loathings.[107] On Nietzsche's reading, Baudelaire's work is decadent not because it overflows with images of organic decay and scenes from the unseemly underbelly of everyday life, but because it stages and expresses the decay of the will and the disintegration of psychic life.[108] Yet the poet's unwilling submission to potent stimuli, or at least his recounting of such instances of surrender, occurs in conjunction with an austere self-command. The tendency to "find charms" in "repugnant objects" is an instance of moral deficiency common to all of us in our fallen state; but it is also the unique gift of the poet, who draws out the allure of the disgusting and makes it an object of art. This poetic perception does not annul the disgusting, as if it were a cover concealing a beautiful essence, but shows how it is in-itself deserving of the artist's attention. Instead of disavowing the tendency to find the charming in the repugnant, Baudelaire cultivates it; through effort, he reworks an inherent failing and turns it into a honed ability.

Baudelaire writes that "the study of beauty is a duel in which the artist shrieks with terror before being overcome."[109] Study, which should be an exercise in self-discipline, culminates in a state of violent submission, wherein beauty overwhelms one naive enough to engage in combat with it. Conversely, the disgusting, which by its nature tends to overpower and can produce unwanted physiological responses – including vomiting – becomes for the poet an object of serene contemplation. With Sade, the disgusting is eroticized and thereby transformed into a source of arousal. The same tendency is to be found in Baudelaire, but it is accompanied by a treatment of the disgusting as an object of disinterested contemplation, whereby we learn to experience a detached pleasure in it, one divorced from our immediate needs and desires. Kant presents disinterestedness as a distinguishing mark of the aesthetic experience of the beautiful; in doing so, he differentiates this experience from those where we seek to take hold of a thing and deploy it to our own ends. According to Schopenhauer, aesthetic contemplation demands a preponderance of intellect over will that is seldom to be found among the *hoi polloi*; and since "the requisite exertion and attention cannot be maintained," even men of genius can sustain their disinterested gaze only for a brief interlude before the will inevitably reasserts itself.[110] But if desire, which for Schopenhauer not infrequently means sexual desire, proves difficult to resist – and quickly throws us back into the inaesthetic world – the disgusting, with its inducement of involuntary physiological reactions, invites a response no less intense than the attraction occasioned by desire. Here, the decadent poet appears to have performed a feat even more impressive than that of the poet occupied solely with the beautiful. In beholding and portraying the disgusting, his senses steadfastly fixed upon it without succumbing to it, he has overcome an instinctive physical revulsion.

With his keen eye for decay, Baudelaire discloses the strange allure of the forces of disintegration at work in both the natural and the social world. In his verse, the rotting of bodies and the degeneration of souls mirror one another; the corruptibility of the flesh is, at once, sign and analogue of the sinfulness of the spirit. To use the language of corruption in portraying the effects of evil can sometimes serve the purpose of depriving evil of reality. In undergoing decay, an entity loses its original cohesiveness; even if it has suffered from adulteration, which implies the addition of extraneous material, the decisive fact remains not the presence of new accretions, but the dissolution of what was once integral. The transition from beauty to ugliness, like the transition from youth to old age, is a matter of entropy, and just like the maintenance of beauty and youth, which requires active resistance to the forces of disintegration, the preservation of goodness and moral purity demands vigilance. In accordance with this line of thought, the fall into evil might be read as a story of lack and loss. This is the story that Rosenkranz tells, who sees the disgusting as closely aligned to evil, yet – by virtue of his subscription to the privationist view – ultimately empties evil of its essence. Baudelaire, however, uses the language of corruption to combat this very understanding. Insisting on the frightful potency of evil, he does not content himself with reflections on the cessation of the pulse of life and the departure of warmth from the body of the recently deceased. His penchant for the image of worms and maggots feeding on the dead derives, in part, from the sense that decomposition is an event with its own internal propulsive force. And just as decay is not a passive process, a gradual loss of organic form, so evil is not a mere absence of good, but a dynamic power that actively undermines the integrity of the soul. This truth finds confirmation in our psychological and physiological responses to the disgusting. The visceral revulsion that it provokes suggests not an awareness of an absent good, the privation of which we judge to be a mark of aesthetic imperfection, but the perception of an all too present evil that forcibly thrusts itself upon us. Whereas the ugly may be dismissed as a mere lack of beauty, the disgusting assaults us with a force that makes its reality difficult to deny. In its power to disturb and to provoke, it forms an indispensable weapon in the arsenal of the poets and novelists of transgression.

Chapter Three

Evil and the Sublime

The sublime participates in a surpassing of limits that uplifts and overwhelms; in the awe that it calls forth, it may even approach the heights of the holy. Yet it is on account of this transgressing of ordinary boundaries that the sublime has been associated with evil. While the beautiful, with its qualities of balance and just proportion, carries connotations of propriety shading into the morally respectable, the sublime – even more so than the grotesque – is an aesthetic of excess. In *Rameau's Nephew*, Diderot's interlocutor asserts that "if it is important to be sublime in anything, it is especially so in evil. You spit on a petty thief, but you can't withhold a sort of respect from a great criminal. His courage bowls you over. His brutality makes you shudder."[1] A slight overstepping of established norms smacks of the improper, but when an act of transgression reaches a point of extremity, it acquires not only a different moral aspect but also a different aesthetic valence.

The portrayal of evil in its grotesque and disgusting guises may serve to subvert established norms, as the cases of Sade and Baudelaire attest, yet there is nothing inherently subversive about drawing an equivalence between evil and ugliness; in fact, it has been the standard procedure of moralists throughout the ages to depict vice as repugnant – although sometimes accompanied by the caveat that it can take on a seductively false appearance. And since the acknowledgement that evil is able to assume the aspect of the beautiful often serves as an admonishment to be vigilant in the face of temptation, the notion that the evil and the beautiful may sometimes coincide, though troubling, does not invariably excite moral outrage. The idea that there may be some point of connection between evil and the sublime proves more offensive; this is due to the fact that the sublime, among all the major aesthetic categories, has the strongest associations with greatness.

In eighteenth-century aesthetic discourse, an evaluative mode of assessing the sublime joined with a phenomenological approach that foregrounded the experience of it as an object of philosophical analysis and psychological enquiry. On the one hand, the study of the sublime participated in the approbation of moral virtues, particularly those associated with masculinity, and the commendation of aesthetic features deemed to produce elevating effects; on the other hand, it invited a precise description of a particular kind of experience and a determination of the subject-object dynamic underlying it. Moralistic-aesthetic evaluation and phenomenological investigation were the two poles around which eighteenth-century discourse on the sublime was configured. The mediation between these poles is at work in the writings of the period's foremost theorists of the sublime, including Burke and Kant. With Burke, the enquiry into the sublime owes less to a desire to ground our aesthetic judgments in universal criteria than to an interest in examining how it is that our encounter with particular objects produces in us specific affective states. His observations concerning our physical reactions to these objects lead him to chart the properties that are prone to call them forth. For Rameau's nephew, we shudder involuntarily before the sublime; Burke also identifies shuddering as an effect of the sublime, especially when it is closely allied to terror. Even though Burke himself does not directly discuss evil in *A Philosophical Enquiry into the Origin of our Ideas of the Sublime and Beautiful*, his argument for the intimate relationship between the terrible and the sublime opens up the problem of the extent to which evil can be said to intersect with the aesthetic category. What Rameau's nephew boldly and recklessly affirms, Burke's *Enquiry* touches on in a more oblique and tentative fashion.

The question of whether or not evil ever warrants being designated as sublime proves most controversial not when applied to fictional narratives or characters, such as Milton's Satan in *Paradise Lost*, but when we are confronted with real instances of human wickedness. The issue takes on an unsettling contemporary relevance when considering the aesthetic status of more recent examples of extreme evil. An examination of the representation of totalitarianism in the work of Hannah Arendt is instructive in this regard. The Romantic and Gothic associations of transgression with genius and the sublime must unravel, it seems, in the face of actual – as opposed to fictive – transgressive acts that, in their extremity, cause us to recoil in horror. What then becomes of those aesthetic theories that insist on the sublime's close connection to the frightful? And if the sublime is, in fact, intertwined with terror, as Burke maintains, what safeguards us from the unseemly judgment that acts of terror are themselves sublime?

Even as Sade draws out the grotesque and disgusting aspects of wickedness, he also presents the performance of wicked acts as sublime in their ecstasy-inducing power; he thereby seeks to exalt and to ennoble a transgressive *modus vivendi* that refuses to respect limits, that finds its highest satisfaction in their deliberate violation. In opposition to such destructive transgressiveness, Burke and Arendt insist on the need for bulwarks against the tide of excess. In the case of Burke, it was the French Revolution, the political embodiment of the pernicious desire to overturn the old order, that most excited his alarm. Arendt took the foremost political danger of the modern age to be the advent of totalitarianism, which she saw as a manifestation of extreme evil without historical precedent. Both thinkers' critical representations of evil are far removed from Sade's ecstatic visions of it. And yet they remain entangled in an aesthetics of the sublime. Reading Arendt's portrayal of totalitarianism in light of Burke's theory of the sublime elucidates the aesthetic dimensions of her depiction of radical evil and the quandaries that this depiction entails. It is first necessary, however, to note the tensions between the aesthetic and the moral in Burke's own work. These tensions are not peculiar to him, but haunt the writings of more than one thinker seeking to represent evil at its outer limits.

Between Elevation and Terror

Although Kant asserts that "the beautiful is the symbol of the morally good," he maintains that it is in the feeling of the sublime, rather than in the perception of the beautiful, that human beings are given an intimation of their supersensible moral vocation. In the face of the external powers of nature, we are forced to "recognize our physical powerlessness," but this confrontation with nature also "reveals a capacity for judging ourselves as independent of it."[2] The element of displeasure operative in the sublime, due to a sense of our impotence, is ultimately subordinated to a sense of triumph, wherein reason exults over both nature and the faculty of the imagination. According to Kant, man's rational pursuit of duty, untainted by self-interest and the search for pleasure, speaks to "the greatness and sublimity of his true vocation."[3] After asking how it is possible "that I can sacrifice the most inner allurements of my drives and all the desires that proceed from my nature to a law that promises me no advantage as a replacement," Kant concedes that the grounds of this sacrifice to the moral law remain an inscrutable mystery.[4] Nonetheless, our experience of the sublime gives "the feeling of a supersensible faculty in us" even if it does not constitute proof of this faculty's existence.[5] For Kant, the disobeying of the moral law – the contravention of good maxims as well as the failure to adopt them – is equivalent to evil. Whereas the sublime elevates us, evil debases and degrades.

In aesthetic discourse, the experience of the sublime has been conceived as both a state of elevation and a state of terror. The former conception predominates with Kant, the latter with Burke. While Burke has sometimes been taken to be representative of eighteenth-century British aesthetics, especially among scholars eager to highlight the novelty of Kant's contributions, his emphasis on the element of terror in the sublime was somewhat at odds with the dominant trend of the time, which was closer to Kant in its tendency to foreground the role of elevation.[6] In his *Enquiry*, Burke set out to make apparent the "remarkable contrast" and "eternal distinction" between the two ideas of the sublime and the beautiful.[7] For Burke, sublimity and beauty are located not only in the psychic constitution of the subject, but also in the properties of objects. Burke shows an attentiveness to the manner in which these properties affect human sensibility, but he also operates with an anthropology wherein the differences between human beings are sufficiently minimal to warrant disregard for divergent aesthetic responses as anomalies. Kant judged Burke's *Enquiry* to be a work of "empirical psychology" that did not attain the level of philosophical universality, a verdict that in some ways accords with Burke's own modest judgment about the limitations of his investigation.[8] As has long been recognized, the merit of his work lies not in its argument for the universality of aesthetic judgments, but in its forceful separation of two aesthetic categories that were not distinguished with sufficient discrimination prior to his *Enquiry*. Past and present critics have suggested that Burke was rather too forceful in his zeal to distinguish; at times, he reduces the beautiful to the cutely minuscule even as he strips the sublime of its pleasurable component. But this overdrawn distinction brings out aspects of the sublime that are muted in Kant's *Critique of the Power of Judgment*. Burke explains that

> whatever is fitted in any sort to excite the ideas of pain, and danger, that is to say, whatever is in any sort terrible, or is conversant about terrible objects, or operates in a manner analogous to terror, is a source of the *sublime*; that is, it is productive of the strongest emotion which the mind is capable of feeling. I say the strongest emotion, because I am satisfied the ideas of pain are much more powerful than those which enter on the part of pleasure.[9]

According to Burke, terror constitutes "the ruling principle of the sublime."[10] As "no passion so effectively robs the mind of all its powers of acting and reasoning as fear," terror brings about a state in which we feel ourselves overwhelmed and incapacitated.[11] For Burke, the sublime always involves "some modification of power"; everything powerful has something terrible about it, even if it is not an immediate threat to us, insofar as it has the potential to cause us harm.[12] When it has lost this potential, as in the case of a strong domesticated animal, it loses its sublimity. Domestication is inimical to the sublime because we feel familiar with what we have brought under our power, whether physically or conceptually. Terror, however, is augmented when we do not discern the nature of what lies before us – hence, the tremendous importance that Burke ascribes to obscurity. He points to the manner in which night arouses our fears since, under the cover of darkness, we can no longer clearly discern "the full extent of any danger."[13] Even vastness and infinity, which Burke identifies as sources of the sublime, owe the influence they exercise on our imaginations not to a pleasure in participating in their grandeur, but to a disconcerting feeling they excite in us. It is thus no surprise that Burke discovers in Milton's portrayal of Satan and Death in *Paradise Lost* the summit of the literary sublime.

In the eighteenth century, leading British theorists treated it as a matter of course that Milton was the poet of the sublime *par excellence*, and the reading of his Satan as a sublime figure became a veritable commonplace in aesthetic discourse. James Beattie, in his *Dissertations Moral and Critical*, published in 1783, writes that "though there are no qualities [of Milton's Satan] that can be called good in a moral view; nay, though every purpose of that wicked spirit is bent on evil, and to that only; yet there is the grandeur of a ruined archangel; there is a force able to contend with the most boisterous elements; and there is boldness, which no power, but what is Almighty, can intimidate"; by virtue of these "astonishing" qualities, "we are often compelled to admire that very greatness by which we are confounded and terrified."[14] Beattie struggles to explain how it is that this character, whom he terms a "sublime idea," can excite "an agreeable astonishment" in us when he himself is "the author of evil."[15] He attempts to resolve the paradox by resorting to the fact that we know him to be "a fictitious being, and a mere poetical hero."[16] This justification sits rather uneasily with the subsequent remarks on the "gloomy satisfaction, or terrifick pleasure" taken in actual, as opposed to merely imaginary, scenes of death and destruction, such as "battles, executions, and shipwrecks."[17] The Romantics went further than Beattie in their praise of the sublimity of Milton's Satan, but laboured under no such interpretive quandary since they maintained that he was more upright than his omnipotent adversary. As we have already seen, this was the position that Shelley advanced in *A Defence of Poetry*, where he asserts that "nothing can exceed the energy and magnificence of the character of Satan in *Paradise Lost*."[18] In this reading, Milton's God cuts a much poorer figure, morally and aesthetically, than his infernal rival.

It is worth considering, here, Burke's uneasiness in describing God himself as sublime. He states that, in his earliest reflections on the matter, he "purposefully avoided" any mention of "the idea of that great and tremendous being, as an example in an argument so light as this," but he also finds it difficult to refrain from speaking of it since his argument finds an important confirmation in our experience of the contemplation of the deity.[19] After suggesting that "a just idea of the Deity" privileges no single property of God at the expense of the others, he adds that, nevertheless, "by far the most striking" attribute, the one that seizes hold of our imagination without reflection, is his limitless power.[20] The awe that we feel in the presence, or imagined presence, of divine power derives not from our disinterested conceptualization, but from our unmediated experience. Indeed, "whilst we contemplate so vast an object," we become sensible of our own smallness and are even "annihilated before him."[21] And because we can have no clear and distinct image of God, even as we ascribe specific superlatives to him, the resistance of this being to any adequate representation amplifies our sense of awe. The resulting terror that we undergo in moments of pious subjection, which Burke hesitatingly connects to the sublime, seems difficult to reconcile with the divine attribute of omnibenevolence and the image of God as a loving comforter.

In addition to Burke's purported reason for not delving more deeply into the relationship between God and the sublime, namely the triviality of his investigation, we should consider his reluctance to introduce God into his *Enquiry* as indicative of a trepidation about the moral ambivalences of his aesthetic project. While Burke denies that the origin of religion is to be found in a superstitious fear, his emphasis on the role of power in bringing about our reverence for God diminishes the significance of the role of goodness. It is the contemplation not of God's love for us, but of his radical otherness, that engenders the sublime; the former, insofar as it makes us feel safe and secure, diminishes rather than enhances our awe. Burke makes an important distinction between admiration of the sublime and love for the beautiful, which is feminized in his account. In his characterization of the beautiful, which Kant also saw as having an intimate connection with the feminine, Burke shows an affection for it, but he also expresses a condescension for its comparative weakness and warns us not to mistake fondness of it with respect for it. He even claims that "love approaches much nearer to contempt than is commonly imagined."[22] The unwanted implication that evil, at least in its potent forms, was not less well suited to call forth the sublime than was the idea of the benevolent deity was sufficiently disconcerting to warrant Burke's stepping gingerly around the topic.

More than a decade prior to Burke's *Enquiry*, John Baillie, in *An essay on the sublime*, had already called attention to the distinction between the virtuous and the sublime. After acknowledging that the two may at certain moments overlap, he goes on to note that "when *Virtue* is at any time *sublime*, it is not that she is the *same* as the *Sublime*, but that she *associates* with it, and from this *Association* each acquires new Charms."[23] With reference to historical examples, Baillie explains, "a *Caligula* commanding Armies to fill their *Helmets* with *Cockle-shells*, is a Power mean and contemptible, altho' ever so absolute; but suppose an *Alexander* laying level Towns, depopulating Countries, and ravaging the whole World, how does the *Sublime* rise, nay tho' *Mankind* be the *Sacrifice* to his *Ambition*!"[24] The relevant distinction between the meanness of Caligula and the sublimity of Alexander resides not in the fact that the former was a vicious tyrant and the latter was not, but in the scope and scale of their respective endeavours. Since "our Idea of *Power* is more or less sublime, as the Power itself is more or less extended," the difference between a relatively mean and a relatively sublime power must be ascertained not with reference to its moral status, but to its extent.[25] At the same time, Baillie's assessment of Caligula indicates the importance of distinguishing the type of power possessed from the manner in which it is exercised. The absoluteness of Caligula's power fails to merit the accolade of the sublime since it is deployed to a trivial and frivolous end. Contrasting Caligula and Alexander, Baillie does not cite an instance of the former's extreme cruelty, of which there are abundant examples, but seizes on a harmless act of capriciousness. In this juxtaposition, Alexander appears as the figure whose endeavours align more closely with death and destruction; indeed, the destructiveness of his undertakings, with the accompanying loss of human life, are proof of a power that earns the designation of the sublime.

In Burke's account of our experience of the sublime, we perceive an object or agent external to us that overpowers us. Like Baillie and Burke, Kant also acknowledges the role of power at work in the sublime, but in contrast to them, he stresses the role of a power within, one that allows us to feel superior to alien forces capable of destroying us; he discerns in the feeling of the sublime a consciousness of our own dignity, which Burke subordinates to the sublime's diminishing effect. At the same time, Kantian aesthetics neglects to take account of the fascination that evil exercises upon human beings, whether as enthralled readers or horrified spectators who cannot look away. Burke, however, shows himself to be more attentive to the psychodynamics of our attraction to the horrific, including its social aspects. Since he seeks to elucidate the relationship between our aesthetic sensibility and our sociality, he devotes attention not only to our disposition towards natural phenomena and works of art, but also to the lived experience of other human beings. In regard to our response to tragedy and to the witnessing of others' adversity, he writes:

> I am convinced we have a degree of delight, and that no small one, in the real misfortunes and pains of others; for let the affection be what it will in appearance, if it does not make us shun such objects, if on the contrary it induces us to approach them, if it makes us dwell upon them, in this case I conceive we must have a delight or pleasure of some species or other in contemplating objects of this kind.[26]

The claim that our pleasure in contemplating the suffering of fictional characters is due to the fact that we know they are fictional is belied by the intense interest we take in actual disasters that have befallen people. Literary works of the imagination, far from being the more engrossing, are often only pale imitations of a more seductive reality. Burke asserts that no matter how well composed and well performed a work of tragedy might be, it would, at the moment of its climax, immediately lose all the members of its audience if they learned that "a state criminal of high rank is on the point of being executed in the adjoining square."[27] Burke reads this not as a mark of our innate cruelty, but as a sign of the complex nature of human sympathy. He suggests, in a rather providential vein, that if to see others in distress were wholly painful, we would flee from the scene of suffering without helping our fellows; as it is, the mixed pleasure we take in their distress induces us to engage in its alleviation, an action that strengthens social bonds and affections.

Burke's further connection of pleasure to grief gives some indication of the latitude that the category enjoys in his work. He observes that "the person who grieves, suffers his passion to grow upon him; he indulges it, he loves it: but this never happens in the case of actual pain, which no man ever willingly endured for any considerable time."[28] Burke sees repetition as fundamental to grief since "it is the nature of grief to keep its object perpetually in its eye" and "to repeat all the circumstances that attend it, even to the last minuteness"; on account of the tendency to recurrence, Burke reasons that "the *pleasure* is still uppermost" in the act of grieving, otherwise we would not continually return to it.[29] Not only do we take pleasure beholding the misfortunes of others; we also delight in reflecting upon our own misery. Burke stresses the role of "delight" in his explication of the sublime, but he consciously invests the word with a meaning it does not have in everyday speech; in his usage, delight, which he classifies as a "species of relative pleasure," refers to "the sensation which accompanies the removal of pain or danger."[30] He even considered devising a neologism to convey what he had in mind when employing this term, but balked at engaging in such innovation on the grounds that the new coinage "would not perhaps incorporate so well with the language."[31]

Yet Burke's insistence that "whatever therefore is terrible, with regard to sight, is sublime too" threatens to undermine not only the role of pleasure, but even the role of delight operative in his reading of the sublime.[32] Is it really the case that anything terrible we behold is a source of delight for us? Elsewhere, Burke acknowledges that "when danger or pain press too nearly, they are incapable of giving any delight, and are simply terrible."[33] But even when we accept this statement as a crucial qualification of the equivalence made between the sublime and the terrible, it disqualifies as sublime only those objects that impinge directly upon us; the very same object may strike another spectator, standing removed from it, as sublime. Apart from this aspect of participatory distance, whether that distance is understood spatially or temporally, Burke does not provide us with a further feature that would allow us to distinguish between the sublime and the "terrible, with regard to sight."

It should not be forgotten, at this point, that Burke himself shrank from the implications of his aesthetic principles, as expressed in the *Enquiry*, when confronted with actual historical phenomena that he found terrible to behold. In his portrayal of the French Revolution, there is a careful avoidance of characterizing the Revolution's excesses as sublime. Burke tells us, in the *Enquiry*, that the state of "astonishment" is "the effect of the sublime in its highest degree."[34] But after proclaiming, in his *Reflections on the Revolution in France*, that "the French revolution is the most astonishing that has hitherto happened in the world," he does not proceed to equate the event and the sublime.[35] On the contrary, he repeatedly calls attention to the disgusting character of the Revolution. In his diatribe against "the literary cabal" of those contemporary French men of letters who seek to bring about "the destruction of the Christian religion," he describes "their whole conversation" – which includes both the content of their atheistical philosophy and the manner of its expression – as "perfectly disgusting."[36] Whereas these enemies of the social order fantasize about the overturning of existing institutions, Burke affirms that, among right-thinking men, "the very idea of the fabrication of a new government, is enough to fill us with disgust and horror."[37] In pointing out that "the evil is radical and intrinsic," Burke makes it clear that the Revolution cannot be corrected, only defeated.[38] In its unwittingly grotesque character, the Revolution displays a tendency to degenerate into the farcical. After describing the deplorable state of the French National Assembly, Burke adds that one cannot help but "turn with horror and disgust from such a profane burlesque."[39] The ludicrous procedures of this legislative body and the absurdity of the undertakings of the revolutionaries are more appropriate to a rowdy fair than to an institution of government. With events caught between the poles of the disgusting and the ridiculous, there remains little place for sublimity in the unfolding of the Revolution. The term "sublime" is noteworthy only for its absence in the *Reflections*; it occurs in but a few passages, as when Burke advocates the infusion and dissemination of "sublime principles," appealed to as an antidote to the Revolution's pernicious effects.[40] At the same time, in his characterization of the Revolution as among the most extraordinary occurrences in human history, Burke cannot help but express his astonishment at the event, which once again aligns it – against his will – with the sublime. He even compares it, in its disruptiveness and in the alarm it excites, to "a miracle in the physical order of things," since such a moral and political disaster has upended the very laws of society.[41]

In the months and years following the publication of the *Reflections*, during which time the Revolution became increasingly radical in its demands and corrosive to the institutions that Burke sought to preserve, he became still more strident in his condemnation. On 11 April 1794, in a speech delivered to the House of Commons at a time when the Reign of Terror had attained a fever pitch, Burke recalls that

> the condition of France at this moment was so frightful and horrible, that if a painter wished to pourtray a description of hell, he could not find so terrible a model, or a subject so pregnant with horror, and fit for his purpose. Milton, with all that genius which enabled him to excel in descriptions of this nature, would have been ashamed to have presented to his readers such a hell as France now was, or such a devil as a modern jacobin; he would have thought his design revolting to the most unlimited imagination, and his colouring overcharged beyond all allowance for the license even of poetical painting.[42]

In the *Enquiry*, Burke frankly acknowledges the delight we take in reading historical narratives about the fall of empires and the calamitous deaths of virtuous men. And, in commenting on what he finds "poetical" in Milton's description of the proudly defiant Satan, who rises up from the lake of fire after being cast down from heaven, he states that it consists "in images of a tower, an archangel, the sun rising through mists, or in an eclipse, the ruin of monarchs, and the revolutions of kingdoms."[43] But when faced with an actual contemporary revolution and ruin of a monarch, Burke not only denounces it on moral and political grounds, but suggests that it is so beyond the pale in the horrors it shows us as to be an unfit object of artistic representation; even "the most unlimited imagination" would be repulsed before its excesses. The withholding of the accolade of sublimity to the Revolution stems not from its failure to instantiate the sources of the sublime, as identified in the *Enquiry*, but from its possessing them "beyond all allowance"; it appears, paradoxically, more sublime than the sublime itself.

Was Burke's refusal to designate the Revolution as sublime a failure of nerve on his part? Was it due to a repression of the disturbing moral implications of an aesthetic theory to which he continued to assent? Was it the result of a prudent rethinking and revision of a prior position whose limitations he now realized? What is certain is the presence of a tension here between Burke's early aesthetic and later political writings.[44] It seems that the close association Burke drew, in his earlier work, between the terrible and the sublime subsequently placed him in the uncomfortable position of being unable to deny, except at the price of contradiction, sublimity to things at once terrible and morally deplorable. In the *Enquiry*, Burke does not argue that one ought to have sublime experiences in response to particular natural phenomena and works of art – though he might very well have felt that a reader who failed to find *Paradise Lost* sublime was rather insensible. The aim of his investigation is to account for our actual experience, not to instruct us in the art of having proper experiences or making correct aesthetic judgments. Unlike Kant, who tends to subordinate feeling to judgment, Burke foregrounds the physiological response, the shudder-inducing encounter, before he explicates the properties that call it forth. Precisely on account of the power of the sublime, it is not something that we can refuse as we please; it forces itself upon us.[45]

If an action or response can be described as moral or immoral only to the extent that it involves freedom of choice without compulsion – a conditional that we may very well deny, but that has nonetheless exercised a profound influence on modern moral thought – then our experience of certain objects of perception as sublime, as Burke explicates it, is open to neither moral praise nor censure. Yet Burke's refusal to designate the Revolution as sublime suggests that whereas the experience of the sublime can be read as the result of an involuntary physiological process, the judgment of whether or not something is sublime has a moral aspect that cannot be reduced to the mechanism of stimulus-response. With its connection to vastness and infinity, the sublime carries lofty overtones, and Burke's later political writings indicate that these should not be transferred over to the morally base. His phenomenological reading of the sublime does not purge the word of its positive moral connotations. Even if the sublime is more akin to a state of terror than to a state of elevation, the term continues to have resonances with that which is exalted. At the sight of the excesses of the Revolution, Burke was thus unwilling to apply the label of the sublime, whose "ruling principle" he held to be "terror," to actual acts of terror. Such a depiction ran the risk of unintentionally elevating what deserved to be denounced, in the strongest terms, as evil.

Representing Radical Evil

The hazards of depicting evil aesthetically have not been lost on those seeking to diminish its allure. Susan Neiman contends that "once evil becomes aesthetic, it's not far from becoming glamorous."[46] She argues that the dangerous tendency to aestheticize evil, exhibited in the writings of the Marquis de Sade, finds its proper corrective in the countervailing tendency to treat it as "boring," exemplified in the work of Hannah Arendt. In *Eichmann in Jerusalem: A Report on the Banality of Evil* – "the best attempt at theodicy postwar philosophy has produced" according to Neiman – Arendt strips evil of its allure in laying bare the mediocrity of one of the chief administrators of the "Final Solution."[47] On account of her exposure of the shallowness of evil, Arendt stands as the foremost representative of the thesis that evil is banal, an idea that underwrites both functionalist accounts of the history of genocide and psychological explanations of atrocities in terms of human beings' readiness to obey authority.[48] Against the temptation to portray evil as profound, Neiman insists that "not evil but goodness should be portrayed with depth and dimension"; she further notes that while Arendt represents perpetrators of atrocity as thoughtless and shallow, "when Arendt described heroes, her use of rhetoric displayed moral passion verging on the sublime."[49] Arendt appears, in this reading, as a thinker who reserves the sublime for the truly heroic and wisely denies it to that which is evil. Yet when we probe more deeply into Arendt's writings and look beyond *Eichmann in Jerusalem*, we see that Arendt's own portrayal of evil slips into an aesthetics of the sublime – at least as Burke characterizes it.

Arendt was not averse to characterizing totalitarianism and other objectionable political phenomena as grotesque, a fact that should already lead us to question her being upheld as an exemplary de-aestheticizer of evil. Nonetheless, to suggest that we might find moments of intersection with the sublime in her representation of evil seems *prima facie* implausible and even offensive. Unlike Burke and Kant, Arendt did not propound a theory of aesthetics, but her recognition of the intimate relationship between politics and artistic performance made her sensitive to the aesthetic dimensions of the political, in both its seductive and its repugnant aspects. In her lectures on Kant's political philosophy, delivered at the New School for Social Research in 1970, Arendt examined the political significance of Kant's writings on aesthetics with special attention to the third *Critique*. But she showed less interest in assessing the validity of Kant's interpretation of the sublime and the beautiful and was more concerned with explicating his reflections on the faculty of judgment. According to Arendt, Kant was the first major thinker to devote serious attention to this faculty, and she saw his work as the point of departure for her own reflections on it.[50] In contrast to her intense engagement with Kant, Arendt's references to Burke are scattered and disconnected. She refers to him on a few occasions in her treatment of imperialism in *The Origins of Totalitarianism*; more notably, in the third and concluding part of the book, on totalitarianism, she mentions his idea of "acting in concert," an idea important to her later theorization of the political.[51]

Although Arendt expressed no notable interest in Burke's aesthetic theory, the parallels between the Burkean sublime and Arendt's representation of radical evil in *The Origins of Totalitarianism* invite us to a closer examination. In *Eichmann in Jerusalem*, the architect of genocide appears in Arendt's portrayal as a witless and altogether mediocre bureaucrat; one of the reasons her argument generated such an outcry was because it was perceived as making him appear all too ordinary.[52] But what of the political system in which Eichmann operated and which enabled his crimes? After pointing to the endurance of ancient classifications of government, Arendt concedes, in *The Origins of Totalitarianism*, that "it seems extremely unlikely" that a new form of rule, never recognized or known before, could suddenly appear after more than "two and half thousand years."[53] She maintains, however, that this unlikely possibility has, in fact, become a reality. Vigorously contesting the categorization of totalitarianism as a modern form of tyranny, Arendt proclaims that this "novel form of government" is "unprecedented."[54] It is, above all, in its "radical evil" that totalitarian government differentiates itself from the recognizable forms of tyranny and authoritarian rule that preceded it. It was Kant who coined the term "radical evil," and Arendt consciously adopts the expression from him as especially apt for describing the new political phenomenon she seeks to understand.[55] Reflecting on how such evil has come into being, her study of totalitarianism mirrors Burke's *Reflections on the Revolution in France*; in both cases, an attempt is made to represent what is taken to be a novel political evil unamenable to traditional concepts and categories.[56]

Arendt herself never refers to totalitarianism as sublime; one cannot even imagine this word on her lips when speaking about the Third Reich. What could be a more perverse abuse of the concept of "*das Erhabene*," in which Kant discerned a mark of human dignity and moral loftiness, than to apply it to the inhumanity of totalitarian government? Yet her description of National Socialism in *The Origins of Totalitarianism* tells a more complicated story.[57] Arendt asserts that "if lawfulness is the essence of non-tyrannical government and lawlessness is the essence of tyranny, then terror is the essence of totalitarian domination."[58] It is not only that totalitarianism terrifies, like so many other horrors in the world, but that terror belongs to it uniquely as its essence; in Burke's language, it is its "ruling principle." Unlike other dictatorships, where terror functions as a means to destroy the opposition, and thus serves some utilitarian purpose, in totalitarianism, "terror becomes total when it becomes independent of all opposition."[59] Instead of slackening after resistance has been eliminated, it accelerates and begins to target those who do not oppose the regime. Following the abolition of the space of freedom that separates them from the leader, even loyal citizens are terrorized. In "a state of affairs in which every citizen feels himself directly confronted with the will of the Leader," the sense of proximity augments anxiety.[60] Throughout history, regimes have inflicted grievous harm upon human beings and have killed large numbers of people, but what makes totalitarianism distinct is that "wherever it has ruled, it has begun to destroy the essence of man."[61] Arendt sardonically observes that "we have learned that the power of man is so great that he really can be what he wishes to be."[62] The realization of this power leads not to utopia, but to catastrophe; in the concentration camps, in particular, "we catch a glimpse into the abyss of the 'possible.'"[63] When Arendt declares that totalitarianism has "exploded" all previous systems of political classification, she indicates the inadequacy of familiar categories in conceptually circumscribing the resulting abyss; it cannot be contained within our moral and political vocabulary.[64] Whereas "murder is only a limited evil," the erasure of the human person and the abolition of human spontaneity and plurality achieved in the camps exceeds recognizable limits.[65] Organized "on the vastest, most improbable scale," these crimes are rendered unbelievable on account of their "very immensity."[66] This surpassing of limits gives totalitarianism an almost fictitious quality. Arendt uses the word "unreality" to describe it and even remarks that the experience of the camps seems like something not of this world, but rather "a story to tell of another planet."[67] Yet, in the midst of references to its unreality, she adds that totalitarianism is "a phenomenon that nevertheless confronts us with its overpowering reality."[68]

Burke claims that "despotic governments, which are founded on the passions of men, and principally upon the passion of fear, keep their chief as much as may be from the public eye. The policy has been the same in many cases of religion. Almost all the heathen temples were dark."[69] The despotic inclination to concealment seems to accord little with the penchant for spectacle and mass participation at work in the Third Reich, with its Nuremberg rallies and its propagandistic representations of the Führer. But Arendt herself perceives in the Nuremberg party days a similarity with "the ritual of secret societies, which also used to frighten their members into secretiveness by means of frightful, awe-inspiring symbols."[70] The fact that "the secret of totalitarian movements is exposed in broad daylight does not necessarily change the nature of the experience," in which the participants feel themselves privy to something terrible and great.[71] Moreover, in both Nazi Germany and the Stalinist Soviet Union, instances of the leader's public appearance are the exception rather than the rule. It is not the leader's visibility, but his separation from the larger community and even from the upper echelons of the movement, that "spread[s] around him an aura of impenetrable mystery which corresponds to his 'intangible preponderance.'"[72] While the private lives of politicians in democracies are paraded on account of their "publicity value," the private lives of leaders of totalitarian movements are kept "absolutely secret."[73] Arendt goes so far as to allege that "the only rule of which everybody in a totalitarian state may be sure is that the more visible government agencies are, the less power they carry."[74] The internal opacity of the totalitarian state, in which the people are unsure of their own position and thus kept in a state of fearful uncertainty, corresponds to its external opacity, in which foreign observers falsely seek rational or utilitarian explanations for the regime's bizarre policy shifts.

It might be objected at this point that totalitarianism, through its obscurantism, gives merely the impression of being sublime to those under its rule; Arendt, however, actually divests totalitarianism of its ostensible sublimity in her explication of the practices and mechanisms of totalitarian government. In showing how the system functions, she does not endow but deprives the leadership and the operations of government of their mysterious aura. According to Burke, clarity is inimical to the sublime; Arendt's exposition, in elucidating the nature of this new system of government, might be read then as destroying the false sublimity of evil. But we must not forget that Arendt's tendency to clarify is offset by an insistence that with totalitarianism we are faced with something which "simply surpass[es] our powers of understanding."[75] This applies especially to the death camps, the most extreme instance of evil, where not only the dehumanizing experience of the victims but the very fact of the camps' existence defies comprehension. In making this claim, Arendt has no intention of engaging in mystification; on the contrary, it would be mystification to imagine that we see clearly in the midst of obscurity. Pre-empting the criticism that she has succumbed to the temptation to mystify evil, Arendt turns the table on her would-be critics in observing that "there is a great temptation to explain away the intrinsically incredible by means of liberal rationalizations. In each one of us, there lurks such a liberal, wheedling us with the voice of common sense."[76] In fact, she maintains that the "common-sense disinclination to believe the monstrous" is encouraged by totalitarianism itself.[77] In the 1950 preface to the first edition of *The Origins of Totalitarianism*, Arendt explains that "comprehension does not mean denying the outrageous, deducing the unprecedented from precedents, or explaining phenomena by such analogies and generalities that the impact of reality and the shock of experience are no longer felt."[78] Although we must not allow ourselves to be overwhelmed by "the shock of experience," the refusal to confront it constitutes an evasion.

In an interview with Günter Gaus from 1964, Arendt described her "shock" on "the day we learned about Auschwitz."[79] She relates that "it was really as if an abyss had opened."[80] The astonishment was due not just to "the number of victims" but to "the method, the fabrication of corpses."[81] Burke identifies "astonishment" as "the effect of the sublime in its highest degree" and describes it as "that state of the soul, in which all its motions are suspended, with some degree of horror."[82] The horror remains relative since the spectator – the beholder of the abyss – has not been directly harmed. Likewise, Arendt asserts that "only the fearful imagination of those who have been aroused by such reports but have not actually been smitten in their own flesh … can afford to keep thinking about horrors."[83] Here, the spectator occupies a privileged position, compared to the victim, since she has not suffered from trauma beyond repair. Following a period of "speechless outrage and impotent horror" upon learning about the Holocaust, Arendt sought to understand how "something which never should have been" became actual.[84] The movement from a state of mute numbness to articulacy is accompanied by an acknowledgement of the abiding importance of this traumatic moment for post-war thought; she notes that "in fear and trembling, have they finally realized of what man is capable – and this is indeed the precondition of any modern political thinking."[85]

In 1961, Arendt was sent on assignment to Jerusalem to report on the trial of Eichmann, whom the Mossad had apprehended in Argentina the previous year. She here had the opportunity to revisit both the problem of totalitarianism and the problem of evil, and this experience played an important role in the development of her subsequent thinking on moral judgment and moral responsibility. The series of articles written about the trial, first published in *The New Yorker* and then republished in the form of *Eichmann in Jerusalem*, has been taken as constituting Arendt's most original contribution to the problem of evil as well as representing her mature view of it. In describing, years after the trial, her initial impression of Eichmann, Arendt wrote that "I was struck by a manifest shallowness in the doer."[86] It is no accident that Arendt seized upon shallowness as a defining feature of Eichmann's personality; this quality was fundamental not only to the accused's character, but to the banality of evil itself as Arendt conceived it. For Burke, among all the spatial orientations, depth has the most affinity with the sublime, and in stressing the absence of depth, Arendt deprives Eichmann of any hint of sublimity. Notwithstanding his role in the genocide of the Jews, he appears not as a "monster" but as a "clown," lacking the rudimentary capacity to think.[87] According to Arendt, it was thoughtlessness, rather than malevolence, that distinguished the nature of his evil and the evil of the majority of those complicit in the Holocaust. In agreement with Augustine, evil is explained, at least in this instance, as due to a kind of deficiency, and this lack – in the form of the absence of thinking – does not serve to exculpate the perpetrator but is precisely that for which he is held responsible. Arendt parts with Augustine, however, in discerning the moral danger in an unquestioning adherence to duty rather than in a refusal to obey or in an act of self-assertion.[88] Ultimately a pathetic and ridiculous figure, Eichmann is even denied the passion of the sadist and the ideological vision of the fanatical believer. The contrast with Arendt's depiction of totalitarianism could hardly be more stark, where the political system appears extraordinary in its monstrosity.

It would be a simplification, though, to imagine that, in her approach to the problem of evil, Arendt moved from an aesthetics of evil in *The Origins of Totalitarianism* to a de-aestheticizing of it in *Eichmann in Jerusalem*. The latter text does not overturn the former, but completes it. This point needs to be emphasized since some of Arendt's most astute interpreters have constructed a trajectory in which an initial conception of evil as radical later yields to a conception of evil as banal.[89] Yet what has changed here is not the conception of evil but the object of analysis; there is a shift from studying totalitarianism as a political system to studying the individuals who were part of this system and made possible its functioning. Arendt sought to avoid falling into the trap of depicting these individuals, whether leaders giving orders or underlings engaged in killing, as figures of "satanic greatness"; she was always scornful of depictions of Hitler and Stalin as incarnations of some daemonic force, and when her former teacher Karl Jaspers drew attention to the risk that her assessment of totalitarianism was liable to inadvertently raise the stature of its leaders, she expressed agreement with his reservations.[90]

Against the unintentional elevation of evil to greatness, Jaspers points out that "bacteria can cause epidemics that wipe out nations, but they remain merely bacteria."[91] In the same letter to Arendt, dated 19 October 1946, Jaspers further insists that "we have to see these things in their total banality, in their prosaic triviality" and notes that his own "more sober outlook" on these matters marks a departure from common opinion.[92]

Immediately after these comments, he asserts that her characterization, in a prior letter to him, of the extremity of the Nazis' crimes suggests that she has "almost taken the path of poetry."[93] The recognition of the power of her language comes with an unconcealed discomfort at the perils this path poses for one committed to patient and methodical enquiry. Jaspers explains that "a Shakespeare would never be able to give adequate form to this material – his instinctive aesthetic sense would lead to a falsification of it – and that's why he couldn't attempt it. There is no idea and no essence here."[94] This passage, in conjuring forth the image of the poet standing before an object of evil that cannot be properly portrayed, calls to mind Burke's assertion that Milton would balk at the prospect of depicting the horrors of the French Revolution; yet the difference between the two pronouncements is not insignificant. For Burke, Milton "would have been ashamed" to treat something "so frightful and horrible" as the Terror as worthy of poetic representation – it cannot be represented because the conscience of the artist and the dictates of propriety disallow it.[95] For Jaspers, it is the "aesthetic sense" itself that renders the poet incapable of offering an adequate representation. Far from being particularly adept at bringing out the truth of the matter, the poet must yield to the more prosaic psychologist and sociologist. While Jaspers does not elaborate on why this is the case, his misgivings stem from the conviction that "the prosaic triviality" of the perpetrators resists translation into the realm of the poetic. Arendt was less inclined to fear the distorting effects of the "aesthetic sense" – and also had a lower regard for the social sciences than did Jaspers – but she too expressed doubt that the works of Shakespeare, Milton, Melville, and Dostoevsky, with their portrayals of "great villains," would be of much avail in understanding the psychology of Nazi perpetrators.[96]

Jaspers's denial of "idea" and "essence" to the perpetrators' crimes resonates with Arendt's emphasis on the vacuity and thoughtlessness of Eichmann; like Jaspers, she seeks to grasp evil in terms of its inherent deficiency. This line of interpretation draws on Augustine's privationist view of evil, in which being is aligned with the good. At the same time, Jaspers's repudiation of essence is at loggerheads with Arendt's fixation on the essence of radical evil. Her essentialist quest is evident in the first edition of *The Origins of Totalitarianism*; it is still more pronounced in the revised edition, published in 1958, in which the repeated references to "essence" in the newly added concluding chapter indicate that totalitarianism must be understood in terms of its unique content, not its lack of content.[97] In Arendt's representation of its crimes and horrors, totalitarianism itself, as opposed to the mediocre people who support it, partakes of the monstrous. Her characterization of it as "explosive" conveys its surpassing of the bounds of what was hitherto conceived as possible. It is a matter not of absence, but of excess. Raymond Aron noted that in reading Arendt, "one risks feeling mysteriously attracted by the horror or the absurdity that is described."[98] The "mysterious attraction" derives, in part, from the sense of encountering an actualized impossibility. After declaring that "when the impossible was made possible it became the unpunishable, unforgivable absolute evil," Arendt adds that such evil is not only unforgivable, but also unintelligible in light of the available philosophical resources.[99] Arendt writes:

> It is inherent in our entire philosophical tradition that we cannot conceive of a "radical evil," and this is true for both Christian theology, which conceded even to the Devil himself a celestial origin, as well as for Kant, the only philosopher who, in the word he coined for it, at least must have suspected the existence of this evil even though he immediately rationalized it in the concept of a "perverted ill will" that could be explained by comprehensible motives. Therefore, we actually have nothing to fall back on in order to understand a phenomenon that nevertheless confronts us with its overpowering reality and breaks down all standards we know.[100]

Arendt's observation that the devil himself was a fallen angel suggests that prior imaginings about diabolical evil were inadequate since they could not conceive of evil independently of some anterior good. Yet her own position remains opposed to any sort of Manichaeism, which posits the dualistic clash of two equally primordial moral principles, and stands closer to the Augustinian tradition, which sees evil emerging out of the abuse of our creaturely freedom. The rather curious reference to the devil's genealogy might seem out of place in the context of Arendt's political analysis of "a novel form of government," but it functions as a reminder that historical reality has exceeded the philosophical imagination. It also indicates Arendt's scepticism towards attempts to apprehend the nature of evil through introducing the figure of the devil rather than providing a careful examination of the actions of human beings. In her review of Denis de

Rougemont's *The Devil's Share*, Arendt asserts that "instead of facing the music of man's genuine capacity for evil and analyzing the nature of man, he [Rougemont] in turn ventures into a flight from reality and writes on the nature of the Devil, thereby, despite all dialectics, evading the responsibility of man for his deeds."[101] One of Arendt's abiding concerns in her reflections on evil is that human beings be held accountable for their actions. Her objections to both psychoanalysis and behaviourism are due to her sense that they absolve of responsibility in reducing us to either a complex of impersonal drives or a series of stimulus-response reactions; the invocation of the devil as a historical agent or force runs the same risk.

For Arendt, Kant showed more insight than both the modern social sciences and the literature of the daemonic in emphasizing the importance of human beings' freedom and their responsibility for their participation in evil. But while praising Kant for having an inkling of the existence of radical evil, Arendt also takes him to task for having "immediately rationalized it."[102] In speaking of radical evil, Arendt adopts Kantian terminology, but she attributes a meaning to the term that is foreign to Kant. When Kant discusses "radical evil," he does not use the term to designate a specific type of evil, its most egregious form present in the intentions and actions of superlatively wicked human beings. It is radical not in the sense of its extremity, but in the sense of its lying at the root (*radix*) of things. A similar meaning is at work in Burke's description of the corrosive effects of the Revolution on French society, when he asserts that "the evil is radical and intrinsic." In Kant, however, radical evil, rather than being rooted in a conjunction of peculiar historical circumstances – as it is in Burke's account of the French Revolution – lies deep within our own being. It refers to a propensity infecting our nature and corrupting the basis of our maxims. Kant claims, in *Religion within the Bounds of Bare Reason*, that the propensity for evil "cannot be *extirpated* through human powers"; the root is too deeply rooted to be uprooted.[103] Nonetheless, Kant intends not to argue for the potency of wickedness, but to emphasize the depth of human freedom and the profound mystery of our capacity to choose between good and evil, both of which always remain available options to us as free moral agents. Arendt concurs with Kant's account of human freedom and moral agency, but she conceives of radical evil as a particular form of actualized evil rather than a propensity in all of us. The mark of radical evil lies not in its deep-seated roots but in its terrifying power to uproot, to extirpate freedom. It is deracinating. Identifying freedom with natality, the human capacity to begin and to bring something new into the world, Arendt conceives of the totalitarian impetus to destroy this capacity, to eliminate all spontaneity, as the elimination of the essence of the human. When and where it succeeds, it makes human beings superfluous. She writes, "men insofar as they are more than animal reaction and fulfillment of functions are entirely superfluous to totalitarian regimes."[104] The destruction of spontaneity and freedom occurs at all levels of totalitarian society, but its most extreme form occurs in the camps, whose "horror can never be fully embraced by the imagination for the very reason that it [life in the concentration camps] stands outside of life and death."[105]

As Arendt explains in *The Human Condition*, "those offenses which, since Kant, we call 'radical evil'" are neither punishable nor forgivable – "they therefore transcend the realm of human affairs and the potentialities of human power."[106] In 1946, more than a decade prior to this pronouncement, Arendt wrote to Jaspers that "the Nazi crimes, it seems to me, explode the limits of the law; and that is precisely what constitutes their monstrousness."[107] Stressing totalitarianism's transgressive character, she interprets its call to duty as itself an act of violation. In totalitarian states, obedience means not just compliance with the commands of superiors, but surrender to an ostensibly higher law. It is in fulfilment of "the law of History" that the Stalinist Soviet Union and in fulfilment of "the law of Nature" that the Third Reich pursue their inhuman political experiments and commit unprecedented atrocities.[108] In the name of a higher law, the most basic standards of decency are disregarded and the most atrocious actions are legitimated. This law, whether that of history or nature, sanctions and enables crimes that "explode the limits of the law." For Arendt, the crimes of totalitarianism are so unprecedented that it is necessary not only to devise new juridical categories in order to prosecute them – as evident in the procedures of the Nuremberg trials – but also to formulate new moral categories in order to classify them. Arendt was certainly not insensitive to the sufferings of the victims of totalitarianism, but what she saw as distinguishing the evil at work in totalitarian regimes could not be arrived at through addressing the amount of suffering inflicted or the number of individuals killed. Such a perspective, even if grounded in a laudable sense of compassion, risked degenerating into a quantitative approach, in which the substantive differences between totalitarianism and other oppressive forms of government were effectively effaced.

Arendt realized that her representation of totalitarianism ran the risk of making it appear so totally other in its mad "unreality" that readers could feel themselves insulated from it; terrifying as it was, it remained an external danger that could be fought with external means. The danger she addresses in *Eichmann in Jerusalem* is this sense of complacency, in which we imagine that simply because we do not harbour wicked intentions, we are therefore incapable of participating in atrocities. In her report on the Eichmann trial, Arendt did not perform an about-face after hearing the platitudes of the accused; rather, she sought to understand him within the framework of totalitarianism that she had articulated in her earlier work. *Eichmann in Jerusalem* should be read not as Arendt's definitive word on the problem of evil, but as the indispensable postscript to her portrayal of radical evil in *The Origins of Totalitarianism*. With her emphasis on the role of thoughtlessness, Arendt indicates that lack of malice is not a sufficient safeguard against doing evil. But this shift of focus does not lead to a rejection of her prior depiction of radical evil. Arendt's later emphasis on thoughtlessness can itself be seen as an elaboration of her earlier pronouncements on how totalitarianism impairs the exercise of individuals' faculties. Arendt asserts that the totalitarian state aims not at implanting deep ideological convictions in people, but at depriving them of the capacity to form convictions altogether.[109] It seeks to make them so passively reactive that any authoritative statement from the state will be accepted and acted upon without rational deliberation. Totalitarianism produces not just fanatical believers, but thoughtless drones who believe whatever they are told to believe and do whatever they are told to do. In fact, even the assent involved in believing can be dispensed with; "the model 'citizen' of a totalitarian state" is "Pavlov's dog," a "bundle of reactions that can always be liquidated and replaced by other bundles of reactions that behave in exactly the same way."[110] Totalitarianism, in reducing individuals to a state of superfluousness, attempts to rob them of the use of their faculties and deny them their supersensible vocation, as Kant terms it.

According to Kant, the experience of the sublime exhibits "a movement of the mind connected with the judging of the object" whereas the enjoyment of the beautiful is predicated upon "calm contemplation."[111]

The Burkean sublime shows neither movement nor calmness, but rather a suspension of reason, in which the spontaneous operation of the faculties is forced to a halt. In giving examples of this experience, Burke refers to human beings' encounters with extreme power in both nature and society. He asserts that when they meet those in positions of power, youth "are commonly struck with an awe which takes away the free use of their faculties."[112] Although elsewhere referring to privation as one of the sources of the sublime, in this example of awestruck youth Burke depicts privation not as its source but as its effect. A fascination with authority may be conducive to the maintenance of the social fabric since it cultivates respect for established social and political institutions, which Burke takes to be a component of civic virtue, but it also can be mobilized in the service of despotism. The loss of citizens' "free use of their faculties" brings with it the danger of the loss of freedom itself. It is this danger become reality that Arendt confronts in her analysis of totalitarianism.

The fact that Arendt's representation of totalitarianism coincides with the features that Burke sees as integral to the sublime and as sufficient for its production might be adduced as proof that Burke's conception of the sublime is not tenable, that he has neglected to identify something crucial that would preserve the sublime from suffering contamination with crimes and atrocities. Notwithstanding its own ambivalences, the Kantian sublime proves more resistant to amoral and immoral applications. But since, according to Kant, no sensible object deserves to be designated as sublime – neither the starry heavens above nor the raging sea below, neither Handel's oratorios nor the pyramids of Giza – the appeal to Kant carries with it a considerable contraction of the sublime whereby it no longer applies to any aesthetic phenomenon whatsoever, understood in the broad sense as referring to objects of *aisthesis.* If we insist that some objects merit being classified as sublime, then the question of the properties that mark these objects as such obtrudes upon us once again. And even if we pull back from Burke's assessment on account of its morally problematic implications, it is important to consider here, more broadly, what remains of evil once it is deprived of the attributes that Burke sees as constitutive of the sublime. If evil is no longer terrifying, powerful, and obscure, then what distinguishes it from the merely unethical? In the only instance that Arendt uses the expression the "banality of evil" in *Eichmann in Jerusalem,* she tellingly describes it as "fearsome, word-and-thought-defying."[113]

On account of the insidious danger it poses to humankind, banal evil, not to speak of radical evil, is frightening in Arendt's reading of it. Conversely, where evil shows itself to be impotent, incapable of harming us at the present moment and incapable of threatening us in the distant future, then it has lost one of its distinguishing marks. The same applies to evil without obscurity, in which it appears readily intelligible. It is seldom the case that evil is ascribed to that which is impotent, transparent, and utterly deficient in fearsomeness, although these same qualities are often applied, unproblematically, to certain forms and agents of moral badness.[114] The argument that evil is just a more extreme form of ordinary moral badness, different in degree, not in kind, neglects to consider the aesthetic dimensions of evil and the aesthetic responses it arouses.

For Arendt, "the real evil is what causes us speechless horror, when all we can say is: This should never have happened."[115] Although Arendt's characterization of evil here might appear purely negative, she acknowledges that evil does not simply repulse with horror but seduces as well. She notes that "evil in the Third Reich had lost the quality by which most people recognize it – the quality of temptation."[116] Within contemporary politics and contemporary theory, the sublime may also be recognized by this quality. A disillusionment with the capacities of a political system to correct abuses and injustices – a recognition, as it were, of the pervasive banality of evil – opens the space for the sublime as a political solution. All too often, perception of its danger proves insufficient in diminishing the fascination with it or the ardour for it; indeed, a sense of danger can even heighten its allure and serve as a further enticement.[117]

If evil never intersects with the sublime, then the sublime never intersects with evil. The danger of maintaining that there are moments of such intersection is that we may unintentionally glamorize or elevate what we deem to be morally reprehensible and seek to condemn; at the same time, in considering the possibility of such an intersection, we also call into question the moral status of the sublime. In the domain of politics, the sublime can serve as a jolt to shake us from our complacency, to make us alive to new possibilities; but it can also function as an anaesthetic that obviates the difficulty of exercising our own judgment, that invites intellectual paralysis and the deferral of moral considerations. It then facilitates the very thoughtlessness that Arendt saw at work in the banality of evil. In this respect, Burke's connection of the sublime with a state of cognitive suspension serves as a better warning of the moral and political dangers of the sublime than the Kantian association of it with the triumph of reason.

But need one really be on guard before the sublime? Or is it only its false imitators that are to be feared? At this point, one might be inclined to vanquish the entire problem by drawing a simple distinction between that which merely appears to be sublime and that which actually is sublime. But once the sublime has been severed from the realm of appearance, broken up into its true and its merely apparent forms, it runs the risk of stepping outside of the aesthetic domain altogether. In rescuing the venerated category from the clutches of immoralism, preserving it from contamination with evil, we risk depriving it of its applicability to specific objects of perception. The integrity of the category of the "pseudo-sublime," like that of the "pseudo-beautiful," depends upon its definition. If something appears to be beautiful, then on what grounds might beauty to be denied to it? What makes its beauty "false"? Is it because, upon closer scrutiny, what first seemed beautiful now reveals itself to suffer from imperfections that make it undeserving of the accolade? This suggests that there are purely phenomenal grounds according to which the appellation can be reasonably withdrawn. The initial verdict is liable to correction through a greater attentiveness to the manner in which an object appears to us. Or should we say that a thing suffers from falsity because it remains deficient in an invisible "inner beauty"? In that case, the aesthetic has expanded beyond the realm of appearance and lost itself in that which no eye can see. Here, moral judgments often supplant aesthetic ones even as the language of aesthetics continues to be invoked.

Another possible solution, which preserves – although less stringently – the sublime from contamination with evil, is to reframe the problem with reference to the kind of person who undergoes a spontaneous experience of the sublime in response to particular phenomena – to accept that the experience of the sublime has specific phenomenological characteristics, themselves devoid of moral value, but to insist that those whose experience of the sublime is excited by certain objects are worthy of commendation or censure depending upon the nature of the excitatory objects. For example, to have the feeling of the sublime in reaction to an atrocity or to a criminal act of violence might be seen as symptomatic of wickedness or some form of mental derangement. In the case of the latter, aesthetics yields to pathology.[118] This pathologizing mode with reference to spontaneous aesthetic experience can also be extended to include considered aesthetic judgment.[119] If to pronounce an aesthetic judgment is to make an involuntary confession about the state of one's soul, it can be read as a sign of spiritual health or mental illness. Symptomatic readings of this kind may deepen our understanding of the complexities of human psychology; they may show us how evaluative judgments are rooted in an individual's psychic constitution, both revealing something about it and explainable through it. Often, however, such readings are themselves screens for moral judgment under the veneer of science. The intrusion of moral judgment may not itself be objectionable – and may very well be welcome – but when unrecognized as such it can lead to unfruitful debates in which arguments about aesthetics occlude matters of moral disagreement. In the case of the sublime, the passion that its false attribution excites points beyond a purely scholarly interest in correct classification or conceptual precision. It bespeaks the sublime's morally laden significance.

Chapter Four

Wicked Spectators

When something we find morally reprehensible is identified as sublime, we tend to react with indignation. If there exists an impermeable barrier separating the aesthetic and the moral, outrage does not seem to be warranted, but if the boundaries between the two are more porous than this sharp distinction allows, it is not surprising that aesthetic judgments can themselves become the objects of moral judgment. The problem of the moral status of aesthetic judgment and aesthetic experience obtrudes upon us most forcefully when we consider responses to instances of evil, actual as well as fictive. How should we critically and affectively respond to them? Can art itself help us to answer this question?

During the eighteenth century, the argument that the theatre exercised an educative function in matters of morality was one of its justifications; leading lights of the age heralded it as a vehicle of enlightenment, one through which the public could be instructed and edified. Theatrical performances were defended both on aesthetic grounds, as a source of refined pleasure and a means to cultivate taste, and on moral ones, since they supposedly had the potential to inculcate a love of virtue and a horror of vice in the hearts and minds of spectators. But it was on account of this touted capacity of the theatre to shape the audience, its power to disseminate ideas and to influence behaviour, that it became a site of contestation. In his *Letter to M. d'Alembert on the Theatre*, published in 1758, Rousseau inveighed against d'Alembert's suggestion that Geneva would benefit from establishing a public theatre. He challenged the verdict that the theatre, in making virtue appear "lovable," functioned as a medium for instilling it in the audience; the argument that it teaches us to shun vice is equally, if not more, dubious.[1] Rousseau writes, "I suspect that any man, to whom the crimes of Phaedra or Medea were told beforehand, would hate them more at the beginning of the play than at the end."[2] Our capacity for pity, which Rousseau elsewhere hails as a much needed corrective to our inveterate egoism, can all too easily be perverted by dramatic stagings of wickedness so that we come to sympathize with those whose deeds we ought to abhor. In decrying the modern playhouse, Rousseau compares the kinds of amusement it affords the public to those of the gladiatorial spectacles held in the Roman amphitheatre. Remarkably, he actually has kinder words for the latter than for the former; while gladiatorial tournaments exacerbated the bloodthirstiness of the people in the days of the Roman Empire, Rousseau maintains that they "animated the courage and valor of the Romans" in the age of the Republic.[3]

Rousseau's animus towards the theatre was grounded in the conviction that it was a source of corruption. He not only argued that theatrical performances perverted the morals of the public; he also maintained that to take pleasure in such performances was itself morally suspect. But for all the novelty of its particular insights, his argument was less a new theorization of the theatre's failings than it was the culmination of a polemic going back centuries to the early Church Fathers and even to Plato. In describing his wayward youth, Augustine narrates his enjoyment of the theatre and the inappropriateness of the feelings that were there excited. He writes:

> But at that time at the theatres I shared the joy of lovers when they wickedly found delight in each other, even though their actions in the spectacle on the stage were imaginary; when, moreover, they lost each other, I shared their sadness by a feeling of compassion. Nevertheless, in both there was pleasure. Today I have more pity for a person who rejoices in wickedness than for a person who has the feeling of having suffered hard knocks by being deprived of a pernicious pleasure or having lost a source of miserable felicity. This is surely a more authentic compassion; for the sorrow contains no element of pleasure.[4]

Augustine finds a moral danger in both the compassion that dramatic productions excite when portraying fictional characters' sufferings and the delight we take in these characters' impermissible indulgences. In regard to the latter, he sees the staging of transgression as an invitation to be complicit in the performance of sin. The taking of pleasure in the wrongdoings of fictional characters is a sign of spectators' wickedness as well as a means of its furtherance.

The attempt to defend the arts against the charge of having morally deleterious effects has assumed various forms in the modern age. In the Enlightenment, the idea that theatrical performances and works of literature were potential sources of moral improvement was prevalent among those *philosophes* who saw in them instruments through which their ideas could be disseminated to the general public. But another possible defence was to separate the spheres of the moral and the aesthetic, and to argue that the standards of the one should not be applied to the other. In Kant's philosophy, aesthetic judgment, like teleological judgment, mediates between the realms of freedom and nature.[5] At the same time, the sphere of the aesthetic follows its own rules and is treated as autonomous vis-à-vis the domains of practical reason and theoretical reason. The aesthetic has – according to Kant – a symbolic relationship to the moral, and disinterested aesthetic experience may even prepare us, in the form of a propaedeutic, to subordinate our self-interest to the morally good.[6] Yet aesthetic judgments and moral judgments are qualitatively distinct from one another, not only in terms of their subject matter but in terms of their epistemic status. Kant approaches art from the perspective of the judge and critic; from the perspective of the artist and creator, a parallel claim for the separation of spheres was being advanced. With the emergence of calls for the autonomy of art and its liberation from the strictures of conventional morality, impediments to the free expression of the artist came to be seen as illegitimate encroachments on the activity of artistic creation. The cult of genius had already paved the way for this development and the notion of *l'art pour l'art* further reinforced it. The treatment of criminal acts as works of art, as we find in De Quincey, marks the logical culmination of this cleavage, one that enables aesthetic judgment to be comfortably cordoned off from moral qualms. This moment, which might be dubbed the liberation of the aesthetic, was quickly followed by an expansion into territory previously ceded to the moral, an aestheticizing movement exhibited in the work of Nietzsche. In his reappraisal of tragedy, which must be understood as both a creative appropriation and a subversion of Schopenhauer's insights into art and nature, Nietzsche opens the way to "an aesthetics of existence" that supplants its previous moralization.[7] Initiating a revaluation of what was hitherto condemned as evil, his transgressive philosophical project carries out a deliberate mixing of the aesthetic and the moral, wherein the latter finds itself increasingly absorbed into the former. The dangers of such a project are not to be denied. Yet the attempt to forcefully separate the aesthetic and the moral carries with it its own moral perils.

The Mirth of Tragedy

In his article on "Curiosity" in the *Philosophical Dictionary*, Voltaire asks us to imagine an angel departing from the heavenly realm and taking up a vantage point from where he observes the inhabitants of hell. He explains, "could we suppose an angel flying on six beautiful wings from the height of the Empyrean, setting out to take a view through some loophole of hell of the torments and contortions of the damned, and congratulating himself on feeling nothing of their inconceivable agonies, such an angel would much resemble the character of Beelzebub."[8] Immediately prior to this condemnation of the pitiless angelic spectator, Voltaire takes Lucretius to task for his claim that we find comfort in beholding the ordeals of others since these remind us of our security from the same evils. At the beginning of the second book of *The Nature of Things*, the poet writes:

> How lovely it is, when the winds lash the great sea into huge
> waves that beset sailors, to gaze out from dry land
> at the tribulations of others – not that we wish them ill,
> but we realize how free we are from the troubles they face.[9]

Voltaire declares that this account fails to identify the actual motive that moves people to fix their gaze on calamities, namely curiosity. Recalling his own experience, he protests that "I solemnly assure you that my pleasure, mingled as it was with uneasiness and distress, did not at all arise from reflection, nor originate in any secret comparison between my own security and the danger of the unfortunate crew."[10] His appeal to "pure curiosity," as he dubs it, opens the way to a distancing from the self, in which immersion in the object leads to a kind of self-forgetting. Voltaire here seeks to counter – in the words of Hans Blumenberg – "the suspicion of reflective self-enjoyment."[11] His devilish angel is not simply unfeeling; rather, he takes satisfaction in his lack of concern for others, and it is this sense of self-regard in his role of indifferent spectator that makes his mode of comportment so inhuman.

In *The World as Will and Representation*, the first volume of which was published in 1818, Schopenhauer also offers a critical gloss on Lucretius's description of the beholder of the tempest-tossed vessel. But whereas Voltaire rejects Lucretius's image because he finds fault with the poet's account of the psychology of the spectator, Schopenhauer actually concurs that "the sight or description of another's sufferings affords us satisfaction and pleasure, just as Lucretius beautifully and frankly expresses it at the beginning of his second book."[12] The problem with this passage is not that it misrepresents the motives and interests of spectators but that the sentiment it expresses is blameworthy; the "kind of pleasure" we derive from such sights "lies very near the source of real, positive wickedness."[13] Such wickedness manifests itself both in the small pleasures we take in the discomfiture of others and in religious doctrines that consign human beings to eternal damnation. In his unfavourable assessment of Dante's *Divine Comedy*, Schopenhauer identifies, in rather pedantic fashion, inconsistencies in the text that point to the poet's sloppiness; he also finds "the extravagant absurdity of the fundamental idea" to be off-putting.[14] But his reservations about the style of the work are subordinate to a deeper critique of the moral impulse that animates it, most objectionable in the first of its three parts. Schopenhauer sees in the *Inferno* the "*apotheosis of cruelty*."[15] He muses that to give the name of "comedy" to this spectacle of suffering can only be ironic:

A comedy indeed! Truly the world would be such a comedy for a God whose insatiable lust for revenge and studied cruelty in the last act gloated over the endless and purposeless torture of the beings whom he uselessly and frivolously called into existence, namely because they had not turned out in accordance with his intention and in their short life had done or believed otherwise than to his liking. Moreover, compared with his unexampled cruelty, all the crimes so severely punished in the *Inferno* would not be worth talking about. Indeed, he himself would be far worse than all the devils we encounter in the *Inferno*; for naturally these are acting only on his instructions and by virtue of his authority.[16]

The cruelty of the being who would orchestrate this hell corresponds to that of the spectator who finds satisfaction at its sight. In addition to railing against the active infliction of suffering on others, Schopenhauer condemns in the strongest terms the spectatorial pleasure taken in such suffering. Attacking Kant's ethics for its rigid condemnation of lying under all circumstances, he asserts that "Kant would have done better to let that special zeal loose against *Schadenfreude*; this, not lying, is the real devilish vice. For it is quite opposite to compassion and is nothing other than impotent cruelty which so gladly sees another suffering that which it is incapable of bringing about itself, and it thanks chance for doing so in its place."[17] Rather than being rated a lesser vice than active cruelty, *Schadenfreude* bears the additional stain of incapacity, as exhibited in the character of the gloating spectator. Schopenhauer does not seek to excuse those interested in watching spectacles of suffering, in the manner of Voltaire, but neither does he uniformly condemn them; what matters is not whether or not one watches, but the mode of comportment towards the suffering being before us.

Schopenhauer devotes attention to both the theatre of everyday cruelty and to dramatic productions staged at the playhouse, an evening visit to which was part of his normal daily regimen. And not surprisingly, given his unabashed pessimism, he shows a particular predilection for works of tragedy. The word "tragedy" refers to a particular form of drama, but it is also used in a much looser sense to refer to any grave misfortune or calamity, and the slippage between these meanings has been decried by aestheticians for confusing an exalted art form with the accidental troubles of everyday life. As Hegel explains, tragedy is not just some "sad story" that engages our sympathy for the misfortunes of the downcast.[18] Schopenhauer, however, claims that "the presentation of a great misfortune is alone essential to tragedy"; he perceives the virtue of tragedy in its description of "the unspeakable pain, the wretchedness and misery of mankind, the triumph of wickedness, the scornful mastery of chance, and the irretrievable fall of the just and the innocent."[19] Schopenhauer's characterization foregrounds the element of suffering, yet in referring to "the triumph of wickedness," he points not only to those who fall prey to the wicked, but to the deeds of the wicked themselves. In keeping with the maxim *homo homini lupus*, oft-repeated in his writings, he discerns the predatory character of human beings at work in behaviours both trivial and murderous, and the tragedian stages the dual role of human beings as perpetrators and victims.

In establishing the proper hierarchy of literary genres, Schopenhauer, like Hegel, awards the laurel to tragedy, but his reasons for doing so diverge sharply from those of his hated rival; he proclaims that "tragedy is to be regarded, and is recognized, as the summit of poetic art, both as regards the greatness of the effect and the difficulty of the achievement. For the whole of our discussion, it is very significant and worth noting that the purpose of this highest poetical achievement is the description of the terrible side of life."[20] Schopenhauer is known for having placed music at the pinnacle of the arts by virtue of the fact that music gives us a "*copy of the will itself*" whereas every other art gives us only "a copy of the Ideas."[21] But while tragedy must yield to music on account of the greater immediacy of the latter, it also enjoys a unique advantage over it and the other arts in its communication of the suffering that lies at the heart of existence.

Schopenhauer's insights into both the vanity of existence and the joys of aesthetic experience are grounded in his metaphysics of the will. He maintains that "the will performs the great tragedy and comedy at its own expense, and is also its own spectator."[22] This conceptualization of the world as a theatrical performance, partly indebted to playwrights such as Shakespeare and Calderón, both shapes and finds expression in the philosopher's reflections on the illusory character of the world and the nature of aesthetic perception.[23] Insofar as the will is the thing-in-itself, and the phenomenal world, in its entirety, is but its objectification, the will may be conceived simultaneously as artist and spectacle. What makes the act of reflexive viewing possible, in which the will becomes its own object, is the appearance of the intellect, a particular manifestation of the will that breaks away from its source in attaining consciousness. Even in breaking away, the intellect continues to be at the service of the will, yet there are brief moments in which its servitude is suspended, most notably in moments of aesthetic contemplation. Schopenhauer accounts for the "aesthetic pleasure" of this experience with reference to "the forgetting of oneself as individual, and the enhancement of consciousness to the pure, will-less, timeless subject of knowing that is independent of all relations."[24] Although he was himself a *bon vivant*, Schopenhauer's philosophy commends the negation of the will, the practice of self-denial that leads to the cessation of desire. But even as he objects to frivolous games, such as whist, whose purpose lies in the excitation of the will, he takes care to secure the fine arts from this charge. Other pleasures are shown to be entangled in the will, but "aesthetic pleasure" actually disassociates us from it. In his characterization of our response to the beautiful, exhibited for example in images of painterly repose, the suffering of the world momentarily vanishes. No longer conscious of his bodily desires or physical pains, the subject of such an experience enters a state of rapt contemplation in which the apprehension of the timelessly true raises him above the restlessness of temporal reality.

Our perennial state of wretchedness leads Schopenhauer to prize these rare instances of escape as well as the spirit of compassion that, through creating a sense of solidarity between us, makes our ongoing misery somewhat more endurable. In giving a phenomenological account of the experience of compassion, Schopenhauer quotes Calderón's line that "between seeing suffering and suffering there is no difference."[25] What is the meaning of positing such an intimate connection, indeed an identity relationship, between a particular experience and the beholding of it? This citation occurs in the context of Schopenhauer's remarks about our sympathies with actual sufferers, not with fictive ones. But the fact that the quote comes from a work of drama makes us wonder how different our affective response is to actual instances of suffering compared to those staged so powerfully as to appear almost indistinguishable from them. Rousseau argues that "the force of natural pity" is so strong that all the vices society perpetuates often prove insufficient to stifle it, and as an example of its deep-rootedness, he cites the case of the murderous Alexander of Pherae, who did not attend tragedies "for fear of being seen weeping with Andromache and Priam."[26] The reference to the tearful tyrant aims to demonstrate the strength of the tendency to identify with others, yet the case is peculiar because Alexander is not identifying, or afraid of identifying, with actually suffering beings but with performers who merely pretend to be suffering, who are just substitutes for historical or mythological personages. Here, Rousseau presents us with the problem of pretence, which can act on our passions more effectively than genuine pain. The distress that such identifications are able to produce, in the context of a dramatic performance, would seem to be disruptive of the repose at play in the contemplation of the beautiful, at least as Schopenhauer presents it. And, in fact, in aligning tragedy with the experience of the sublime – rather than with that of the beautiful – Schopenhauer does not fail to recognize that the viewer of scenes of violent upheaval is not simply at ease, but exhibits an internal bifurcation, indicative of "the twofold nature of his consciousness"; at one and the same time, "he feels himself as individual, as the feeble phenomenon of will" and "as the eternal, serene subject of knowing, who as the condition of every object is the supporter of this whole world."[27] Tragedy allows us to see through the barriers between self and other, yet the proper aesthetic response to the suffering victim on the stage is not the dissolving of the barrier that separates spectator and actor, the dissolution of the *principium individuationis* through a process of identification, which occurs in a genuine act of compassion and which merits, on Schopenhauer's reading, the designation of the morally good. Even when moved to shuddering before the sufferings of the drama's characters and to his own likeness to them as a fellow fragile being, the beholder of a performance of tragedy – at least one having an aesthetic experience worthy of the name – takes "pleasure in the sight of what directly opposes the will."[28] In quieting the will, art functions, for Schopenhauer, not as a spur to action but as a suspension and even annulment of it.[29]

After expressing his praise for *Hamlet* as an exemplar of the tragic on account of the ubiquity of "the sublime element" in the play, Schopenhauer states that "now if knowledge reaches the point where the vanity of all willing and striving dawns on it and the will consequently abolishes itself, it is then that the drama becomes really tragic and hence truly sublime and attains its supreme purpose."[30] The argument that tragedy has a morally educative function, in the sense that it leads to the cultivation of virtue, remains foreign to Schopenhauer. He does not think that tragedy teaches us to be more compassionate, that in displaying the plight of those on stage we learn to pity the unfortunate. From his own personal experience, he knew that his frequent visitations to the playhouse had not made him a better person. Moreover, according to his doctrine of the intelligible character, our moral constitution is not subject to changes occurring in the phenomenal world; it is immutable and remains the same from birth to death. The theatre cannot alter our character, for better or for worse, but then neither can anything else in the world; at most, it teaches us how to conform to it. To translate Schopenhauer's doctrine into the language of psychoanalysis, the triumph of the reality principle does not alter the nature of the instincts. Yet tragedy teaches us a weighty truth about our existence, and this truth is an eminently moral one; unlike the other arts, which merely quiet the will temporarily, the purpose of tragedy lies in directing us to the abolition of the will, in leading us "to turn our will away from life, to give up willing and loving life."[31] The truth that the world deserves to be renounced is indirectly shown in the unfolding of the action of the tragic drama. Sometimes it is also given express articulation in the utterances of its characters; formulations of it are to be found in the world-weary speeches of Hamlet, Macbeth, and the aged Oedipus.

In aesthetic experience, as Schopenhauer conceives it, the intellect finds itself so absorbed in an object of contemplation that willing temporarily ceases; in ascetic experience, through the practice of self-denial, the will to live is itself negated. For Schopenhauer, these are two qualitatively different experiences that correspond to distinct individual types; the former is the element of the man of genius, the latter that of the saint or holy man. Yet the spectator of tragedy, whose experience in the act of viewing a staged drama is obviously an aesthetic rather than an ascetic one, nonetheless learns to recognize the wisdom of the saint's renunciation of the world and undergoes a momentary urge to pursue the same redemptive path. In speaking of the abolition of the will in identifying tragedy's "supreme purpose," Schopenhauer slips out of the language of aesthetics and employs a vocabulary more closely tied to that used in his treatment of morals, with its more extreme advocacy of life-negation. It is in tragedy that the aesthetic and the moral come closest to intersecting.

Milton, in the preface to *Samson Agonistes*, affirms that "tragedy, as it was anciently compos'd, hath been ever held the gravest, moralest, and most profitable of all other Poems."[32] Milton's appraisal of tragedy's moral import accords with Schopenhauer's view, but it is opposed to the assessment of the pessimist's most ingenious and wayward philosophical pupil. While Nietzsche shared Milton's high regard for tragedy, he did so for reasons removed from, indeed antithetical to those of the Englishman. Instead of finding tragedy to be something "grave," he saw it as an instance of resistance to "the spirit of gravity," in which the individual and the community rise above the weight of existence and exult in overcoming the heaviness of things; and while acknowledging tragedy's educative role in shaping the Greek community, he reads it not as the "moralest" form of art, but as the one most conducive to justifying the world through its aestheticization.

Already in his first book, *The Birth of Tragedy*, published in 1872, we see Nietzsche extricating himself from Schopenhauer's philosophy even as his principal concepts and categories of analysis remain indebted to it. At the outset of this work, Nietzsche departs from the dominant philosophical tradition with its adoption of the vantage point of the critic in preference to that of the artist; instead of asking how the work appears to the audience and how the consummate critic ought to judge it, he foregrounds those neglected forces that move the artist in the act of creation – it is in this context that he introduces the well-known duality of the Apollonian and the Dionysian. But even in introducing this perspectival shift, with its attentiveness to the dynamics of the creative process, Nietzsche does not omit consideration of the position of the viewer; rather, it is in moving back and forth between two registers, the creative and the spectatorial, that he attains a fuller picture of tragedy than do his philosophical predecessors.

According to Nietzsche, Greek tragedy testifies to the Hellenes' penetrating insight into the terrors of existence. Gazing steadfastly into the abyss, they come to acknowledge the hardness of man's lot and the implacable power of fate, a recognition of the nature of things that dispels a facile and shallow optimism. At the same time, Nietzsche does not equate the Greeks' "pessimism" with bleakness or melancholia. In his characterization of Sophocles's handling of the myth of Oedipus, Nietzsche asserts that "as a poet he [Sophocles] first shows us a marvelously tied knot of a trial, slowly unraveled by the judge, bit by bit, for his own undoing."[33] Instead of perceiving in this dramatic irony a despair at the limitations of the wisest man's wisdom, Nietzsche notes that "the genuinely Hellenic delight at this dialectical solution is so great that it introduces a trait of superior cheerfulness (*Heiterkeit*) into the whole work, everywhere softening the sharp points of the gruesome presuppositions of this process."[34] More surprising still, he claims that "in *Oedipus at Colonus* we encounter the same cheerfulness, but elevated into an infinite transfiguration."[35] In what does the cheerfulness of tragedy reside, which shows us the sufferings of heroic men and women? One might imagine that *Oedipus at Colonus*, among all works of Greek tragedy, comes closest to expressing the pessimistic truth that nothingness is preferable to being; Schopenhauer, for one, was well disposed to the antinatalist pronouncements of the tragic chorus, which accorded with his own life-negating outlook and which he quotes with approval.[36] Nietzsche offers a variation of this utterance, where Silenus exclaims to the enquiring King Midas, "what is best of all is utterly beyond your reach: not to be born, not to *be*, to be *nothing*. But the second best for you is – to die soon."[37] What is noteworthy, for Nietzsche, is that the poet, after authoring words of despair, and the auditors, after hearing them, did not embrace resignation as Schopenhauer recommended; on the contrary, through tragedy, the Greeks come to embrace life all the more fervently. This spirit of affirmation is evident in tragedy's Dionysian aspect, with its intoxicating power, as well as its Apollonian one, with its delight in the oneiric play of forms.

Speaking of "the metaphysical comfort" that tragedy imparts to us, Nietzsche asserts that "life is at the bottom of things, despite all the changes of appearances, indestructibly powerful and pleasurable."[38] A sense of life's potency serves as a balm to the wounded spirit that feels all too keenly the travails of existence. Nietzsche treats the wisdom of Silenus not as an ending but as a point of departure that spurs the Greeks on to an affirmative vision, a vision at once honest in its confrontation with painful truths and celebratory in its capacity to translate them into the language of song and dance. In his description of the tragic chorus, which was originally "the chorus of satyrs, a chorus of natural beings," Nietzsche writes, "with this chorus the profound Hellene, uniquely susceptible to the tenderest and deepest suffering, comforts himself, having looked boldly right into the terrible destructiveness of so-called world history as well as the cruelty of nature, and being in danger of longing for a Buddhistic negation of the will. Art saves him, and through art – life."[39] The salvation that tragedy brings about is not the liberation from the will, but a reconciliation to existence in spite of all its pains, injustices, and terrors. Seduced to life through the enchanting power of art, the ancient Greek finds himself after the tragic performance less alienated from the world and more at home in it. Nietzsche discerns "danger" not in this moment of seduction, but in the "Buddhistic negation of the will," which Schopenhauer saw as tragedy's proper aim.[40]

Like Schopenhauer, Nietzsche interprets tragedy as a spectacle of suffering, but he also sees it as a staging of transgression that excites the sympathies of the audience. Even when they entail dire – and justly merited – punishments, these transgressions inspire awe. In *The Birth of Tragedy*, Nietzsche makes no mention of Aristotle's much debated idea of *hamartia*, sometimes translated as "tragic flaw" or "tragic error." His own interpretation of the actions that lead to the downfall of the tragic protagonist stands opposed, however, to one that explains it in terms of some form of deficiency, moral or otherwise, and ties it instead to a sublime excess. Linking Oedipus's crimes of patricide and incest with his solving of the riddle of the sphinx as acts destructive of "the most sacred natural orders," Nietzsche argues that the knowledge that allows Oedipus to vanquish the monster is inseparable from his own monstrous deeds – "the myth seems to wish to whisper to us that wisdom, and particularly Dionysian wisdom, is an unnatural abomination"; it grants a superhuman power even as it necessarily brings about the destruction of its over-wise bearer.[41] The same "unnatural" moment is present in the myth of Prometheus, whose theft of fire, "the true palladium of every ascending culture," breaks the power of nature over us.[42] Following their recognition that "the best and highest possession mankind can acquire is obtained by sacrilege," the Greeks come to endow sacrilege itself with a "*dignity*" worthy of commemoration in dramatic performance.[43] In Wagner's estimation, Aeschylus's *Prometheus* cycle stood at the pinnacle of Greek tragedy; it disclosed to its spectators "the riddle of their own actions," let them "fuse" with "their god," and allowed them "in noblest, stillest peace to live again the life which a brief space of time before, they had lived in restless activity and accentuated individuality."[44] In accord with Wagner's veneration of *Prometheus Bound*, Nietzsche also praises Aeschylus for showing us "the glory of activity" – although the tragic hero remains, throughout the drama, sadly immobilized in his bounded state.[45] He contrasts the transgression of Prometheus with the transgression of Eve, whose fall comes about through an incapacity to withstand temptation rather than through the contestatory pursuit of that which is prohibited. The masculine character of the former is antithetical to the distinctively feminine vices central to the biblical narrative. Nietzsche writes, "what distinguishes the Aryan notion is the sublime view of *active sin* as the characteristically Promethean virtue."[46] This reading, with its antisemitic and sexist overtones, owes something to Wagner and Schopenhauer; at the same time, in his emphasis on activity, Nietzsche departs from Schopenhauer's notion of the bondage of the will and comes to exalt acts that threaten to undermine the social and natural order of things. Against the Augustinian reduction of sin to deficiency, Nietzsche's distinction between two kinds of sin, one born of susceptibility and one born of initiative, anticipates his later critique of decadence – where decadence entails an inability to resist reacting to external stimuli – as well as his positive revaluation of "active" evil.

Citing the closing stanza of Goethe's "Prometheus," Nietzsche praises the lyric poem as "the veritable hymn of impiety."[47] And while he sees a convergence between the German lyrist and the Greek tragedian in their demands for justice, before which neither men nor gods are exempt, he also expresses an unconcealed satisfaction in the defiant tone of Goethe's impious apostrophes, even apart from any appeal to a higher ethical principle. In Nietzsche's account, favourable depictions of defiant and even sacrilegious transgressors are not unique to the moderns, but appear in the oldest extant Greek tragedies, as the case of *Prometheus Bound* attests. His sense of an intimate relationship between transgression and tragedy is succinctly articulated in his later work, where transgression appears not only as a subject of dramatic representation but as the motive force in tragedy's creation. In *The Gay Science*, Nietzsche posits that "in their desire to invent some dignity for sacrilege and to incorporate nobility in it, they [the Greeks] invented *tragedy*."[48] As in *The Birth of Tragedy*, Nietzsche once again contrasts this sacrilegious impulse with the abhorrence of sin operative in the Jewish tradition. What the Jews take to be evil, the Greeks laud as heroic even in their acknowledgement of its impropriety. But he goes further in locating the impulse to exalt transgression as constitutive of tragic art itself. In place of the dialectic of the Apollonian and the Dionysian, around which *The Birth of Tragedy* was configured, Nietzsche here stresses a single motive, the ennobling of sacrilege, as decisive for tragedy's invention.

The pleasure in beholding works of tragedy applies to the viewing of both acts of transgression and scenes of suffering. In the former case, the heroism invested in sacrilegious deeds makes us shudder with delight before the audacity of the transgressor; it encourages us even to identify with him. In the latter case, the beautiful form given to moments of pain testifies to the power of art to redeem the ostensibly unendurable. Apart from a pleasure in the play of forms, Nietzsche also identifies – more provocatively – another motive that draws us to dramatic spectacles of suffering, namely cruelty. In *The Birth of Tragedy*, this motivation is alluded to in the reflections on the Dionysian, presented at times as barbarous in its untamed destructiveness. In Nietzsche's account, the Dionysian effaces the space of appearance separating individuals from one another, an effacement that can be understood as constitutive of community through the engendering of a mystical communion. The ecstatic moment, in which the subject steps outside of itself, is also, however, an act of disruption; its indescribable pleasure, which resides in the release from the constraining limits of selfhood, is joined with a terror at the prospect of the disorienting loss of self.[49] This transgression of limits, which the Greeks themselves recognized as a danger to self and society when confronted with the bloody and self-mutilating revels of their barbarian neighbours, already hints at a pleasure in destruction. Yet the Dionysian remains highly ambivalent in this text since its destructiveness, apparent in the annihilation of the distinctions between individuals and the binding of them together in suffering, seems, at times, to have more in common with compassion, which Schopenhauer conceives as bringing about the dissolution of the principle of individuation, than with cruelty. In Nietzsche's later writings, however, he begins to probe more deeply into the ways in which cruelty creeps into and even animates art.

Schopenhauer, in his reading of Lucretius, unveils the elements of self-interest and cruelty present in the spectatorship of shipwreck; as a follower of Kant, however, he insists upon the centrality of disinterestedness to aesthetic experience. Nietzsche concurs with the judgment that cruelty is at work in many of our spectatorial pleasures, but he also fiercely attacks the alignment of the aesthetic and the disinterested. Heidegger attributes Nietzsche's critique of disinterestedness to the pernicious influence of Schopenhauer, whom he treats as a kind of faulty lens through which Nietzsche glimpses only a distorted version of Kant's aesthetics; he proposes that Nietzsche and Kant are, despite all appearances to the contrary, actually in agreement with one another.[50] But Nietzsche himself was aware of the divergence between the meaning of disinterestedness in Kant and Schopenhauer, and his reconfiguration of aesthetic experience amounts to a rejection of both thinkers' accounts. His remarks strike more directly at the latter than at the former only because Nietzsche comes to define his position in opposition to the one out of which it first emerged. Even where Schopenhauer is not explicitly mentioned, he still lurks in the background, the unnamed interlocutor of a polemical, internal dialogue. Taken in isolation, Nietzsche's pronouncement that "in music the passions enjoy themselves" sounds almost banal.[51] But it needs to be understood as a deliberate rebuttal of Schopenhauer's aesthetics with its attempt to subordinate the passions to the intellect; whereas the older pessimist sees art as pacifying the passions, the philosopher of Dionysus interprets it as a vehicle for their mobilization. More daringly, he perceives cruelty itself as among the passions at work in the generation of art and informing the aesthetic reception of it. The destructiveness of the tragic impulse occurs in conjunction with a celebration of nature's creative forces, wherein the healthy individual and community feel themselves to be participants. If Schopenhauer's interpretation of tragedy as leading to resignation were correct, then tragedy would be "a symptom of decay" (*ein Symptom des Verfalls*), not the stimulant to life that it actually is.[52] As Nietzsche proclaims in *Twilight of the Idols*, "the heroic man praises his own being through tragedy – to him alone the tragedian presents this drink of sweetest cruelty."[53] In the same text, he explains that "if there is to be art, if there is to be any aesthetic doing and seeing, one physiological condition is indispensable: frenzy."[54] This includes, quite explicitly, "the frenzy in destruction" and "the frenzy of cruelty."[55] What Schopenhauer seeks to hold apart, Nietzsche presses together; the purpose of this operation is not to muddy conceptual waters, but to reveal the inadequacy of prior conceptual distinctions that artificially separate what belongs together – both naturally and experientially. Cruelty, far from being alien to aesthetic experience, forms an integral part of it – although it may be evident only in a sublimated form that eludes easy detection.[56]

The quest to ferret out cruelty in unlikely places animates Nietzsche's inquiries into things he seeks to exalt as well as those he wishes to condemn; he finds cruelty, although in radically different forms, operative in the antithetical moralities of the Homeric epics and the Pauline epistles. In regard to the latter, Nietzsche claims that he was the first to bring to light the subterranean roots of Christianity, to show that its exaltation of love is resentment in disguise. He adduces, as a telling instance of the Christian spirit of hatred and vengefulness, an extended passage from Tertullian's tract on spectacles, in which the theologian expresses delight at the future prospect of the enemies of Christ suffering shameful torments on the day of judgment. Among those whose anticipated torment Tertullian relishes are the "play-actors" and "the tragedians, louder-voiced in their own calamity."[57] Against this punitive tendency, Nietzsche calls into question the notion of moral responsibility, which undergirds the conviction that justice demands the chastisement of "sinners." Zarathustra warns us, in his speech "On the Tarantulas," to "mistrust all in whom the impulse to punish is powerful"; indeed, he proclaims "for *that man be delivered from revenge*, that is for me the bridge to the highest hope, and a rainbow after long storms."[58] This denunciation of the spirit of vengefulness does not preclude, however, a rehabilitation of cruelty.

Arendt writes, in regard to Tertullian's finding joy in the sufferings of the damned, that "the first to be really scandalized by this was Nietzsche."[59] This claim is more than a little dubious. In *The Decline and Fall of the Roman Empire*, Gibbon's unfavourable judgment of Tertullian, with its attribution of "resentment" to him, anticipates Nietzsche's assessment in its decisive point – notwithstanding pronounced differences in style and mode of expression between the two men.[60] And before Schopenhauer and the *philosophes* of the eighteenth century expressed their horror at the cruel visions of the religious imagination, more tender-hearted Christians – often believers in the doctrine of universal salvation – were alarmed that their fellow advocates of the religion of neighbour-love should delight in the thought of the interminable agony of their neighbours. What is novel about Nietzsche's treatment of Tertullian is not that he found his views scandalous; if there is anything new in it, it lies, rather, in the fact that he was more contemptuous of the impotence and the slavishness underlying Tertullian's fantasy than dismayed by its cruelty – although even on this point he was preceded by the ancient pagans. In *De Spectaculis*, Tertullian acknowledges that there are no direct prohibitions in scripture against visiting the circus or attending the theatre, as there are commandments forbidding murder, idolatry, and adultery, but he insists that "every show is an assembly of the wicked" and ought to be shunned on that account alone.[61] Yet his denunciation of the impieties of circus spectacles and dramatic performances culminates in a startling inversion; instead of decrying the spectatorship of suffering, Tertullian expresses his anticipatory pleasure in beholding the future agonies of those currently occupying the position of spectators. After abstaining from the theatre for a lifetime, the blessed finally assume the role of the audience as they witness the verdicts of the last judgment, a show far greater than any to be staged by human hands. In a stunning reversal of fortunes, the most powerful men, who on earth subjected those beneath them to their authority, find themselves in a perpetual state of helplessness and abjection. In Nietzsche's eyes, Tertullian's vision is a fantasy of the oppressed, one that dishonestly masks a thirst for power with appeals to justice and love. Whereas Greek tragedy affirms life in all its harshness, the Christian drama of judgment resentfully indicts terrestrial existence and humankind's highest specimens.[62]

The argument that "morally corrupt pleasure" involves the enjoyment of the sufferings of others has served as a point of departure for recent scholarly investigations seeking to determine the moral status of aesthetic pleasure.[63] It underlies the judgment that where this enjoyment is lacking when watching tragedies performed on the stage, we need not – and do not – feel guilty. But this assessment tells us less about the moral status of tragedy than it does about contemporary assumptions, values, and dispositions. Although it might seem intuitively right to many of us moderns, it is at odds with the views of both Nietzsche and the early Church Fathers. For Tertullian, Augustine, and leading early modern Puritans, the watching of tragedies and comedies was sinful not because the members of the audience delighted in the characters' unhappiness but because they found happiness in the triumphs of their transgressions – frequently of an illicit, romantic nature. Moreover, the failure to feel guilty about partaking in such pleasure was itself seen as indicative of a kind of moral corruption, the atrophy or warping of conscience. Conversely, Nietzsche maintains that cruelty is a vital component of aesthetic experience, but instead of seeing it as something morally corrupt, he identifies it as part of the psychic constitution of healthy individuals; it is only the decadent who wish to root it out.

As a self-proclaimed advocate of the affirmation of life, Nietzsche polemicizes against this decadent impulse, the most sustained philosophical articulation of which appears in the work of Schopenhauer. And as a psychologist of art and religion, he attempts to divulge the complex role that cruelty – directed towards both others and ourselves – plays in the pleasures of spectatorship, thereby showing that neither the aesthetic nor the religious are removed from it. At times, these pleasures have a decidedly masochistic resonance, as when we identify with individual sufferers and yet, instead of averting our eyes, gladly immerse ourselves in their pain and make it our own. Nietzsche presents us with the following scenario in *Daybreak*, in which he considers the possible motivations of the creator in undertaking the creation of our world:

> And supposing it was a god of love [who created the world]: what enjoyment
> for such a god to create *suffering* men, to suffer divinely and superhumanly from

the ceaseless torment of the sight of them, and thus to tyrannise over himself! And even supposing it was not only a god of love, but also a god of holiness and sinlessness: what deliriums of the divine ascetic can be imagined when he creates sin and sinners and eternal damnation and a vast abode of eternal affliction and eternal groaning and sighing![64]

In *On the Genealogy of Morals*, published in 1887, Nietzsche once again takes up the problem of cruelty as it relates to the divine spectator. But instead of offering a speculative psychotheology, as in *Daybreak*, he puts forward a hypothesis about the historical origins of the gods, according to which human beings invented gods in order to make suffering bearable and intelligible. Human suffering, much of which occurs away from the gaze of other mortals, often appears senseless; but the gods, who play the part of divine spectators, behold these pains and are gratified at the sight of them. Since our suffering contributes to their amusement, it is not, in fact, bereft of purpose. Rather than augmenting our miseries, as Schopenhauer imagined, cruelty allows pleasure to be extracted from misfortune and, in this fashion, paradoxically redeems it. This applies to both the imagined cruelty of the gods and the actual cruelty of men. Nietzsche writes:

> The *Greeks* still knew of no tastier spice to offer their gods to season their happiness than the pleasures of cruelty. With what eyes do you think Homer made his gods look down upon the destinies of men? What was at bottom the ultimate meaning of Trojan Wars and other such tragic terrors? There can be no doubt whatever: they were intended as *festival plays* for the gods; and, insofar as the poet is in these matters of a more "godlike" disposition than other men, no doubt also as festival plays for the poets.[65]

The Greek gods find entertainment value both in the spectacle of human suffering and in the sight of human folly; when the former is incurred as a result of the latter, this proves especially agreeable to their malicious sense of humour. Their cruelty should not surprise us since, as Nietzsche posits, these gods are themselves "reflections of noble and autocratic men, in whom *the animal* in man felt deified."[66] Such noble types, whom the slavish and ignoble come to denounce as evil, are predatory by nature. In describing these types in heroic terms, Nietzsche goes beyond disputing the morality underwriting negative Christian assessments of them; he aestheticizes "wicked men," portrays them as sublime exemplars, thereby lifting them and their deeds from the sphere of moral condemnation into the realm of artistic affirmation. Achilles and Odysseus, whom Dante consigned to the second and the eighth circle of hell respectively, are restored with their pre-Christian lustre. In his depiction of the exploits of warrior castes and races – among whom are included "the Roman, Arabian, Germanic, Japanese nobility, the Homeric heroes, the Scandinavian Vikings" – Nietzsche does not downplay their terribleness; on the contrary, he claims that once these "uncaged beasts of prey" are let loose, they wreak havoc on their enemies and all those unfortunate enough to find themselves in their path; he envisions them as "triumphant monsters who perhaps emerge from a disgusting procession of murder, arson, rape, and torture, exhilarated and undisturbed of soul, as if it were no more than a students' prank, convinced they have provided the poets with a lot more material for song and praise."[67] Their destructive undertakings are admittedly frightful; they are also ideal material for poetic eulogy and memorialization.

The idea that the violent and the horrific are not unsuitable as objects of artistic representation is already at work in *The Birth of Tragedy*, but their celebration remains somewhat tempered by the mollifying influence of Schopenhauer. The questioning of moral values is, however, already underway, a questioning that opens the path to the more radical and aggressive "revaluation of all values" that Nietzsche proclaims in the late 1880s. In the 1886 preface to *The Birth of Tragedy*, Nietzsche notes what he judged to be his first book's missteps as well as its felicitous points of departure. In his retrospective assessment, entitled "Attempt at a Self-Criticism," he expresses chagrin at the ponderous style, the sentimentality, and the logical incoherences of "this questionable book," yet he also lauds it for setting out on untrodden pathways.[68] Foremost among its innovations is what Nietzsche refers to as its "*antimoral* propensity"; in opposition to the moralistic metaphysics of Schopenhauer, Nietzsche here advances "a philosophy that dares to move, to demote, morality into the realm of appearance – and not merely among 'appearances' or phenomena (in the sense assigned to these words by Idealistic philosophers), but among 'deceptions,' as semblance, delusion, error, interpretation, contrivance, art."[69] The recognition that such deceptions are among the conditions of existence leads to the repudiation of all moral systems that seek to root out "art" in search of a truth supposedly free from semblance. Discerning in the hostility to art a masked hostility to life, Nietzsche declares that "nothing could be more opposed to the purely aesthetic interpretation and justification of the world which are taught in this book than the Christian teaching, which is, and wants to be, *only* moral and which relegates art, *every* art, to the realm of *lies*."[70] Two years later, in his autobiography *Ecce Homo*, Nietzsche notes that "aesthetic values" are "the only values recognized in *The Birth of Tragedy*."[71] Is this reading belied by the text itself? After all, Nietzsche himself praises, in this work, the Aeschylean veneration of justice, which functions as a moral value and not exclusively an aesthetic one. Nonetheless, Nietzsche's characterization of his youthful intervention rightly underscores its departure from Schopenhauer and the moral philosophers who preceded him in its subordination of the problem of morality to the problem of art.

Schopenhauer claims that the idea "that the world has only a physical and not a moral significance is a fundamental error, one that is the greatest and most pernicious, the real *perversity* of the mind. At bottom, it is also that which faith has personified as antichrist."[72] Nietzsche's denial of the world's moral significance and his reduction of metaphysics to physiology mark his thinking as eminently perverse in Schopenhauer's sense. It is only fitting that the philosopher who espouses such a position should come to don the mantle of the Antichrist and conclude his autobiography with the rallying cry "*Dionysus versus the Crucified*."[73] But to what extent does the repudiation of Christian values amount to a repudiation of moral values *tout court*? It should be noted that the famous declaration that "there are no moral phenomena at all, but only a moral interpretation of phenomena," as given in an epigram from *Beyond Good and Evil*, does not commit Nietzsche to the surrender of moral value judgments.[74] Notwithstanding his vaunted "immoralism" and his rejection of the dichotomy of "good and evil," he does not hesitate to label things as good and bad. The campaign against morality is not a campaign against moral evaluations as such – inescapable for beings such as ourselves, whether or not they are erroneous – but targets, instead, the invented world imagined to ground them. With its denial of the thing-in-itself and its refutation of a "real world" that lies behind the phenomenal one, Nietzsche's attack on metaphysics leads to a dismantling of the concept of reality – or at least a dominant philosophical understanding of it in which it is pitted against appearance.[75] In Nietzsche, the aesthetic absorbs the moral and the metaphysical alike. Yet aesthetic values are not deemed to be objective or even to stand on less shaky legs than moral ones. "Nothing," Nietzsche tells us in *Twilight of the Idols*, "is more conditional – or, let us say, narrower – than our feeling for beauty."[76] Nietzsche does not wish to argue for the autonomy of art; he is not even invested in showing that "the aesthetic" possesses conceptual coherence as a philosophical category.[77] He intends rather to undermine the autonomy of morality or, to be more precise, those particular moralities that obligate "unconditionally." The elevation of the aesthetic, and the mixing of the aesthetic and the moral, serve to erode the integrity of the latter. The vindication of art and appearance destabilize traditional morality and open the way to a radical revaluation.

Nietzsche's "aestheticist" enterprise has affinities with the pursuits of contemporary French aesthetes, to whom he was not very well disposed. He equates the slogan *l'art pour l'art* with the exclamation, "The devil take morality!"[78] To this extent, he shows some sympathy for it, but he also disparages its proclaimers for their lack of purpose, for their failure to understand that art must be placed in the service not of itself but of life; this *lebensphilosophisch* caveat marks the limits of Nietzsche's aestheticism and provides the context in which it is articulated. According to Nietzsche, the French decadents wallow in their own impotence, and their compositions are symptomatic of both sickness and weakness of will – as is their susceptibility to the diseased music of Wagner. Art, however, in its healthy manifestations, expresses and enhances the joyous affirmation of the self. It is precisely this which Greek tragedy attains and which is too often lacking in the art of the modern age.

Crime and the Connoisseur

Nietzsche writes, in *Beyond Good and Evil*, that "the lawyers defending a criminal are rarely artists enough to turn the beautiful terribleness of his deed to his advantage."[79] This pronouncement, which one might be tempted to dismiss as a blithe attempt at provocation, finds an echo in Nietzsche's reflections on contemporary criminality. While he often treats criminals as degenerates, he sometimes suggests that they are actually superior souls who suffer adversely under unfavourable conditions; and he does not balk at making allowances for the most spectacular in their ranks. In a letter to Strindberg, dated 7 December 1888, Nietzsche expressed his admiration for the criminal Prado, who was found guilty of murder and who had been sentenced to death in Paris less than a month before. To the consternation of the playwright, who had registered in a previous letter his reservations about the philosopher's esteem for criminal types, Nietzsche praises Prado as "superior to his judges, even to his lawyers, in self-control, wit, and exuberance of spirit."[80] Shortly after his collapse in Turin in early January, when Nietzsche had lost all remaining inhibitions, he even declared, in a missive to Burckhardt, that "I am Prado."[81] In *Dialectic of Enlightenment*, Horkheimer and Adorno state that "like Juliette he [Nietzsche] admired 'the beautiful terribleness of the deed,' even though, as a German professor, he differed from Sade in rejecting criminality" on account of the baseness of its motives.[82] But while this rejection applies to the most common forms of criminal activity, it is not applicable to criminality's highest specimens.

The suggestion that the purported beauty of a crime ought to have any bearing on our verdict of it, whether given in a court of law or in the court of private moral judgment, seems misguided, if not altogether perverse. In making this suggestion, Nietzsche places the sharp distinction between the aesthetic and the moral in question. The erasure of the boundary between the two forms part of his larger project of a revaluation of all values aimed at overturning the most venerated moral ideals of the past two millennia. Against this erasure, it might seem that the appropriate rearguard action would be to argue all the more strongly for their separation; in order to prevent the blurring of good and evil, and the attendant moral confusion that Nietzsche invites – at least according to his critics – a strict and clearly articulated distinction is needed.

The establishment of an airtight separation of the aesthetic and the moral carries, however, its own dangers. The amusing and sometimes disquieting consequences of their delimitation are made apparent in De Quincey's *On Murder Considered as One of the Fine Arts*, first published in *Blackwood's Magazine* in 1827. The main body of this piece consists of a lecture given to a society of "Murder-Fanciers," the transcript of which, we are told, has somehow fallen into the hands of a certain "X.Y.Z.," a framing narrative that allows – through a double removal – De Quincey to pursue dangerous ideas without implicating himself too directly in the views there espoused.[83] In his presentation of "the Williams' Lecture on Murder" to The Society of Connoisseurs in Murder, the unnamed lecturer pays homage to John Williams, the culprit responsible for a killing spree that rocked East London in December 1811. In his raids on two family residences in the span of a fortnight, which resulted in seven fatalities, Williams ignited a panic that swept through the city, subsiding only with the public exhibition of his dead body on New Year's Eve. We hear relatively little about either of these cases in the Williams' Lecture and are treated instead to an account of murders of more dubious provenance, with considerable attention devoted to the slaying of prominent modern philosophers. After narrating the murders of Spinoza and Malebranche, and the near scrapes with death of Descartes and Kant at the hands of homicidal brigands, the lecturer declares that "I have traced the connexion between philosophy and our art, until insensibly I find that I have wandered into our own era."[84] Apart from the curious fact that philosophers seem to be in greater danger of succumbing to death by homicide, the nature of this "connexion" remains far from clear. Moreover, since most of these narratives, in their mingling of fact with conjecture and downright invention, are themselves of questionable historical accuracy, they make the reader wonder if there is any meaningful connection between them at all. But in drawing philosophy and murder together, although in an arch and comical fashion, De Quincey intimates the philosophical significance of his fantastical reflections.

As Aristotle seeks to determine the rules for the construction of a tragedy in the *Poetics*, treating the genre as an object worthy of the philosopher's interest, De Quincey meditates on murder as an act with its own artistry, without which killing degenerates into a deed devoid of aesthetic merit. After all, "something more goes to the composition of a fine murder than two blockheads to kill and be killed – a knife – a purse – and a dark lane."[85] This meditation rests on a strict conceptual distinction, which, notwithstanding the allusions to Aristotle, owes more to the philosophy of the moderns than to that of the ancients. The unnamed lecturer proclaims, "everything in this world has two handles. Murder, for instance, may be laid hold of by its moral handle, (as it generally is in the pulpit, and at the Old Bailey;) and *that*, I confess, is its weak side; or it may also be treated *aesthetically*, as the Germans call it, that is, in relation to good taste."[86] The invocation of the Germans signals the lecturer's acquaintance with the most fashionable trends in current philosophical thought, which De Quincey saw as having an antagonistic relationship to commonsensical understandings of the world. It was Baumgarten who redefined the term "aesthetic" so as to align it with the beautiful and the study of taste, and it was Hegel who provided the most systematic philosophical exposition of the fine arts, but De Quincey's work does not draw upon either of them. His distinction between the aesthetic and the moral owes more to Kant than it does to Kant's German forerunners and successors.

Even as he acknowledges Kant's enduring contributions to philosophy, De Quincey presents him as a figure of disenchantment who intensifies the anxiety that ours is "in some sense a world of deception."[87] In an autobiographical fragment devoted to an explication of Kant's transcendental idealism, the author of the *Critique of Pure Reason* is described as promulgating "a philosophy of destruction," an assessment that calls to mind Moses Mendelssohn's characterization.[88] De Quincey notes that while this philosophy has proved fertile in giving rise to various sects in Germany, "all its truths are barren."[89] The barrenness of the system mirrors that of its author. In the Williams' Lecture on Murder, Kant appears as so devitalized – the lecturer compares the "old, arid, and adust metaphysician" to a mummy – that his escape from death seems almost superfluous.[90] But notwithstanding this unfavourable portrayal, De Quincey's reliance on the distinction between the "two handles" of the aesthetic and the moral indicates less a mockery of Kant – although the acceptance of the distinction sometimes leads to rather unsavoury results – than an admission of its utility in separating things that are too often left undiscriminated.[91]

During his brief tenure, beginning in 1818, as an editor of the *Westmorland Gazette*, a newspaper that devoted considerable space to noteworthy crimes and court trials, De Quincey was ever watchful for sensational events that might pique his readers' interest.[92] As a publicist attentive to the likings of his audience, he recognized that certain crimes exercised a greater fascination over the general public, and he was curious as to what precisely made some cases more captivating than others. He was also self-conscious enough to reflect upon the grounds of his own interest in things morally abhorrent. The treatment of Williams's murder spree as representing the height of the art reflects De Quincey's sentiment that there was something singular about his crimes that made them spectacular. In the essay of 1827, the narrations of the murders of philosophers, or at least their near brushes with would-be murderers, along with a description of other more far-fetched instances of homicide, including an account of a protracted boxing match between a professional pugilist and a baker, are so whimsical as to distract from the seriousness of the underlying idea. In a second supplementary paper, published in 1839, most of which is devoted to the thoughts and doings of a particularly eccentric murder-fancier named Toad-in-the-hole, the ridiculous element is still more pronounced than in the original. It is rather to the "Postscript" of 1854 that we must turn to find a sustained and less oblique discussion of actual murders, with a concentration on the Williams murders and with brief narrations of two additional cases of homicide that had achieved notoriety in the press of the day.

At the beginning of the "Postscript" to *On Murder Considered as One of the Fine Arts*, De Quincey expresses his exasperation with those who found his two prior pieces off-putting. He writes that "it is impossible to conciliate readers of so saturnine and gloomy a class, that they cannot enter with genial sympathy into any gaiety whatever, but, least of all, when the gaiety trespasses a little into the province of the extravagant."[93] After dismissing those "churls" incapable of taking pleasure in imaginative forays, the author defends himself against the charge that, in the original essay, "the general gaiety of the conception, went too far."[94] Against this objection, we find the rather curious defence that "the very excess of the extravagance, in fact, by suggesting to the reader continually the mere aeriality of the entire speculation, furnishes the surest means of disenchanting him from the horror which might else gather upon his feelings."[95] The presentation of the Williams' Lecture as serving the ends of disenchantment rests on a tacit acknowledgement that "the horror" of murder already has something enchanting about it; otherwise, the process of disenchantment would be otiose. Is De Quincey's intention to disenchant the horrific, to deprive it of its sublime effects by treating the act of murder in an extravagant fashion? If this were his aim, the sense of more than one reader that he lends it new charms suggests that he was not altogether successful in this endeavour. In defending his earlier excesses, De Quincey invokes "A Modest Proposal," as if Swift's satire on the inhumane treatment of the Irish and the misguided policies targeting the poor mirrored his own procedure in *On Murder Considered as One of the Fine Arts*.[96] But if De Quincey is giving us a work of satire, what exactly is being satirized? Instead of rejecting the tendency to aestheticize, he appears, in the "Postscript," to sanction it, to show that a moral repugnance towards wicked acts is compatible with a recognition of their aesthetic appeal. Indeed, it is only the "saturnine and gloomy" who are unable to enjoy the prospect of considering crimes as works of art.

The references to murderers' artistry in the Williams' Lecture might be brushed aside as an unserious, ironic "extravagance," but De Quincey's characterization, in the much less fanciful "Postscript," of actual homicides that occurred four decades earlier indicates that his aesthetics of crime was not confined to the fantastic. In fact, De Quincey's short story "The Avenger," his most sustained engagement with murder in the form of fiction, is less explicitly aestheticizing than are his non-fictional writings. De Quincey describes, in the "Postscript," Williams as having "consummated so complex a tragedy" as if he were a dramatist who had authored the murderous affair.[97] In his reflections on the distinguishing marks of the foremost tragedies, Aristotle gives pride of place to the construction of plot, an assessment that accords with his high regard for Sophocles's *Oedipus Tyrannus*. But for De Quincey, Williams's genius resides not in emplotting, but in plotting. His stealthy entrance into the residence of the Marr family evinces a frightful cunning, and the brutality with which he finishes off adult and infant alike speaks to the cold-blooded single-mindedness with which he pursues his task. But since the culprit is caught after his second homicidal escapade, and since De Quincey even dilates on the sloppiness with which the murder weapons were handled after the crime, Williams cannot be said to have executed the perfect murder.[98] The failure to dispose of one of the murder weapons, the mistake that will ultimately prove fatal for the killer, is an elementary error. And the fact that potential victims eluded Williams on two separate occasions does him little credit as an assassin, whatever good fortune we might attribute to the escapees. Moreover, prior to raiding the Williamson house and murdering its inhabitants, he does not seem to have given much thought to the manner of his own escape; at least, the awkwardness of his exit exhibits little proof of forethought. What seems to excite De Quincey's imagination, however, is the sheer audacity of the undertaking and the extremity of the achievement, with its near annihilation of an entire household. Just as a work of literature can be hailed for its greatness, notwithstanding the presence of defects and imperfections, when it demonstrates a boldness of conception and an unexampled ambition in design, so the act of murder can be excused for its blunders where its originality attains the rank of the unprecedented. A great work of art is not one that is free from mistakes, but one that breaks the mould, that goes beyond anything hitherto imagined or executed. It is the valorization of excess rather than a delight in the precision of the murderous craft that informs De Quincey's aestheticizing. Here, De Quincey shows his debts to the modern Romantic conception of genius, with its disregard for convention and its low estimation of the faultless following of pre-given models.

The designating of Williams as "the great artist" might give the impression that he orchestrated events in accordance with his will, but he appears in the "Postscript" less as the director of the drama than as one more actor on the stage – the engine, no doubt, of the tragedy, but also a plaything of fortune whose success and failure hinge on circumstances beyond his control.[99] In describing Williams's actions in one room of the house and the simultaneous actions of a journeyman attempting to flee in another, De Quincey sets up a parallelism between the undertakings of the killer in search of booty and the potential victim struggling to extricate himself from the premises. Employing the language of tragedy, he compares their oppositional movements to the "strophe" and the "antistrophe" of the tragic chorus.[100] The mirroring of their conflicting strivings lends the scene a tension and a symmetry fitting for a work of art. In this instance, it is not Williams but De Quincey himself who proves to be the tragedian; the narrator, in the act of representing the murder, transforms the moment of crime into a poetic drama with its own internal structure, one unknown to any of the actors participating in it.[101] Even where the details of the case are carefully surveyed and brought together in such a manner as to correspond to the actual sequence of events, De Quincey's rewriting of the criminal act aims less at a perfect fidelity to the past than at bringing the deadly deed back to life. Sustaining the interest of the reader, in line with the requirements of good fiction, trumps a commitment to facts, especially where these do little to intensify the tension of the drama.

The act of aestheticizing has affinities with the act of poetic creation insofar as it involves the remaking of something, the transformation of the inaesthetic into the aesthetic. That is why the term "aestheticizing" is applied to the representation of objects deemed to be not properly aesthetic; it connotes a distortion, the treatment of a thing in a fashion that does not accord with its nature. Seldom do we refer to the aestheticizing of a painting or even the aestheticizing of a flower since these are usually considered properly aesthetic objects to begin with. An act of evil seems, however, to be of a different order. At the same time, wickedness has proved to be among the most fertile fields in bringing forth objects well suited to artistic representation. Here, it is important to differentiate two distinct, though sometimes interrelated, levels of aestheticizing. On the first level, to aestheticize means to present an object under the aspect of a particular aesthetic category, such as the beautiful or the sublime; on the second, it means to present an object as itself a work of art. When De Quincey speaks of the beauty of crime, this does not in itself commit him to the latter presentation; a crime may be beautiful in the same way that works of nature, which are not the product of artifice, are beautiful. But in his description of the criminal as an artist, which means conceiving of crime as a constructed work with its own author, De Quincey takes a second step in the aestheticizing of evil.[102] This reconfiguration challenges conventional understandings of what counts as art.[103] It also alters the meaning of evil acts – or at least a certain distinguished class of them – through a process of interpretive dissociation. The critic who considers the artistic excellencies of a particular murder has dislodged it from the realm of moral judgment and subjected it to a standard of assessment independent of it; the positing of this standard, which rubs against the dictates of convention, constitutes a reinvention of the terms according to which judgment operates. Where the critic assumes the role of narrator, one who describes what he beholds or imagines himself to behold in placing himself at the scene of a crime, the evaluative act and the reconstructive act fuse together. The narrating spectator, far from being a passive observer who registers the aesthetic merits and demerits of a performance, remakes the scene of the crime in his own imagination; in endowing it with the qualities proper to a literary narrative, he imparts to it a structural coherence of which no actor in the drama has any awareness. He alone hears the song of the chorus – its strophe and antistrophe – to which the actors themselves remain deaf, a song that is of his own making and that can only find a voice through him, through his own articulation.

In assessing the aesthetic composition of the scene of the crime, which means in actuality to recompose it aesthetically, De Quincey does not give equal attention to all the participants in the drama in the interest of some ideal of equilibrium. Compared to the perpetrator, the victims play an ancillary role. Whereas the former provides the impetus to the entire affair, setting everything that follows in motion, the victims are the human material upon which the perpetrator plies his art. In insisting that the best murders are those in which the victims are "good men," the presenter of the Williams' Lecture claims that "the final purpose of murder, considered as a fine art, is precisely the same as that of Tragedy, in Aristotle's account of it, viz. 'to cleanse the heart by means of pity and terror.' Now, terror there may be, but how can there be any pity for one tiger destroyed by another tiger?"[104] Yet De Quincey's depictions of murder are seldom punctuated with outbursts of pity; rather, this affect is set aside in favour of the sang-froid that distinguishes the analytical aesthete. He does not savour the sufferings of the victim in the fashion of the sadist, but neither does he show himself overwhelmed with grief at their misfortunes. And if there are expressions of concern for the welfare of others, insofar as we are invited to imagine the horror that the victims or potential victims experience in the face of impending death, these are themselves subordinated to or placed in the service of the feeling of terror, which De Quincey expertly excites in his recreation of the murder scene. This is evident in the account of Williams's murder of the Marrs, with its report of the butchery of the whole family and the escape of the servant girl Mary, a retelling that rivals, in the atmosphere it evokes and the sense of suspense it generates, the most engrossing narratives of Poe. No less than the foremost masters of Gothic fiction, De Quincey here shows his skill in summoning the sublime.[105]

The evocation of terror in the "Postscript" supplants the earlier hyperbolic excesses that, through the insertion of the ridiculous into an otherwise macabre subject matter, counteract potential sublime effects. The change of tone from the two earlier pieces invites us to consider the prefatory remarks of the first essay and to think through the extent to which aesthetic appreciation implies endorsement, as these remarks intimate. In his polemic against gladiatorial games, Lactantius writes:

> Now, if merely to be present at a murder fastens on a man the character of an accomplice, – if barely to be a spectator involves us in one common guilt with the perpetrator; it follows of necessity, that, in these murders of the amphitheatre, the hand which inflicts the fatal blow is not more deeply imbrued in blood

than his who sits and looks on: neither can *he* be clear of blood who has countenanced its shedding; nor that man seem other than a participator in murder who gives his applause to the murderer, and calls for prizes in his behalf.[106]

This quotation, which precedes the Williams' Lecture, operates as a disclaimer of sorts, distinguishing the one who introduces it from the unnamed lecturer speaking to the other members of The Society of Connoisseurs in Murder. It is possible, however, to accept Lactantius's judgment, in which an individual's presence in the amphitheatre is understood as tantamount to countenancing, without extending it to encompass the spectatorship of other scenes of violence and destruction, where watching should not be conflated with moral sanction. Indeed, the distinction between the moral and the aesthetic "handle," which the original lecture introduces, serves to diffuse Lactantius's objection at the outset, to show that aesthetic appreciation and moral disapproval are not incompatible. Whereas the 1827 essay gives us an over-the-top panegyric to murderous deeds, the "Postscript" exhibits restraint in its expressions of admiration and proves more sparing in its "applause" and exclamatory laudations; yet the same underlying principle, the conception of the murderer as an artist and murder as a work of art, persists unimpaired.

Already at the beginning of the Williams' Lecture, we are given a more morally ambiguous case of spectatorship than the attendance of gladiatorial games presents us with, namely the viewing of the outbreak of a fire in a densely populated urban space. The games in the Coliseum constitute a veritable theatre of cruelty, one that human beings themselves have constructed and orchestrated; the fire ignited in the city appears, conversely, as a spontaneous and unbidden act of nature. Yet in both cases the spectacle of destruction lends itself to cheering and jeering. The people on Oxford Street watching the inferno – which in De Quincey's account turns out to be a highly disappointing one, unworthy of the name, since it peters out before it even gets going – are presented as sorely disappointed at the poor showing, and the poet Coleridge, who abandons a lecture he was giving on Plotinus in order to enjoy the blaze, expresses his indignation that something so promising "turned out so ill."[107] The case of Coleridge notwithstanding, it would be misguided to reduce the decision to watch the fire with a rooting for its intensification; it is certainly possible to look upon it in hope of its speedy extinguishing – although the lecture makes no mention of any attendees so inclined. And yet the presence of some pleasure residing in the sight of a conflagration, keeping us transfixed before it, forces us to ask what kind of pleasure it is.

In Dostoevsky's *Devils*, the narrator of the novel describes night fires as "a challenge to the destructive instincts."[108] We are told that the same soul who "would rush into the flames to save a child or an old woman from burning" cannot help but admire the site of such destruction.[109] The delight in the fire cannot be equated with a delight in the sufferings of its victims; reflection on the material losses they suffer, not to speak of the sight of their burns, fills the same spectator with horror and compassion, though he nonetheless feels, in watching the blaze, a thrill in its spreading and a secret wish for it to spread further still. Goethe's Mephistopheles, in claiming that fire is the sole element that he has been able to reserve for himself, points to its inherently destructive nature.[110] But fire is also "Faustian"; it can be read as a symbol of transgression, even a manifestation of it in the realm of nature, insofar as it does not respect its confines but threatens to cross over into adjacent space. The seemingly innocent delight in the play of its flickering forms is perhaps not so far removed from the lust to see it take on new shapes as it absorbs foreign bodies into itself, damaging and even annihilating them. If it is not possible for moral concern and aesthetic pleasure to exist simultaneously, if they both jostle against one another in a struggle to occupy limited psychic space, then the succession between the two, the rapid alternation from one to the other, must be understood as an instance of conflict rather than disconnection; indeed, Dostoevsky intimates that our delight is itself rooted in a dangerous passion and thus cannot be confined to the realm of the aesthetic narrowly conceived. In drawing out the tension internal to the enjoyment of sights of devastation, he indicates that we make things too easy for ourselves when we imagine that our impulse to empathize with and to help others insulates us from the dangers posed by "the destructive instincts" lurking within. In Dostoevsky's novel, the fact that the night fire being described is not a natural calamity but the product of a criminal act, the work of revolutionary arsonists, adds a further dimension to the moral complexities of the pleasure at its sight. The desire to see the fire spread aligns the spectator, perhaps against his will, with that of the criminal who ignited the blaze.

De Quincey, in treating an interest in the perpetuation of the fire aesthetically and sharply separating it from moral sentiments at odds with it, offers a way of sanitizing our spectatorial pleasure in things terrible and unworthy of approbation. This sanitizing operation is still more pronounced in his discussion of our retrospective judgment of acts of devastation. After a fire has been extinguished or a murder spree has ended and "after the first tribute of sorrow to those who have perished" has been paid, our thoughts readily turn to "the scenical features (what aesthetically may be called the comparative *advantages*)" of the tragedy.[111] We are told that this way of looking at things finds "an inevitable and perpetual ground in the spontaneous tendencies of the human mind"; the naturalization of the inclination to aestheticize functions in this context as an exculpation of it.[112] Whereas Dostoevsky gives us an image of internal conflict, De Quincey treats the aesthetic and the moral as two parallel tracks that do not suffer disruptive moments of intersection. The extremity of the position he advocates, and the irony with which he at times expresses it, destabilizes the dichotomy he sets up and threatens to dissolve the distinction he introduces. Yet even as he lampoons the results of his own procedure, he continually reconstitutes the two spheres, defending their separateness and independence. Writing more than a century before De Quincey, Addison, in an article of *The Spectator*, noted:

> There are, indeed, but very few who know how to be idle and innocent, or have a Relish of any Pleasures that are not Criminal; every Diversion they take is at the Expence of some one Virtue or another, and their very first Step out of Business is into Vice or Folly. A Man should endeavour, therefore, to make the Sphere of his innocent Pleasures as wide as possible, that he may retire into them with Safety, and find in them such a Satisfaction as a wise Man would not blush to take.[113]

With the expansion of the terrain of the aesthetic, the sphere of what are counted as "innocent Pleasures," or at least pleasures considered morally permissible, undergoes a corresponding enlargement. Can an unexpurgated Shakespeare be enjoyed in good conscience? Is a Bowdler required to ensure that the bard's plays accord with the dictates of propriety? The conviction that censored abridgements are themselves a mark of philistinism, especially in the case of acknowledged masterpieces, is itself a sign of increasing latitude granted to aesthetic pleasure and artistic licence. But this development, when it goes too far, leads to a reconsideration of the parameters of art and a questioning of its insulation from the realm of the moral. In pointing out the role of cruelty in aesthetic pleasure, Nietzsche shows that our enjoyment of works of art is not so innocent as we sometimes imagine; on this score, there is a peculiar convergence between the viewpoint of the radical immoralist and that of the paranoid puritan, who discerns in every pleasure the taint of sin. Yet the result of Nietzsche's exercise in unveiling is not to discredit such pleasures, to draw us away from them as the moralist urges, but to force us to recognize how things that we decry as immoral are inextricably bound up with our deepest joys and highest virtues. Both the creation and the enjoyment of art are rooted in animalistic impulses, are the product of these impulses' sublimation, not their negation. De Quincey takes a very different tack, but the end products of the two thinkers' aestheticizing procedures have appeared sufficiently similar to obscure the difference between them. The aestheticizing of crime has functioned as an incitement to the emulation of it, and it has found objectors on this score. A more subtle and insidious effect of aestheticizing is that it gives us licence to discount the morally dubious aspects of the interest we take in criminal acts, since this interest can be treated as purely aesthetic and therefore bereft of moral import. Such a procedure enables us to treat crime as alluring in its shudder-inducing terror even as we strongly condemn it on strictly moral grounds; the condemnation averts the charge of sanctioning crime while it simultaneously opens the way to its glamorization.

The spread of sensationalistic accounts of violent criminality in print journalism was contemporaneous with the rise of Gothic fiction, and, as the traffic between the two attests, their parallel ascendancy was no coincidence. In the American context we see, in the move from the early eighteenth to the early nineteenth century, formulaic accounts of murder, almost telegraphic in their concision, give way to more elaborate narratives that, far from shying away from gorier particulars, foreground them, with the expectation that it is precisely a murder's most horrific aspects that will be of greatest interest to the general reader.[114] Instead of designating the criminal as an artist, as we find in De Quincey, the most common conceit in this emergent literature – one that continues today in the genre of "true crime" – is the portrayal of the criminal as a kind of monster whose actions appear senseless to normal human beings. This stance is occasionally adopted in De Quincey's own reflections on Williams, as when he refers to him as a "monster" and "one born of hell."[115] But rather than dislodging or undercutting the assessment of Williams as a great artist, the depiction of him as a monster curiously merges with it since both of these roles are shown to be productive of the sublime. In the "Postscript," Williams appears as an agent of the aesthetic, an instrument – holding the reader in a state of suspenseful enthralment – through which sublime effects are generated. Seized by a power that fascinates even as it repulses, we find that we cannot tear ourselves away from reading about that which we profess to abhor. The profession may very well be sincere, but it often functions as a way to distance ourselves from taking pleasure in things that it would be, according to our own moral lights, inappropriate to take pleasure in.

The aestheticizing of crime as it occurs in the genre of true crime literature diverges from the form it takes in De Quincey's work with its adoption of the posture of the detached aesthete. Yet it often reproduces, in unreflective and less self-conscious forms, the same aesthetic refashioning and narrative remaking of the criminal act in accordance with the standards of literary fiction, a procedure that sometimes leads to an unwitting elevation of the criminal and his or her deed. *On Murder Considered as One of the Fine Arts* should be understood as unveiling this aestheticizing tendency, operative in the Gothic fiction and sensationalistic journalism of De Quincey's day; it is not so much that De Quincey devises a novel way of looking at crime as that he unmasks a process already well underway. The fact that criminals are not explicitly identified as artists in the popular press and that such an identification would be met with indignant outcries does not alter the fact that much reportage participates in the "sublimification" of criminal acts.[116] It should be recalled, moreover, that the antipode of this treatment of criminals as vehicles of the sublime, namely the representation of them as all too ordinary, as "banal," has also proved controversial since it diminishes the distance separating "monsters" from normal human beings. In De Quincey's case, the "extravagant" portrayal of murder is no *reductio ad absurdum* that leads to a renunciation of the aestheticizing tendency on account of its unseemly consequences. Not the disavowal but the conscious adoption of an aesthetic vantage point distinguishes his mode of presentation from that of its less lucid counterparts.

As Foucault writes in *Discipline and Punish*, "from the adventure story to de Quincey, or from the *Castle of Otranto* to Baudelaire, there is a whole aesthetic rewriting of crime, which is also the appropriation of criminality in acceptable forms. In appearance, it is the discovery of the beauty and greatness of crime; in fact, it is the affirmation that greatness too has a right to crime and that it even becomes the exclusive privilege of those who are really great."[117] Like the artistic genius, whose prerogative it is to disregard the rules of composition and who finds commendation for refusing to adhere to that which binds lesser artists, "those who are really great" are granted a corresponding licence in the sphere of action, entitled to still bolder forms of transgression than those vouchsafed to poet and painter. Gesturing to the significance of this "affirmation" of greatness, Foucault puts his finger on key moments in the trajectory of the "aesthetic rewriting of crime"; at the same time, his formulation of the dichotomy is overdrawn, and potentially misleading, in its distinction between what he characterizes as the apparent and the actual. Nietzsche makes the case that actions inappropriate for some are meritorious when performed by others. While he denies the existence of a "doer" behind the "deed" in his attempted deconstruction of the subject, he maintains that certain doers are entitled, by virtue of their strength, to commit deeds that their inferiors are not.[118] No doubt, the notion that "greatness too has a right to crime" is evident in the emergent literature of transgression, but it also faced resistance in a democratizing age in which the category of greatness was met with increasing suspicion. It is with full consciousness of this shift in sentiment that Nietzsche, and Carlyle before him, struggle to reinvest greatness with reality and to refute its egalitarian debunkers. Moreover, what Foucault dismisses as mere appearance, deceptive in its seeming obviousness, nonetheless captures an important aspect of the literary valorization of criminality. Even as the category of greatness suffers erosion, the celebration of transgression finds a new lease on life. It finds a place not only in the musings of self-styled "aristocratic radicals," but also in the political programs of socialists and anarchists of various stripes intent on demolishing distinctions of rank.

Foucault refers to this intellectual genealogy as if he were external to it; at least, he does not situate himself in relation to it. But his own work can be understood as engaged in a coterminous project; the reconceptualization of transgression that animates the nineteenth-century "aesthetic rewriting of crime" continues apace in his own reinscription of it in post-structuralist terms. Indeed, "the discovery of the beauty and greatness of crime," which he identifies only to dismiss as a thing of subsidiary importance, finds a mirror in his reflections on transgression, wherein the breaching of limits is invested with renewed significance and sublimity. In his 1963 essay "A Preface to Transgression," dedicated to Bataille, Foucault never refers to "evil," a word that Bataille himself audaciously reclaims and repurposes for his own transgressive ends. This linguistic mobilization enables a kind of "hypermorality" – as Bataille dubs it – which is marked by a heightened vigilance in the detection of evil.[119] For Foucault, however, transgression "must be detached from its questionable association to ethics if we want to understand it."[120] This detachment, not unlike De Quincey's parsing of crime into the aesthetic and the moral, is not without ethical significance. Even as he seeks to invest transgression with a transformative potency, Foucault rewrites it in an "acceptable form" so as to prevent it from being associated with something base or negative.

Insisting on transgression's difference from and even opposition to negation, Foucault asserts that "it is the solar inversion of satanic denial. It was originally linked to the divine, or rather, from this limit marked by the sacred it opens the space where the divine functions."[121] Notwithstanding the anti-Romantic thrust of Foucault's intervention, with its questioning of revelatory origins and unitary beginnings, this characterization repeats the Romantic gesture that transforms the Satanic into the Promethean. And like the *via negativa*, which resists predication of the divine, Foucault's own pronouncements on transgression, vertiginous as the spiral whose image he invokes as its spatial analogue, do not amount to a definition of the concept in question but reveal the inadequacy of existing concepts in apprehending its serpentine undulations. His assertions, punctuated with a lengthy series of unanswered but suggestive questions about the nature of transgression, assume a rhapsodic tone that evokes a sense of liberation and affirmation although the content of what is being affirmed is indeterminate; Foucault even speaks of "an affirmation that affirms nothing."[122] The generality of the terms deployed makes it difficult to discern precisely what kinds of transgressive acts are worthy of approbation. What remains clear is that the generative power attributed to transgression distinguishes it from an act of negation that exhausts itself in erasing or cancelling out what stands against it. As with Nietzsche, who distinguishes Eve's passive lapse into sin from Prometheus's act of self-conscious opposition, Foucault valorizes transgression on account of its contestatory spirit. And as with De Quincey, who treats crime not merely as a breach of the law but as a kind of artistic performance, Foucault's reading of transgression as both ineffable and radically transformative participates in an aesthetics of the sublime. The performer, however, is here wholly absorbed into the performance. There is, in his essay, no mention of the transgressor; it is as if transgression occurred without a subject behind it or an agent initiating it. Emancipated from the vestiges of an ontology of the subject and unloosened from its sordid associations with the criminal and the evil-doer, transgression is set free in a space that lies beyond the law and stands outside the conventions of morality. But this beyond and outside surreptitiously expand at the expense of that which is positioned as external to them. What poses as a detachment from the ethical is, in its inversion and recasting of a category once synonymous with evil, itself a subversion of ethics.

Epilogue

In the past, heretics anxiously guarded themselves against charges of unorthodoxy. They were motivated not solely by fear of persecution; nor were their attempts to find confirmation in the ancient scriptures the product of disingenuous calculation. As terrifying as the threat of thumbscrews and the rack was the idea of originality, the lonely thought that their convictions deviated from the truths that were propounded before them. The fear that these convictions were without a noble lineage, or even any lineage at all, led them to conceal the novelty of new insights, both from others and from themselves. Today, conversely, there is no shortage of those who present themselves as iconoclasts and transgressors of inherited values; striving to find the new for its own sake, they are not infrequently condemned to remain derivative. And where novelty wanes, where seemingly new ideas are absorbed into what we come to accept as all too familiar, the power to provoke and to unsettle also diminishes. The invocation of Sade in certain circles stems from a desire to reinvest transgression with its former potency, to reclaim its subversive power and resist its domestication; but this invocation comes at the price of its association with wickedness. In order to preserve transgression from such an association, a sanitizing operation is often required that once again threatens to defang it and deprive it of its force.

I have sought, in the present work, to examine various representations of transgression and the diverse, indeed conflicting ends that they have been made to serve. And I have treated them as implicated – not only in their effects but in their formulations – in an ongoing axiological reconfiguration. In making sense of the rehabilitation of transgression in the modern era, it is important to acknowledge the extent of its internal tensions and to take account of the persistence of rival valuational assessments that stand in opposition to it. Applied to the present moment, an attentiveness to its ramifications allows us to better map out the variegated topography of the contemporary moral landscape and the place – or rather the places – that evil occupies within it. While the revaluation of transgression, already well underway in the eighteenth century, has concurrent repercussions in the realms of the moral and the aesthetic – and therefore suggests some sort of connection between the two, howsoever mediated – the precise nature of the connection remains a matter of uncertainty and dispute, especially where evil is concerned. The attempts of avowedly transgressive thinkers to assimilate morality to aesthetics are sometimes couched in the language of freedom and self-expression; yet, on account of their evident and even advertised subversiveness, these exercises in destabilization have also contributed to the suspicion that any blurring of the lines between the moral and the aesthetic is hazardous. Moreover, portrayals of wickedness in popular culture, not infrequently attended by a romanticization of evil acts and evil-doers, make it seem that an aesthetic treatment of evil, whatever viewing pleasures it calls forth, is tantamount to a distortion of it. I do not intend to diminish the dangers posed by glamorizations of evil in contemporary culture – some of these may be, if not benign, then relatively inconsequential whereas others are a serious cause for concern. Rather, I want to note that especially dubious forms of aestheticizing should not lead us into thinking that the solution is to build a wall separating the moral from the aesthetic. On the contrary, the problem of evil is to be rethought through an examination of our perceptions of it and the moral intuitions intertwined with them.

In this endeavour, a consideration of our images of evil, rather than our conceptualizations of it, facilitates an elucidation of evil's aesthetic modalities. When we reflect upon evil, what leaps to mind is not a concept but a set of images, ones that are often affectively charged; we are more likely to think of individuals, actions, and even places (such as Auschwitz) rather than a definition. To ask about evil is to ask, whether intentionally or not, for a body of proper names – the names of serial killers, terrorists, dictators, war criminals. Our tendency to think through concepts with reference to examples is one philosophy is well acquainted with and has been combatting for centuries. It finds one of its earliest subjections to critical scrutiny in Plato's dialogues, where Socrates grills his interlocutors about a given concept, of which they are unable to arrive at a satisfactory definition since they can come up only with particular instances of the concept in question. Without gainsaying the merits of the Socratic project and the questioning of self-certainties and complacencies it entails, we might – rather than seeking to subsume particulars under the umbrella of universals – more profitably consider how it is that certain particulars and universals have come to be associated with and disassociated from one another. Taking images of evil seriously means being open to the possibility that these images tell us as much or more about our morality as the arguments we mobilize to justify our judgments and standpoints.

While the argument that moral philosophy is one thing and aesthetics another – that they have different objects of enquiry and thus need to be conceived as two relatively autonomous discursive spheres – is not implausible when they are abstracted from history, it runs aground once we begin considering the historical formation of particular moralities and aesthetic sensibilities. Indeed, the insistence on an insuperable division between the moral and the aesthetic may itself be understood in aesthetic terms. The desire for, sometimes even the fixation on, unambiguous demarcations indicates not only an epistemic ideal but an aesthetic one; at times, it betrays a questionable insistence on purity and an intolerance for messiness. I say this not in order to pathologize a liking for clear distinctions or to deny its role in the advancement of knowledge, but to call attention to the obtrusion of the aesthetic even in moments of its disavowal. In protecting the integrity of the moral from the encroachments of the aesthetic, we risk denaturing what we seek to defend, cutting it off from embodied experience and depriving it of its nourishing cultural roots. At the very least, the maintenance of this strict partition when carried into the field of history occludes an understanding of the vicissitudes of our notions of good and evil with all their aesthetic entanglements. Whether or not the moral ultimately belongs to a separate sphere, one that is conceptually distinct and with its own inherent integrity and logic, the adoption of a historical vantage point teaches us that to treat it in isolation from aesthetic categories, responses, and interests – howsoever "disinterested" aesthetic judgment might present itself as being – prevents us from apprehending the genesis, development, and modification of moral positions and modes of comportment. A genealogy of morals that seeks to dig beneath the concepts that dominate the surface of moral discourse would do well, then, to integrate within itself a genealogy of aesthetics.

Notes

Introduction

1 Responding to Eric Voegelin's critical review of *The Origins of Totalitarianism*, Arendt asserted, in defence of her characterization of the horrors of totalitarianism, that "a description of the camps as Hell on earth is more 'objective,' that is, more adequate to their essence than statements of a purely sociological or psychological nature." Arendt, "A Reply," p. 404.

2 At the outset of *A Philosophy of Evil*, Lars Svendsen stresses the distinction between evil as "a *moral* category" and evil as "an *aesthetic* object." The maintenance of this distinction is crucial to his attempted "'rehabilitation' of the concept of evil" (p. 9).

3 While evil and violence should not be conflated, the overlap between them is not negligible. The topic of the aestheticizing of violence has generated significant scholarly work, whose insights are often relevant to problems pertaining to the aesthetics of evil. See Black, *The Aesthetics of Murder*; Eide, *Terrible Beauty*; Halttunen, *Murder Most Foul*; and Sheehan, *Modernism and the Aesthetics of Violence*.

4 Phillip Cole argues that "evil is not a philosophical concept, certainly not a psychological one, and not even a religious one. It is a mythological concept that has a role to play in grand narratives of world history." Cole, *The Myth of Evil*, p. 23.

5 See Taylor, *Sources of the Self*, and Blumenberg, *Legitimacy of the Modern Age*.

6 In her critical assessment of characterizations of genius as masculine, Christine Battersby maintains that "the Romantic conception of genius is particularly harmful to women. Our present criteria for artistic excellence have their origins in theories that implicitly and explicitly denied women genius." Battersby, *Gender and Genius*, p. 23.

7   Hans Jonas, *The Imperative of Responsibility*, p. 27.

8   Hobbes, *Leviathan*, bk. I, chap. XIII, p. 186.

9   Bernstein, *Radical Evil*, p. 226.

10   As Neiman explains, "the problem of evil can be expressed in theological or secular terms, but it is fundamentally a problem about the intelligibility of the world as a whole. Thus it belongs neither to ethics nor to metaphysics but forms a link between the two." Neiman, *Evil in Modern Thought*, pp. 7–8.

11   Important points of reference for my analysis include Mikhail Bakhtin's *Rabelais and His World*, Terry Eagleton's *The Ideology of the Aesthetic*, Wolfgang Kayser's *The Grotesque in Art and Literature*, and Winfried Menninghaus's *Disgust*.

12   This tendency, evident in Nietzsche, remains operative in much post-structuralist thought and its contemporary offspring. See Megill, *Prophets of Extremity*.

13   Representative of this tendency is the entry on "transgression" in the *Encyclopedia of Disability*, ed. Albrecht. Transgression is here described as "a form of resistance involving the crossing of limits or boundaries. It is not antagonistic or aggressive, nor does it involve a contest in which there is a victor; rather, transgression is playful and creative." This rehabilitation and even domestication of transgression is striking given that the entry goes on to reference Foucault's invocation of the Marquis de Sade, a figure whose transgressiveness was more than a little "aggressive."

1 Genius and the Spirit of Transgression

1   Diderot, *Rameau's Nephew*, p. 38.

2   Ibid., pp. 37–8.

3   Diderot, *Oeuvres*, vol. 1: *Philosophie*, p. 1313.

4   Characterizations of Hitler and Stalin as geniuses were commonplace in the Third Reich and the Stalinist Soviet Union respectively, and this is not surprising given the active promotion of cults of personality in both states. With the addition of the attributive adjective "evil," the label of genius was also taken up by critics; this continued in the immediate postwar period and beyond. At times, the designation has even been applied to these men's more influential underlings, as evident, for example, in the title of Willi Frischauer's biographical study *Himmler: The Evil Genius of the Third Reich*.

5   Arendt, *Origins of Totalitarianism*, p. 305.

6   Ibid., p. 305.

7   Citations of Milton's work are from Milton, *Complete Poems and Major Prose*.

 8 Augustine, *Works of Saint Augustine*, vol. 1/13, p. 354.

 9 Ibid., p. 440.

10 William Empson, writing more than half a century ago, noted that "most critics are now agreed that there is a gradual calculated degradation of Satan, but this bit of understanding gets obscured by a hunger to argue that he is very bad from the start." Empson, *Milton's God*, p. 71. Empson's assessment understates, however, the moral gravity of Satan's will to disobey God, an impulse that animates his course of action at every major turn in *Paradise Lost*.

11 Lewis, *Preface to Paradise Lost*, p. 95.

12 A.J.A. Waldock questions the weight accorded to these insertions, arguing that "the demonstration" of Satan's noble qualities exhibited in his speeches must be granted priority over the mere "allegations" of the deflationary narrator. Waldock, *Paradise Lost and Its Critics*, p. 78. Against this interpretation, Stanley Fish reads the dynamic between Satan's words and those of the narrator as vital to the poem, in which Milton anticipates our response to the devil's sublime orations and shames us for our susceptibility to his rhetoric. Fish, *Surprised by Sin*, pp. 6–9.

13 Kierkegaard, *On Authority and Revelation*, p. xviii.

14 The seeming paradox that this pronouncement is made by one of the nineteenth-century's greatest theorists of subjectivity, one of its most stalwart defenders of the individual, and one who himself did not assume a very deferential posture in relation to the church of his forefathers, need not detain us here although it does raise interesting questions about the tensions within his thought – tensions that an appeal to the pseudonymous character of his writings cannot alone resolve. It is perhaps further worth noting that the search for authenticity and a penchant for authoritarianism, with its call to submission, is by no means alien to the tradition of "existentialism." A consideration of the later Heidegger's reconceptualization of thinking as a pious listening to the call of being is not altogether out of place in this context.

15 Mill, *On Liberty and Other Writings*, p. 68.

16 Ibid., p. 69.

17 Ibid., p. 78.

18 Nietzsche, *Human, All Too Human*, p. 51.

19 Young, *Conjectures on Original Composition*, pp. 11–12.

20 Ibid., p. 13.

21 Ibid., p. 13.

22 Ibid., p. 14.

23 Horace, *Satires and Epistles*, p. 114.

24 "Whereas mediocrity for Horace implies the inability to observe rules and thus to maintain tradition, for the eighteenth-century genius, mediocrity arises from the reliance on imitation that makes such a conservative tradition possible." Fleming, *Exemplarity and Mediocrity*, pp. 27–8.

25 Young, *Conjectures on Original Composition*, p. 15.

26 Ibid., p. 24.

27 Augustine, *Confessions*, pp. 22–3.

28 Augustine asks the vainglorious, "Why are you proud, man? God became humble for your sake. Perhaps, it would shame you to imitate a humble man; at least imitate a humble God." Augustine, *Tractates on the Gospel of John*, p. 254.

29 Young, *Conjectures on Original Composition*, p. 16.

30 Ibid., p. 6.

31 Ibid., p. 7.

32 Rousseau, *Discourse*, p. 25.

33 Ibid., pp. 25–6.

34 Ibid., p. 15.

35 Rousseau, *Confessions*, p. 5.

36 Shaftesbury, *Characteristics*, p. 93.

37 Ibid., p. 241.

38 Ibid., p. 93.

39 Ibid., p. 93.

40 Goethe, *Essays on Art and Literature*, p. 3. Jochen Schmidt describes the comparison of the artist to God and the accompanying transposition of attributes from the deity to the genius as a conscious act of "blasphemous secularization." Schmidt, *Geschichte des Genie-Gedankens*, p. 193.

41 Goethe, *Essays on Art and Literature*, p. 3.

42 Ibid., p. 9. In the poem "Reunion," written almost half a century later, Goethe refers to "the wings of rosy dawn" (*morgenroten Flügeln*), which convey the lover to the awaiting lips of the beloved. Goethe, *Selected Poems*, pp. 214–15. The reference occurs immediately after a pronouncement declaring that God no longer needs to create since his creatures now have the power to bring the world into being.

43 Goethe, *Essays on Art and Literature*, p. 5.

44 Ibid., p. 9.

45 Ibid., pp. 9–10.

46 Ibid., pp. 9–10.

47 Line citations of *Faust* are from Goethe, *Faust I & II*.

48 Goethe, *Selected Poems*, p. 29.

49 Wellbery, *The Specular Moment*, p. 309. Departing from interpretations in thrall to what he calls "the theological-materialistic schema of artistic creation," Wellbery explicates the ways in which "Prometheus" functions as a form of linguistic self-enactment; he writes, "the poem itself accomplishes the process about which it speaks; as act of speech it realizes the emancipatory program of Enlightenment" (p. 293).

50 The appropriative spirit is present throughout Goethe's creative career, marked by a series of productive assimilations of the works of past masters. The *West-Eastern Divan*, with its modern refashionings of medieval Persian material and its respectful rivalry with the poet Hafez, is exemplary in this respect.

51 Stressing the anti-Augustinian spirit of the poem, Christian Weber interprets Prometheus's retrospection as "a polemical parody" of the recollective introspection of the *Confessions*, which leads Augustine to acknowledge the vanity of his life and his dependency on God. Weber, "Goethes *Prometheus*," p. 110.

52 Schlegel, *Friedrich Schlegel's Lucinde*, p. 67.

53 Goethe, *From My Life (Parts One to Three)*, pp. 469–70.

54 This argument is advanced in Darrin M. McMahon's *Divine Fury*, p. 76. This important study uncovers developments in our ideas of genius from antiquity to the present.

55 Blake, *Marriage of Heaven and Hell*, p. 35.

56 According to Harold Bloom, "The specific difficulty in reading *The Marriage of Heaven and Hell* is to mark the limits of its irony: where does Blake speak straight?" Bloom, *Ringers in the Tower*, p. 55. Notwithstanding the subtlety of Bloom's analysis, with its attentiveness to the dialectical complexities of the work, this search for the unironic author in the text strikes me as not altogether fruitful. Blake's voice is to be found not in a specific assertion or specific assertions of *The Marriage of Heaven and Hell* – it is to be found in all of them; the truth of his vision resides less in its unironic parts than in its ironic totality.

57 Focusing on *The Marriage of Heaven and Hell*, I do not venture into the domain of Blake's later writings or address the problem of the continuities and ruptures between this piece and his later works.

58 As David V. Erdman points out in his reading of *America*, the speech of the quasi-Satanic Orc offers a "poetic paraphrase of The Declaration of Independence." Erdman, *Blake*, pp. 24–5.

59 Blake, *Marriage of Heaven and Hell*, p. 35. Here as elsewhere, I have retained Blake's rather idiosyncratic punctuation and capitalization.

60 Ibid., p. 34.

61 Ibid., p. 34.

62 Ibid., p. 34.

63 Ibid., pp. 37–8.

64 Ibid., p. 36.

65 Ibid., p. 37.

66 Blake provided illustrations for an edition of Young's *Night Thoughts*, first published in 1797. It is difficult to determine with any precision, however, the extent to which Young influenced Blake's ideas on genius. For an analysis of Blake's illustrations, see Tambling, *Blake's Night Thoughts*.

67 Its hieratic tone notwithstanding, *The Marriage of Heaven and Hell*, with its double-voicedness and internalized dialogism, shares features of the "novelistic" as Mikhail Bakhtin defines it in *The Dialogic Imagination*.

68 For an exposition of Blake's views of artist, artwork, and audience in terms of his expressivist theory, see Eaves, *Blake's Theory of Art*. Eaves explains that "when Blake calls for originality we must understand that he means the complete self-expression of the complete self in imagination" (p. 72).

69 Blake, *Marriage of Heaven and Hell*, p. 34.

70 Ibid., p. 36.

71 Blake's use of "overflow" as a symbol of expression and creation anticipates Nietzsche, whose *Thus Spoke Zarathustra* begins with its eponymous hero's "overflowing" and "going under."

72 Blake, *Marriage of Heaven and Hell*, p. 35.

73 Such an acknowledgement does not detract from the special position that Milton occupied in Blake's thought. In *Milton: A Poem*, Blake even presents the poet himself as an epic protagonist.

74 Blake, *Marriage of Heaven and Hell*, p. 43.

75 Ibid., p. 44.

76 Ibid., p. 34.

77 Lewis, *The Great Divorce*, pp. vi–viii.

78 Ibid., p. viii.

79 Ibid., p. i.

80 On the points of convergence between the two poets, with specific reference to "overcoming negations," see Bidney, *Blake and Goethe*.

81 Goethe, *Scientific Studies*, p. 166.

82 Ibid., pp. 155–6.

83 Ibid., pp. 245–6.

84 See Nisbet, "*Das Dämonische*," pp. 259–81.

85 Goethe, *From My Life (Part Four)*, p. 597.

86 Nicholls, *Goethe's Concept of the Daemonic*. Nicholls places particular emphasis on the influence of Plato's daemonology on Goethe's thought.

87 Goethe, *From My Life (Part Four)*, p. 598.

88 Goethe, *Sämtliche Werke. Briefe, Tagebücher und Gespräche. Band 12 (39). Johann Peter Eckermann: Gespräche mit Goethe*, p. 364.

89 These two faces of the daemonic correspond respectively to two different kinds of genius, which Peter Kivy calls "the possessor" and "the possessed." See his *The Possessor and the Possessed*.

90 Goethe, *From My Life (Part Four)*, p. 597.

91 Goethe, *Gespräche mit Goethe*, p. 456.

92 Lewis, *Screwtape Letters*, p. ix.

93 Hegel, *Lectures on Fine Art*, vol. 1, p. 160.

94 On the particular evils that Mephistopheles manifests and the different personae he adopts in the drama, see Anderegg, "Wie böse ist der Böse?"

95 As Lewis states in *Mere Christianity*, pride is "the complete anti-God state of mind" and the worst of the vices beside which all others are "mere fleabites in comparison" (p. 107).

96 Arnold, *Essays in Criticism*, p. 99.

97 The connection to the daemonic is apparent not only in Byron's greatness as a writer, but also in his restlessness, irresistibility to women, and death at a relatively young age. Goethe, *Gespräche mit Goethe*, pp. 250, 459, 660.

98 Southey, *Poetical Works*, p. 769.

99 Shelley, *A Defence of Poetry*, p. 290.

100 Shelley, "Essay on the Devil," p. 266.

101 Ibid., p. 269.

102 Ibid., p. 269.

103 Ibid., p. 270.

104 Ibid., p. 270.

105 Ibid., p. 270.

106 As Judith Shklar explains, "the victims must redeem mankind. The virtues most becoming to them are fortitude and pride, and it is these that are usually ascribed to them. Pride may be a deadly sin for those who preach faith and

meekness, but it recommends itself to those who put cruelty first." Shklar, *Ordinary Vices*, p. 15.

107 Schopenhauer, *Essays and Aphorisms*, p. 139.

108 A concern with pain and suffering is also evident in the more ambitious synthetic philosophical projects of recent decades, such as Derek Parfit's "Triple Theory," which seeks to unite consequentialist, Kantian, and contractualist theories. According to Parfit, "we can deserve many things, such as gratitude, praise, and the kind of blame that is merely moral dispraise. But no one could ever deserve to suffer." Parfit, *On What Matters*, vol. 1, p. 272.

109 Augustine, *Concerning the City of God*, p. 995.

110 Ibid., p. 14.

111 Taylor, *A Secular Age*, pp. 78–9.

112 Shelley, "A Refutation of Deism," p. 135.

113 Shelley, *A Defence of Poetry*, pp. 282–3.

114 Ibid., p. 283.

115 Scrivener, *Radical Shelley*, pp. 252–3.

116 Dawson, *The Unacknowledged Legislator*, p. 225.

117 Ibid., pp. 225–43.

118 Shelley, *A Defence of Poetry*, p. 295.

119 Balzac, *Père Goriot*, p. 85.

2 Symbols of the Morally Bad

1 In his assessment of Shakespeare's "monstrous farces, which are called tragedies," Voltaire declares that the English playwright "had a strong and fertile genius, full of naturalness and sublimity, without the slightest spark of good taste or the least knowledge of the rules." Voltaire, *Letters on England*, p. 92.

2 Kant, *Critique of the Power of Judgment*, pp. 227–8.

3 Lombroso, *Criminal Man*, pp. 202–5.

4 Stoker, *Dracula*, p. 342.

5 Arendt, *Origins of Totalitarianism*, p. 447.

6 Ibid., p. 450.

7 Rosenkranz, *Aesthetics of Ugliness*, p. 25.

8 Sartre, *Saint Genet*, p. 498.

9 Hegel, *Lectures on Fine Art*, vol. 1, p. 332.

10 Ibid., p. 338.

11 Ibid., p. 335.

12 Ibid., 338.

13 Ibid., 340.

14 Ibid., p. 341.

15 Ibid., p. 341.

16 Hegel, *Philosophy of History*, p. 158.

17 On the history of this prejudicial assessment, see Mitter, *Much Maligned Monsters*. In accounting for instances of unsympathetic reaction, Mitter points to the role played by Christian demonology and "frightening imagery of demons and hell" (pp. 9–10). The assimilation of Indian divinities to malformed devils made aesthetic revulsion and moral alarm the appropriate response to depictions of them.

18 Hegel, *Lectures on Fine Art*, vol. 1, p. 438.

19 Ibid., p. 223.

20 Ibid., p. 222.

21 Hegel himself maintained that India "has always been the land of longing and appears to us still as a kingdom of wonders, an enchanted world (*eine verzauberte Welt*)." Hegel, *Vorlesungen*, p. 174.

22 Beckford, *Vathek*, p. 4.

23 Ibid., p. 6.

24 Ibid., p. 6.

25 Ibid., pp. 6, 13.

26 Ibid., p. 18.

27 Lewis, *Screwtape Letters*, p. 145. *Tundale's Vision*, composed in the twelfth century, offers a gallery of the torments of the damned culminating in the sight of "the Prince of Shadows," a mammoth beast who sucks souls into his immense mouth and devours them. Gardiner, *Visions of Heaven and Hell*, pp. 177–8.

28 Bakhtin, *Rabelais and His World*, pp. 278–82.

29 This mixture is already to be found in perceptions of it in the early modern period, prior to its merger with the fantastic and supernatural in Gothic literature. As Wolfgang Kayser notes, "by the word *grottesco*, the Renaissance, which used it to designate a specific ornamental style suggested by antiquity, understood not only something playfully gay and carelessly fantastic, but also something ominous and sinister in the face of a world totally different from the familiar one – a world in which the realm of inanimate things is no longer separated from those of plants, animals, and human beings, and where the laws of statics, symmetry, and proportion are no longer valid." Kayser, *The Grotesque in Art and Literature*, p. 21.

30 Châtel, *William Beckford*, p. 135.

31 Beckford, *Vathek*, 94.

32 Ibid., 94.

33 In supplementary stories to *Vathek*, Beckford attempted to go further still in his portrayal of acts of extremity. The narrator of "The Story of Prince Barkiarokh" begins the account of his misdeeds with the line, "My crimes are even greater than those of the Calif Vathek." Beckford, *The Episodes of Vathek*, p. 65.

34 Hegel, *Lectures on Fine Art*, vol. 1, p. 159.

35 Ibid., p. 160.

36 Beckford, *Vathek*, p. 8.

37 Ibid., pp. 73–4.

38 Robert J. Gemmett maintains that "the humor is fundamentally incongruous to the tale" and that "the work is, on the whole, fundamentally serious." Gemmett, *William Beckford*, pp. 96–7. He thus sees the characters as heroic figures, albeit deeply flawed ones. In response to this assessment, R.D. Stock exclaims, "This is what comes of seeing the humor as extrinsic!" Stock, *The Holy and the Daemonic*, p. 295. But while Stock recognizes the centrality of the protagonists' buffoonery to their adventures, in emphasizing what a poor showing evil makes in *Vathek*, he downplays the text's subversiveness.

39 This quotation serves as an epigraph to Lewis's *Screwtape Letters*.

40 Borges, *Selected Non-fictions*, p. 238.

41 In his history of Fonthill, Gemmett describes it as "a kindred creation to *Vathek*, a piece cut from the same artistic fabric and also inextricably associated with the creator's complex personal life." Gemmett, *Beckford's Fonthill*, p. 23.

42 Coleridge, *Collected Works*, vol. 11, p. 61.

43 Marquis de Sade, *Crimes of Love*, p. 14.

44 Ibid., p. 14.

45 Krafft-Ebing, *Psychopathia Sexualis*, p. 53.

46 Hegel, *Lectures on Fine Art*, vol. 1, p. 338.

47 Sade, *Philosophy in the Boudoir*, p. 75.

48 d'Holbach, *Oeuvres*, vol. 2, pp. 355–67.

49 de Beauvoir, *The Marquis de Sade*, p. 59.

50 Noting that "Sade's thinking on this point was not quite coherent," Beauvoir still maintains that "nature retains her sacred character for Sade: indivisible and unique, she is an absolute, outside of which there is no reality" (*The Marquis de Sade*, pp. 61–3). But even if nature is appealed to in Sade, it is just as often used, abused, and dismissed. Far from finding the sacred in nature, Sade's philosophy

seems bent on extirpating the sacred everywhere it finds it; one of its driving forces is profanation.

51 As Pierre Klossowski explains, "sodomy is formulated by a specific gesture of countergenerality, the most significant in Sade's eyes – that which strikes precisely at the law of the propagation of the species and thus *bears witness to the death of the species in the individual*. It evinces an attitude not only of refusal but of aggression; in being the simulacrum of the act of generation, it is a mockery of it." Klossowski, *Sade My Neighbor*, p. 24.

52 Bakhtin, *Rabelais and His World*, pp. 317–18.

53 Hegel, *Lectures on Fine Art*, vol. 1, pp. 343–4.

54 Ibid., p. 215.

55 Ibid., pp. 214–15.

56 Sade, *Juliette*, pp. 68–72.

57 Sade, *Philosophy in the Boudoir*, p. 82.

58 "This transformation of all sexual expression, including Sade's, into something healthy was thus consistent with the idea that sexual, even perverse instinct informs the most normal kinds of behavior." Dean, *The Self and Its Pleasures*, p. 135.

59 On the history of this canonization and appropriation, with a focus on changes in the introductions to various editions of Sade's published works, see McMorran, "Introducing the Marquis de Sade," pp. 133–51.

60 Lying, for example, cannot be raised to the level of a categorical imperative without falling into contradiction.

61 Horkheimer and Adorno, *Dialectic of Enlightenment*, p. 74.

62 Ibid., p. 74.

63 Nietzsche, *Twilight of the Idols*, p. 483.

64 For an informative treatment of the moral status of bodily waste in the Middle Ages, see Martha Bayless's *Sin and Filth in Medieval Culture*, which offers a wealth of examples from the fifth century onwards in which the devil is linked with excrement and excretion.

65 Rosenkranz, *Aesthetics of Ugliness*, pp. 196–7.

66 Ibid., p. 191.

67 Ibid., p. 190.

68 Ibid., pp. 214–15.

69 Ibid., p. 215.

70 Ibid., pp. 214–15.

71 Ibid., p. 192.

72 Ibid., p. 197.

73 Ibid., p. 197.

74 Sade, *120 Days of Sodom*, p. 59.

75 Ibid., p. 31.

76 Ibid., p. 31.

77 Sade, *Philosophy in the Boudoir*, p. 46.

78 Sade, *Juliette*, p. 344.

79 Ibid., p. 8.

80 Ibid., pp. 20, 40.

81 Ibid., pp. 217–18.

82 "Il faut toujours en revenir à de Sade, c'est-à-dire à *l'homme naturel*, pour expliquer le mal." Baudelaire, *Oeuvres diverses*, p. 88.

83 Baudelaire, *Flowers of Evil*, p. 5.

84 Ibid., p. 5.

85 Ibid., p. 5.

86 How are we to distinguish moments of devilish intervention from all-too-human lapses? In accounting for the role of the devil in *The Flowers of Evil*, Jonathan Culler writes, "What is most diabolical about the Devil, I am tempted to conclude, is that we can never be sure when he is at work." Culler, *Baudelaire's Satanic Verses*, p. 16.

87 Rosenkranz, *Aesthetics of Ugliness*, p. 49.

88 Ibid., p. 49.

89 On this aspect of Baudelaire's work, see Rollins, *Baudelaire et le Grotesque*; Chao, *Rethinking the Concept of the Grotesque*; and Swayne, *Grotesque Figures*.

90 Baudelaire, *Flowers of Evil*, p. 61.

91 Ibid., p. 60.

92 Ibid., p. 71.

93 With specific reference to "A Carcass," but with application to Baudelaire's wider poetry of putrefaction, Winfried Menninghaus writes that "from *itself* and *the very beginning*, desire aims, in scarcely hidden form, at precisely the imagination of the putrefying body as something excessively alive – if not as the cipher of sexuality itself." Menninghaus, *Disgust*, p. 138.

94 Baudelaire, *Flowers of Evil*, p. 53.

95 Ibid., p. 52.

96 Ibid., p. 65.

97 Ibid., p. 65.

98 The connections between sadism and masochism in Baudelaire are explicated in Blin, *Le Sadisme de Baudelaire*, pp. 37–47.

99 Hegel, *Phenomenology of Spirit*, p. 2.

100 The lack of resolution in Baudelaire's portrayal of the interaction of contraries not only applies to his reflections on disgust and desire. With reference to Baudelaire's "double vision," Françoise Meltzer writes that the poet attempts "to depict a world of contrary, disjunct events without giving in to the normalized unity and depth of a stereoscope." Meltzer, *Seeing Double*, p. 113.

101 Schopenhauer, *The World as Will and Representation*, vol. 1, p. 367.

102 Baudelaire, *Paris Spleen*, pp. 41–2.

103 Ibid., p. 43.

104 Baudelaire, *Baudelaire on Poe*, p. 73.

105 Ibid., p. 126. It is not that Poe has discovered a fundamental truth, but rather that he has remembered it. In appealing to the doctrine of original sin, Baudelaire shows an affinity with earlier Christian thinkers such as Pascal, whose despair at human beings' impotence and incapacity for happiness without divine grace resonates with the sentiments and convictions of the poet. For both men, the notion of "the universality of corruption" is vital to their understanding of human nature and man's place in an inhospitable cosmos. Dubray, *Pascal et Baudelaire*, pp. 91–107.

106 Baudelaire, *Baudelaire on Poe*, p. 126.

107 Nietzsche, *Twilight of the Idols*, p. 487.

108 Nietzsche's critical reception of Baudelaire was tied to both his ongoing polemic against Wagner and his attempt to clarify the nature of decadence, a concept with which he was intensively occupied in the late 1880s. See Le Rider, "Nietzsche et Baudelaire," pp. 85–101.

109 Baudelaire, *Paris Spleen*, p. 3.

110 Schopenhauer, *Parerga and Paralipomena*, vol. 2, pp. 419–20.

3 Evil and the Sublime

1 Diderot, *Rameau's Nephew*, p. 93.

2 Kant, *Critique of the Power of Judgment*, p. 145.

3 Kant, "On the Common Saying," p. 71.

4 Kant, "On a Newly Arisen Superior Tone," p. 68.

5 Kant, *Critique of the Power of Judgment*, p. 134.

6 On this particular point, at least, leading British thinkers (including Kames, Reid, and Hume) were more in accord with Kant than with Burke.

 7 Burke, *A Philosophical Enquiry*, p. 124.

 8 Kant, *Critique of the Power of Judgment*, p. 38.

 9 Burke, *A Philosophical Enquiry*, p. 39.

10 Ibid., p. 58.

11 Ibid, p. 57.

12 Ibid., p. 64.

13 Ibid., pp. 58–9.

14 Beattie, *Dissertations Moral and Critical*, pp. 612–13.

15 Ibid., p. 613.

16 Ibid., p. 614.

17 Ibid., p. 615.

18 Shelley, *A Defence of Poetry*, p. 290.

19 Burke, *A Philosophical Enquiry*, pp. 67–8.

20 Ibid., p. 68.

21 Ibid., p. 68.

22 Ibid., p. 67. Terry Eagleton identifies the difficulties that this piece of aesthetic psychology poses for Burke's larger political project. "The political paradox is plain: only love will truly win us to the law, but this love will erode the law to nothing. A law attractive enough to engage our intimate affections, and so hegemonically effective, will tend to inspire in us a benign contempt." Eagleton, *Ideology of the Aesthetic*, p. 55.

23 Baillie, *Essay on the sublime*, p. 26.

24 Ibid., p. 20.

25 Ibid., p. 21.

26 Burke, *A Philosophical Enquiry*, p. 45.

27 Ibid., p. 47.

28 Ibid., p. 37.

29 Ibid., p. 37.

30 Ibid., pp. 36–7.

31 Ibid., p. 36.

32 Ibid., p. 57.

33 Ibid., p. 40.

34 Ibid., p. 57. This characterization of astonishment is reiterated later in the text (p. 136).

35 Burke, *Reflections on the Revolution*, p. 154.

36 Ibid., pp. 276–7.

37 Ibid., p. 181.

38 Ibid., p. 386.
39 Ibid., p. 230.
40 Ibid., p. 257.
41 Ibid., p. 243. Burke's fellow anti-revolutionary Joseph de Maistre makes a similar comparison in his *Considerations on France*, where he declares that "the French Revolution and everything now happening in Europe is just as marvellous in its own way as the instantaneous fructification of a tree in the month of January" (p. 4).
42 Burke, *Speeches*, vol. 4, pp. 164–5.
43 Burke, *A Philosophical Enquiry*, p. 62.
44 There is a considerable body of literature on the relationship between Burke's *Enquiry* and his *Reflections on the Revolution in France*; the most sustained exposition is to be found in Tom Furniss, *Edmund Burke's Aesthetic Ideology*. On Furniss's reading, "Burke seeks to reinterpret the Revolution as a false sublime, or as an example of the way the sublime in its highest degree can run out of control" (p. 119). Likewise, in his reading of the intersections between Burke's politics and aesthetics, Ronald Paulson refers to Burke's sense of the "pseudo-sublimity" of the French Revolution. Paulson, "Burke's Sublime," p. 251. With reference to Burke's aforementioned speech before the Commons, Paulson interprets it as an attempt to articulate the difference between the "true sublime" and the "false sublime," wherein the latter operates as a "perversion" of the former (p. 249). It is important to note, however, that Burke himself never makes this distinction explicit in his *Reflections*, nor does he provide us with a standard according to which the sublime's true and false forms could be differentiated. Scholars have thus had difficulty determining in what precisely this so-called falsity consists, at least according to the parameters of the sublime as set forth in the *Enquiry*. According to Stephen K. White, the creation of "the false sublime" is "the true aesthetic-affective innovation of the revolution," which comes about as a result of the sublime's "humanization." White, *Edmund Burke*, pp. 74–7. While White's reflections on the process of humanization contain interesting insights into changes the Revolution wrought, there is little in the *Enquiry* itself that suggests that a "humanized sublime" is an inauthentic one.
45 An element of compulsion may also be constitutive of our perception of the beautiful. As Mikel Dufrenne writes, "the aesthetic object causes us to yield to it, rather than accommodating itself to us." Dufrenne, *Phenomenology of Aesthetic Experience*, p. 427. Nonetheless, the feeling of being overpowered is more apparent in the sublime.

46 Neiman, *Evil in Modern Thought*, p. 302.

47 Ibid., p. 300.

48 For a functionalist approach to the Holocaust, see *From Weimar to Auschwitz* by Hans Mommsen, who also wrote the introduction to the German edition of *Eichmann in Jerusalem*. In *Obedience to Authority*, Stanley Milgram refers to Arendt's banality of evil thesis, for which he found confirmation in his own laboratory experiments.

49 Neiman, *Evil in Modern Thought*, p. 302.

50 Arendt, *Lectures*, p. 4.

51 Arendt, *Origins of Totalitarianism*, p. 474. While Arendt was much more well disposed to the American Revolution than to the French Revolution, she did not share Burke's unremittingly negative view of the latter. See Arendt, *On Revolution*.

52 The accuracy of this depiction has been disputed since Arendt first reported on the trial and has been challenged more recently by Stangneth's *Eichmann before Jerusalem*.

53 Arendt, *Origins of Totalitarianism*, p. 461.

54 Ibid., p. 461.

55 Kant introduced this term in *Religion within the Bounds of Bare Reason*, published in 1793.

56 In regard to the challenges of representing the Holocaust, Saul Friedlander disputes the claim that the Holocaust is unrepresentable, but he adds that "we are dealing with an event which tests our traditional representational and conceptual categories, an 'event at the limits.'" Friedlander, "Introduction," pp. 2–3.

57 Bernstein writes that "the problem one faces in speaking about evil bears a strong family resemblance to the way in which Kant speaks of the sublime. But there is nothing sublime about radical evil." Bernstein, *Hannah Arendt and the Jewish Question*, p. 149. After this emphatic denial of commonality between the two, Bernstein does not specify, however, what exactly makes radical evil wholly alien to the sublime.

58 Arendt, *Origins of Totalitarianism*, p. 464.

59 Ibid., p. 464.

60 Ibid., p. 405.

61 Ibid., p. viii.

62 Ibid., p. 456.

63 Ibid., p. 437.

64 Ibid., p. 461.

65 Ibid., p. 442.

66 Ibid., p. 439.

67 Ibid., p. 444.

68 Ibid., p. 459.

69 Burke, *A Philosophical Enquiry*, p. 59.

70 Arendt, *Origins of Totalitarianism*, p. 378.

71 Ibid., p. 378.

72 Ibid., p. 373.

73 Ibid., p. 373.

74 Ibid., p. 403.

75 Ibid., p. 441.

76 Ibid., pp. 439–40.

77 Ibid., p. 437.

78 Ibid., p. viii.

79 Arendt, "What Remains?," p. 13.

80 Ibid., p. 14.

81 Ibid., p. 14.

82 Burke, *A Philosophical Enquiry*, p. 57.

83 Arendt, *Origins of Totalitarianism*, p. 441.

84 In an unpublished note from June 1950, Arendt defines radical evil as "das, was nicht hätte passieren dürfen." Arendt, *Denktagebuch*, p. 7.

85 Arendt, "Organized Guilt," p. 132.

86 Arendt, *Life of the Mind*, p. 4.

87 Arendt, *Eichmann in Jerusalem*, p. 54.

88 As Simona Forti puts it, "Eichmann, we might say, is the anti-Stavrogin. Even from a philosophical point of view, he is the mirror-image opposite of Dostoevsky's anti-heroes, in the sense that he performs evil not by transgressing the law for the sake of evil but by fully observing the law, regardless of its content." Forti, *New Demons*, p. 193.

89 Elisabeth Young-Bruehl provides a version of this narrative in her biography *Hannah Arendt: For Love of the World*, pp. 367–71. This narrative has attained a position approaching orthodoxy in Arendt scholarship although it has not been without prominent dissenters. Perhaps the most cogent attempt to read Arendt's concepts of radical evil and banal evil as intertwined, rather than temporally successive and oppositional, can be found in Bernstein's important study *Radical Evil*. At the same time, Bernstein maintains that Arendt rejected "any mythological or aesthetic attempt to characterize the intentions of the perpetrators of radical evil" (p. 215). The juxtaposition of the mythological and the aesthetic gives the impression that these

two categories implicate one another; but not all aestheticizing is mythologizing. And even if it is true that Arendt did not treat evil "intentions" aesthetically, this does not preclude an aesthetic treatment of the political forms that radical evil assumes.

90 *Hannah Arendt/Karl Jaspers Correspondence*, p. 69.
91 Ibid., p. 62.
92 Ibid., p. 62.
93 Ibid., p. 62.
94 Ibid., p. 62.
95 Burke, *Speeches*, vol. 4, p. 164.
96 Arendt, "Some Questions," p. 74.
97 In his review of the first edition of *The Origins of Totalitarianism*, Raymond Aron expressed doubts about the essentialist strand in Arendt's interpretation. Aron, "The Essence of Totalitarianism," pp. 366–76. With the incorporation of the essay "Ideology and Terror: A Novel Form of Government" into the second edition, this essentialism becomes still more central to Arendt's book.
98 Aron, "The Essence of Totalitarianism," p. 366.
99 Arendt, *Origins of Totalitarianism*, p. 459.
100 Ibid., p. 459.
101 Arendt, "Nightmare and Flight," p. 134.
102 Arendt, *Origins of Totalitarianism*, p. 459.
103 Kant, *Religion within the Bounds of Bare Reason*, p. 41.
104 Arendt, *Origins of Totalitarianism*, p. 457.
105 Ibid., p. 444.
106 Arendt, *The Human Condition* p. 241.
107 *Hannah Arendt/Karl Jaspers Correspondence*, p. 54.
108 Arendt, *Origins of Totalitarianism*, pp. 461–3.
109 Ibid., p. 468.
110 Ibid., p. 456.
111 Kant, *Critique of the Power of Judgment*, p. 131.
112 Burke, *A Philosophical Enquiry*, p. 67.
113 Arendt, *Eichmann in Jerusalem*, p. 252.
114 Among the major philosophers, Kant stands out as one who does not hesitate to label seemingly tepid forms of badness as evil. But it is this moral "rigorism," as he himself dubs it, that has made his pronouncements seem especially severe and unpalatable to many.
115 Arendt, "Some Questions," p. 75.
116 Arendt, *Eichmann in Jerusalem*, p. 150.

117 In the work of Slavoj Žižek, for example, we are confronted with a deliberately provocative call to violent action and even "terror," in which the sublime is sought out and embraced. Žižek does not seek to downplay the risk that this entails, since the acknowledgment of it excites rather than dampens revolutionary fervour. See Žižek's introduction to Robespierre, *Virtue and Terror*, and Žižek, *Violence*. In his critical assessment of the configuration of violence, trauma, and the sublime in Žižek's work, Dominick LaCapra reads it in terms of "a transcendentally legitimated, fatalistic modernism whereby excess *must* overwhelm all limits." LaCapra, *History, Literature, Critical Theory*, p. 155.

118 A pathologizing approach is at work in Erich Fromm's *The Anatomy of Human Destructiveness*, where the moral depravity of "the necrophilous personality" is linked to a preoccupation with death, excrement, violence, and the machinic. Futurism, as presented in Marinetti's *Futurist Manifesto*, is listed as an example of a necrophilous aesthetic.

119 In the nineteenth century, the relationship between aesthetics and illness becomes a matter of considerable philosophical and scientific interest. In a work first published in 1854, the music critic Eduard Hanslick identifies "the aesthetic" and "the pathological" as two oppositional ways of listening to music, wherein the latter is associated with a primitive, undiscriminating surrender to intoxicating feelings. Judgments that arise out of such feelings are to be read symptomatically since they tell us nothing substantive about the experienced musical composition itself. Hanslick, *Vom Musikalisch-Schönen*, pp. 88–9.

4 Wicked Spectators

1 Rousseau, *Politics and the Arts*, p. 22.

2 Ibid., p. 23.

3 Ibid., p. 17.

4 Augustine, *Confessions*, pp. 36–7.

5 The determination of the nature of this mediation exercises a considerable influence on post-Kantian thought. Schiller's program of "aesthetic education," Schelling's placing of art at the pinnacle of philosophy in his *System of Transcendental Idealism*, and Schlegel's theorization of romantic poetry are all attempts to bridge the gap between freedom and nature in aesthetic terms.

6 Kant, *Critique of the Power of Judgment*, p. 151.

7   According to Foucault, the Greeks aimed "to constitute a kind of ethics which was an aesthetics of existence." Foucault, *The Foucault Reader*, p. 343. The same impulse, inspired in large part by his encounter with the Greeks, animates Nietzsche's work.

8   Voltaire, *Philosophical Dictionary*, vol. 4, p. 46.

9   Lucretius, *De Rerum Natura*, p. 48.

10 Voltaire, *Philosophical Dictionary*, vol. 4, p. 45.

11 Blumenberg, *Shipwreck with Spectator*, p. 38.

12 Schopenhauer, *The World as Will and Representation*, vol. 1, p. 320.

13 Ibid., p. 320.

14 Schopenhauer, *Parerga and Paralipomena*, vol. 2, p. 441.

15 Ibid., p. 443.

16 Ibid., p. 442.

17 Schopenhauer, *Two Fundamental Problems of Ethics*, p. 228.

18 Hegel, *Lectures on Fine Art*, vol. 2, p. 1198.

19 Schopenhauer, *The World as Will and Representation*, vol. 1, pp. 252–4.

20 Ibid., p. 252.

21 Ibid., p. 257.

22 Ibid., p. 331.

23 Lerchner, "Die Welt als Vorstellung," pp. 53–75.

24 Schopenhauer, *The World as Will and Representation*, vol. 1, p. 199. This constitutes "the subjective side" of aesthetic experience; "the objective side," which I do not discuss, refers to Schopenhauer's quasi-Platonic theory of ideas.

25 Schopenhauer, *Two Fundamental Problems of Ethics*, p. 231.

26 Rousseau, *Discourse*, p. 37.

27 Schopenhauer, *The World as Will and Representation*, vol. 1, pp. 204–5.

28 Schopenhauer, *The World as Will and Representation*, vol. 2, p. 433.

29 Following Jacques Rancière, Claire Bishop writes that "the binary of active/passive always ends up in a deadlock: either a disparagement of the spectator because he does nothing, while the performers on stage do something – or the converse claim that those who act are inferior to those who are able to look, contemplate ideas, and have critical distance on the world." Bishop, *Artificial Hells*, pp. 37–8. Among those who favour the latter claim, Schopenhauer provides one of the more extreme instances. Unlike Schiller, who locates political potentialities in the aesthetic, Schopenhauer stresses what is individual and what is subjectively universal in the moment of aesthetic contemplation; in doing so, he leaves no room for mediation, social or political, between the

individual and a larger collective. But it is in this mediated space, where a community emerges as an agent of transformation, that disinterested spectatorship transitions to participatory art.

30 Schopenhauer, *Parerga and Paralipomena*, vol. 2, p. 600.

31 Schopenhauer, *The World as Will and Representation*, vol. 2, p. 433.

32 Milton, *Complete Poems and Major Prose*, p. 549.

33 Nietzsche, *Birth of Tragedy*, p. 68.

34 Ibid., p. 68.

35 Ibid., p. 68.

36 Schopenhauer, *The World as Will and Representation*, vol. 2, pp. 586–7.

37 Nietzsche, *Birth of Tragedy*, p. 42.

38 Ibid., p. 59.

39 Ibid., p. 59.

40 Pointing out the early Nietzsche's debts to Schopenhauer and Wagner in his interpretation of Greek tragedy, Julian Young argues that "the Greeks, Nietzsche suggests, were really Schopenhauerians." Young, "Richard Wagner," p. 237. But while Nietzsche shows that the Greeks were far removed from naive optimism, their peculiar brand of Hellenic pessimism is differentiated from the Buddhistic pessimism that characterizes Schopenhauer's worldview. The antinatalist wisdom of Silenus does not tell us the whole story; it must be paired with the lament of Achilles, who prefers even the toiling life of the day labourer to the shadow existence of the underworld.

41 Nietzsche, *Birth of Tragedy*, p. 69.

42 Ibid., p. 71.

43 Ibid. p. 71.

44 Wagner, *Art-Work of the Future*, p. 34.

45 Nietzsche, *Birth of Tragedy*, p. 69.

46 Ibid., p. 71.

47 Ibid., p. 70.

48 Nietzsche, *Gay Science*, p. 188.

49 "In Dionysian ecstasy, in being outside oneself, one transgresses the limit that ordinarily would delimit one's self, one's individuality, one's subjectivity. The Dionysian state is one of being impelled beyond the limit, driven on beyond the very limit that would delimit every state of the individual." Sallis, *Crossings*, p. 54.

50 Heidegger, *Nietzsche*, vol. 1, pp. 107–13.

51 Nietzsche, *Beyond Good and Evil*, p. 274.

52 Nietzsche, *Werke. Kritische Gesamtausgabe.* Abteilung 8, Band 3, p. 204. This assessment occurs in an unpublished note from 1888 with the heading "Was ist tragisch."

53 Nietzsche, *Twilight of the Idols*, p. 530.

54 Ibid., p. 518.

55 Ibid., p. 518.

56 Aesthetic experience provides an occasion to reflect upon our moral intuitions and categories; this applies especially to its more violently disruptive forms. Such reflection can be enlisted in service of a deconstructive genealogy or a self-reflective strengthening of the moral imagination. Marian Eide writes that "in linking moral capacity and the violent aesthetic, I argue neither that the violent aesthetic teaches readers to be moral, nor that it threatens to damage virtue, but rather that it provokes exactly these divided reactions in readers who wonder if they are damaged or improved by the text's brutality, who are inspired by the text to take up moral questions." Eide, *Terrible Beauty*, pp. 20–1.

57 Tertullian, "The Shows," p. 91.

58 Nietzsche, *Thus Spoke Zarathustra*, pp. 211–12.

59 Arendt, "Some Questions," p. 73.

60 Gibbon writes, "the Christians, who, in this world, found themselves oppressed by the power of the Pagans, were sometimes seduced by resentment and spiritual pride to delight in the prospect of their future triumph." After quoting the same passage from *De Spectaculis* that Nietzsche cites in *On the Genealogy of Morals*, he adds that "the humanity of the reader will permit me to draw a veil over the rest of this infernal description, which the zealous African pursues in a long variety of affected and unfeeling witticisms." Gibbon, *Decline and Fall*, p. 27.

61 Tertullian, "The Shows," p. 81.

62 In speaking of Zarathustra's ideal of the overman, Nietzsche tells us that those who deem themselves good would find in this most exalted type the exemplar of evil – "the good and the just would call his overman *devil.*" Nietzsche, *Ecce Homo*, p. 787.

63 Simone Neuber uses the term "morally corrupt (aesthetic) pleasure" to refer to "any (aesthetic) pleasure that relates intrinsically to the unhappiness of others." Neuber, "Morally Corrupt Aesthetic Pleasure?," p. 91.

64 Nietzsche, *Daybreak*, p. 114.

65 Nietzsche, *On the Genealogy of Morals*, p. 505.

66 Ibid., p. 529.

67 Ibid., pp. 476–7.

68 Nietzsche, *Birth of Tragedy*, pp. 17–20.

69 Ibid., pp. 22–3.

70 Ibid., p. 23.

71 Nietzsche, *Ecce Homo*, p. 727.

72 Schopenhauer, *Parerga and Paralipomena*, vol. 2, p. 201.

73 Nietzsche, *Ecce Homo*, p. 791.

74 Nietzsche, *Beyond Good and Evil*, p. 275.

75 Nietzsche, *Twilight of the Idols*, pp. 485–6.

76 Ibid., p. 525.

77 In polemicizing against Wagner, Nietzsche declares that "aesthetics is nothing but a kind of applied physiology." Nietzsche, *Nietzsche contra Wagner*, p. 664. The importance attributed to the body in the configuration of the aesthetic is also at work in his theorization of morality. In *Prophets of Extremity*, Allan Megill opposes the "aestheticist" Nietzsche to the "naturalist" Nietzsche (pp. 29–33). The distinction is not invalid, but in treating the two positions as oppositional, Megill does not consider Nietzsche's attempts to close the gaps between them. Even the categories of the Apollonian and the Dionysian, as introduced in *The Birth of Tragedy*, are conceived as natural impulses prior to assuming the form of art impulses. Megill's tying of the transgressiveness of Nietzsche's project to his "aestheticism" rightly brings out a crucial dimension of it. But in seeking out connections with later thinkers (Heidegger, Foucault, and Derrida) who were much more suspicious of "biologism" than was Nietzsche himself, Megill downplays the extent to which Nietzsche's reflections on the aesthetic were tied to his "naturalism."

78 Nietzsche, *Twilight of the Idols*, p. 529.

79 Nietzsche, *Beyond Good and Evil*, p. 275.

80 Nietzsche, *Selected Letters*, p. 329.

81 Ibid., p. 347.

82 Horkheimer and Adorno, *Dialectic of Enlightenment*, p. 79.

83 De Quincey, *On Murder*, pp. 8–9.

84 Ibid., p. 24.

85 Ibid., p. 10.

86 Ibid., pp. 10–11. The same distinction is made, with explicit reference to the Germans, in Carlyle's 1840 lectures on hero worship, where he states that "the *Vates* Prophet, we might say, has seized that sacred mystery rather on the moral side, as Good and Evil, Duty and Prohibition; the *Vates* Poet on what the

Germans call the aesthetic side, as Beautiful, and the like." Carlyle, *Works*,
p. 81.

87 De Quincey, *Works*, vol. 10, ed. Alina Clej, p. 173.

88 Ibid., p. 163.

89 Ibid., p. 163.

90 De Quincey, *On Murder*, pp. 23–4.

91 What else De Quincey's ideas on aesthetics owe to Kant is not easy to determine since he has surprisingly little to say about Kantian aesthetics. While he devotes attention to the first *Critique* and even to a number of shorter pieces, such as "Perpetual Peace," he does not discuss the *Critique of the Power of Judgment*. He mentions Kant's "Observations on the Feeling of the Beautiful and Sublime," but describes it as "determinately shallow and trivial." De Quincey, *Works*, vol. 7, ed. Robert Morrison, p. 51. Scholarly studies attempting to draw out the Kantian influences on De Quincey's aesthetics are thus largely speculative and, while often containing intriguing insights, must be approached with some degree of caution.

92 "His conduct of the paper was a characteristic blend of high-minded idealism, obsessive concern for detail and lively sensation-mongering." Lindop, *The Opium Eater*, p. 228.

93 De Quincey, *On Murder*, p. 95.

94 Ibid., p. 95.

95 Ibid., p. 95.

96 A brief reference to "A Modest Proposal" also precedes the 1827 essay, most probably inserted by the then editor of *Blackwood's Magazine* rather than by De Quincey himself.

97 De Quincey, *On Murder*, p. 103.

98 Ibid., pp. 134–6.

99 Ibid., p. 99.

100 Ibid., p. 126.

101 With reference to this scene, Nigel Leask writes that "this self-conscious choric narrative has the effect of highlighting Williams' 'artistry.'" Leask, "Toward a Universal Aesthetic," p. 115. It would be more apt, however, to say that this narrative highlights De Quincey's artistry, evident in his refashioning of the event to meet the demands of tragic art.

102 In accounting for what motivates De Quincey and other writers to "portray criminals as artists," Joel Black writes, "violent acts compel an aesthetic response in the beholder of awe, admiration, or bafflement. If an action evokes an

aesthetic response, then it is logical to assume that this action – even if it is murder – must have been the work of an artist." Black, *Aesthetics of Murder*, p. 39. Such an assumption, in order to be logical, rests on two presuppositions – that every artwork is the work of an artist and, more controversially, that whatever calls forth an aesthetic response is necessarily an artwork.

103 According to Frank Lentricchia and Jody McAuliffe, "since about 1800, the serious artist is the would-be criminal violator of the order of things." Lentricchia and McAuliffe, *Crimes of Art and Terror*, p. 18. On this reading, the aestheticizing of crime corresponds to the criminalizing of art, in which great art is conceived as radically transgressive in its destruction or intended destruction of the existing order.

104 De Quincey, *On Murder*, p. 32.

105 De Quincey showed an interest in Gothic literature from his youth onwards. On the applicability of the designation "Gothic" to his own work, see Bridgwater, *De Quincey's Gothic Masquerade*, pp. 60–74.

106 De Quincey, *On Murder*, p. 9.

107 Ibid., p. 11.

108 Dostoevsky, *Devils*, p. 582.

109 Ibid., p. 582.

110 "If I had not kept fire for myself, / there would be nothing I could call my own." Goethe, *Faust I & II*, 1,377–8.

111 De Quincey, *On Murder*, p. 97.

112 Ibid., p. 97.

113 *The Spectator*, vol. 3, no. 411, pp. 538–9.

114 On the history of this development, with the accompanying transformation of the murderer from "common sinner" to "moral monster" to "mental alien," see Halttunen, *Murder Most Foul*.

115 De Quincey, *On Murder*, pp. 104, 107.

116 One need only recall the reaction to Stockhausen's description of the terrorist attacks on the World Trade Center as "the greatest work of art that exists for the whole cosmos." Stockhausen, "'Huuuh!' Das Pressegespräch am 16. September 2001," p. 77. This depiction was roundly criticized in the media for its insensitive treatment of the victims of the tragedy and for its apparent celebration of the perpetrators as artistic geniuses. Stockhausen later clarified, but also defended his description as a misunderstood reference to the work of "Lucifer," whom he identified as "the cosmic spirit of rebellion" whose creative activity takes the form of anarchic destruction. In referring to Lucifer, Stockhausen

sought to show that he was far from morally condoning the terrorist attacks even as he alluded to art's participation in transgression and the role of destructiveness in the artistic process. Needless to say, this clarification did little to assuage his critics, who felt that he had callously transformed an evil act demanding the most severe moral condemnation into an aesthetic phenomenon.

117 Foucault, *Discipline and Punish*, pp. 68–9.
118 Nietzsche, *On the Genealogy of Morals*, p. 481.
119 Bataille, *Literature and Evil*, p. ix.
120 Foucault, *Language, Counter-Memory, Practice*, p. 35.
121 Ibid., p. 37.
122 Ibid., p. 36.

Bibliography

Anderegg, Johannes. "Wie böse ist der Böse? Zur Gestalt des Mephisto in Goethes 'Faust.'" *Monatshefte* 96.3 (2004): 343–59.

Arendt, Hannah. *Denktagebuch*. Edited by Ursula Ludz and Ingeborg Nordmann. Munich: Piper, 2002.

- *Eichmann in Jerusalem: A Report on the Banality of Evil*. New York: Penguin, 1994.
- *Essays in Understanding, 1930–1954*. Edited by Jerome Kohn. New York: Schocken Books, 1994.
- *The Human Condition*. Chicago: University of Chicago Press, 1998.
- *Lectures on Kant's Political Philosophy*. Chicago: University of Chicago Press, 1982.
- *The Life of the Mind*. New York: Mariner, 1981.
- "Nightmare and Flight." In Arendt, *Essays in Understanding*, 133–5.
- "Organized Guilt and Universal Responsibility." In Arendt, *Essays in Understanding*, 121–32.
- *The Origins of Totalitarianism*. New York: Harcourt, 1994.
- "A Reply to Eric Voegelin." In Arendt, *Essays in Understanding*, 401–8.
- *On Revolution*. New York: Viking, 1963.
- "Some Questions of Moral Philosophy." In Arendt, *Responsibility and Judgment*, edited by Jerome Kohn, 49–146. New York: Schocken Books, 2003.
- "'What Remains? The Language Remains': A Conversation with Günter Gaus." In Arendt, *Essays in Understanding*, 1–23.

Arnold, Matthew. *Essays in Criticism: First Series*. Chicago: University of Chicago Press, 1968.

Aron, Raymond. "The Essence of Totalitarianism according to Hannah Arendt." *Partisan Review* 60.3 (1993): 366–76. Originally published as "L'essence du totalitarisme," *Critique* (1954).

Augustine. *Concerning the City of God against the Pagans*. Translated by Henry Bettenson. New York: Penguin, 2003.

–   *Confessions*. Translated by Henry Chadwick. Oxford: Oxford University Press, 2009.

–   *Tractates on the Gospel of John, 11–27*. Translated by John W. Rettig. Washington, DC: Catholic University of America Press, 2003.

–   *The Works of Saint Augustine: On Genesis*. Vol. 1/13. Edited by John E. Rotelle. Translated by Edmund Hill. New York: New City Press, 2002.

Baillie, John. *An essay on the sublime*. London: 1747.

Bakhtin, Mikhail. *The Dialogic Imagination: Four Essays*. Edited by Michael Holquist. Translated by Caryl Emerson and Michael Holquist. Austin: University of Texas Press, 1981.

–   *Rabelais and His World*. Translated by Helene Iswolsky. Bloomington: Indiana University Press, 1984.

Balzac, Honoré de. *Père Goriot*. Translated by Burton Raffel. New York: W.W. Norton, 1994.

Bataille, Georges. *Literature and Evil*. Translated by Alastair Hamilton. London: Calder and Boyars, 1973.

Battersby, Christine. *Gender and Genius: Towards a Feminist Aesthetics*. Bloomington: Indiana University Press, 1989.

Baudelaire, Charles. *Baudelaire on Poe: Critical Papers*. Edited and translated by Lois Hyslop and Francis E. Hyslop, Jr. State College, PA: Bald Eagle Press, 1952.

–   *The Flowers of Evil*. Translated by James McGowan. Oxford: Oxford University Press, 1993.

–   *Oeuvres diverses*. Vol. 6 of *Oeuvres Complètes de Charles Baudelaire*. Edited by F.-F. Gautier and Y.-G. Le Dantec. Paris: Éditions de la Nouvelle Revue Française, 1918–37.

–   *Paris Spleen*. Translated by Louise Varèse. New York: New Directions, 1970.

Bayless, Martha. *Sin and Filth in Medieval Culture: The Devil in The Latrine*. New York: Routledge, 2012.

Beattie, James. *Dissertations Moral and Critical*. New York: Garland, 1971.

Beauvoir, Simone de. *The Marquis de Sade*. Edited and translated by Paul Dinnage. London: John Calder, 1962. Originally published as "Faut-il brûler Sade?" in *Privilèges* (1955).

Beckford, William. *The Episodes of Vathek*. Translated by Frank Marzials. Sawtry, UK: Dedalus, 1994.

–   *Vathek*. Oxford: Oxford University Press, 2013.

Bernstein, Richard. *Hannah Arendt and the Jewish Question*. Cambridge: Polity, 1996.

–   *Radical Evil: A Philosophical Interrogation*. Malden: Polity, 2002.

Bidney, Martin. *Blake and Goethe: Psychology, Ontology, Imagination*. Columbia: University of Missouri Press, 1988.

Bishop, Claire. *Artificial Hells: Participatory Art and the Politics of Spectatorship*. New York: Verso, 2012.

Black, Joel. *The Aesthetics of Murder: A Study in Romantic Literature and Contemporary Culture*. Baltimore: Johns Hopkins University Press, 1991.

Blake, William. *The Complete Poetry and Prose of William Blake*. Edited by David V. Erdman. New York: Anchor Books, 1988.

– *The Marriage of Heaven and Hell*. In Blake, *The Complete Poetry and Prose*, 33–45.

Blin, Georges. *Le Sadisme de Baudelaire*. Paris: Librairie José Corti, 1948.

Bloom, Harold. *The Ringers in the Tower: Studies in Romantic Tradition*. Chicago: University of Chicago Press, 1971.

Blumenberg, Hans. *The Legitimacy of the Modern Age*. Translated by Robert M. Wallace. Cambridge, MA: MIT Press, 1985.

– *Shipwreck with Spectator: Paradigm of a Metaphor for Existence*. Translated by Steven Rendall. Cambridge, MA: MIT Press, 1997.

Borges, Jorge Luis. *Selected Non-fictions*. Edited by Eliot Weinberger. Translated by Esther Allen, Suzanne Jill Levine, and Eliot Weinberger. New York: Penguin, 1999.

Bridgwater, Patrick. *De Quincey's Gothic Masquerade*. Amsterdam: Rodopi, 2004.

Burke, Edmund. *A Philosophical Enquiry into the Origin of our Ideas of the Sublime and Beautiful*. New York: Columbia University Press, 1958.

– *Reflections on the Revolution in France*. Stanford: Stanford University Press, 2001.

– *Speeches of the Right Honourable Edmund Burke*. Vol. 4. London: Longman, Hurst, Rees, Orme, and Brown, 1816.

Carlyle, Thomas. *The Works of Thomas Carlyle*. Vol. 5: *On Heroes, Hero-worship and the Heroic in History*. Edited by Henry Duff Traill. Cambridge: Cambridge University Press: 2010.

Chao, Shun-Liang. *Rethinking the Concept of the Grotesque: Crashaw, Baudelaire, Magritte*. New York: Legenda, 2010.

Châtel, Laurent. *William Beckford: The Elusive Orientalist*. Oxford University Studies in the Enlightenment. Oxford: Voltaire Foundation, 2016.

Cole, Phillip. *The Myth of Evil*. Edinburgh: Edinburgh University Press, 2006.

Coleridge, Samuel Taylor. *The Collected Works of Samuel Taylor Coleridge*, vol. 11: *Shorter Works and Fragments*. Edited by H.J. Jackson and J.R. de J. Jackson. Princeton: Princeton University Press, 1995.

Culler, Jonathan. *Baudelaire's Satanic Verses*. London: University of London, 1994.

Dawson, P.M.S. *The Unacknowledged Legislator: Shelley and Politics*. Oxford: Oxford University Press, 1980.

De Quincey, Thomas. *On Murder*. Oxford: Oxford University Press, 2009.

– *The Works of Thomas De Quincey*. Edited by Barry Symonds. London: Pickering & Chatto, 2000–3.

Dean, Carolyn J. *The Self and Its Pleasures: Bataille, Lacan, and the History of the Decentered Subject*. Ithaca: Cornell University Press, 1992.

Diderot, Denis. *Oeuvres,* vol. 1: *Philosophie*. Edited by Laurent Versini. Paris: Robert Laffont, 1994–7.

– *Rameau's Nephew and D'Alembert's Dream*. Translated by Leonard Tancock. London: Penguin, 1976.

Dostoevsky, Fyodor. *Devils*. Translated by Michael R. Katz. Oxford: Oxford University Press, 2008.

Dubray, Jean. *Pascal et Baudelaire*. Paris: Classiques Garnier, 2011.

Dufrenne, Mikel. *The Phenomenology of Aesthetic Experience*. Translated by Edward S. Casey, Albert A. Anderson, Willis Domingo, and Leon Jacobson. Evanston: Northwestern University Press, 1973.

Eagleton, Terry. *The Ideology of the Aesthetic*. Malden: Blackwell, 1990.

Eaves, Morris. *Blake's Theory of Art*. Princeton: Princeton University Press, 1982.

Eide, Marian. *Terrible Beauty: The Violent Aesthetic and Twentieth-Century Literature*. Charlottesville: University of Virginia Press, 2019.

Empson, William. *Milton's God*. Westport: Greenwood, 1961.

Encyclopedia of Disability. Edited by Gary L. Albrecht. Thousand Oaks: Sage, 2005.

Erdman, David V. *Blake: Prophet against Empire*. Princeton: Princeton University Press, 1977.

Fish, Stanley. *Surprised by Sin: The Reader in "Paradise Lost."* London: Macmillan, 1997.

Fleming, Paul. *Exemplarity and Mediocrity: The Art of the Average from Bourgeois Tragedy to Realism*. Stanford: Stanford University Press, 2009.

Forti, Simona. *New Demons: Rethinking Power and Evil Today*. Translated by Zakiya Hanafi. Stanford: Stanford University Press, 2015.

Foucault, Michel. *Discipline and Punish: The Birth of the Prison*. Translated by Alan Sheridan. New York: Vintage, 1995.

– *The Foucault Reader*. Edited by Paul Rabinow. New York: Pantheon, 1984.

– *Language, Counter-Memory, Practice: Selected Essays and Interviews*. Edited by Donald F. Bouchard. Translated by Donald F. Bouchard and Sherry Simon. Oxford: Blackwell, 1977.

Friedlander, Saul. "Introduction." In *Probing the Limits of Representation: Nazism and the "Final Solution,"* edited by Saul Friedlander, 1–21. Cambridge, MA: Harvard University Press, 1992.

Frischauer, Willi. *Himmler: The Evil Genius of the Third Reich*. Boston: Beacon, 1953.

Fromm, Erich. *The Anatomy of Human Destructiveness*. London: Cape, 1974.

Furniss, Tom. *Edmund Burke's Aesthetic Ideology: Language, Gender and Political Economy in Revolution*. Cambridge: Cambridge University Press, 1993.

Gardiner, Eileen, ed. *Visions of Heaven and Hell before Dante*. New York: Italica, 1989.

Gemmett, Robert J. *Beckford's Fonthill: The Rise of a Romantic Icon*. Norwich: Michael Russell, 2003.

- *William Beckford*. Boston: Twayne, 1977.

Gibbon, Edward. *The History of the Decline and Fall of the Roman Empire*. Vol. 2. Edited by J.B. Bury. London: Methuen & Co., 1901.

Goethe, Johann Wolfgang von. *Essays on Art and Literature*. Edited by John Gearey. Translated by Ellen von Nardroff and Ernest H. von Nardroff. Princeton: Princeton University Press, 1994.

- *Faust I & II*. Edited and translated by Stuart Atkins. Cambridge, MA: Suhrkamp/Insel, 1984.

- *From My Life: Poetry and Truth (Parts One to Three)*. Edited by Thomas P. Saine and Jeffrey L. Sammons. New York: Suhrkamp, 1987.

- *From My Life: Poetry and Truth (Part Four). Campaign in France 1792. Siege of Mainz*. Edited by Thomas P. Saine and Jeffrey L. Sammons. New York: Suhrkamp, 1987.

- *Sämtliche Werke. Briefe, Tagebücher und Gespräche*. Edited by Dieter Borchmeyer et al. Frankfurt am Main: Deutscher Klassiker Verlag, 1985–2013.

- *Scientific Studies*. Edited and translated by Douglas Miller. New York: Suhrkamp, 1988.

- *Selected Poems*. Edited by Christopher Middleton. Boston: Suhrkamp/Insel, 1983.

Halttunen, Karen. *Murder Most Foul: The Killer and the American Gothic Imagination*. Cambridge, MA: Harvard University Press, 1998.

Hannah Arendt/Karl Jaspers Correspondence, 1926–1969. Edited by Lotte Kohler and Hans Saner. Translated by Robert and Rita Kimber. New York: Harcourt Brace Jovanovich, 1992.

Hanslick, Eduard. *Vom Musikalisch-Schönen: Ein Beitrag zur Revision der Ästhetik der Tonkunst*. Darmstadt: Wissenschaftliche Buchgesellschaft, 2010.

Hegel, G.W.F. *Hegel's Aesthetics: Lectures on Fine Art*. Translated by T.M. Knox. Oxford: Oxford University Press, 1988.

- *Phenomenology of Spirit*. Translated by A.V. Miller. Oxford: Oxford University Press, 1977.

- *The Philosophy of History*. Translated by J. Sibree. New York: Dover, 1956.

- *Vorlesungen über die Philosophie der Geschichte*. Edited by Eva Moldenhauer and Karl Markus Michel. Frankfurt: Suhrkamp, 1970.

Heidegger, Martin. *Nietzsche*. Vols. 1 and 2. Translated by David Farrell Krell. New York: HarperCollins, 1991.

Hobbes, Thomas. *Leviathan*. London: Penguin, 1985.

d'Holbach, Paul-Henri Thiry. *Oeuvres philosophiques*. Edited by Jean-Pierre Jackson. Paris: Alive, 1998–2001.

Horace. *Satires and Epistles*. Translated by John Davie. Oxford: Oxford University Press, 2011.

Horkheimer, Max, and Theodor W. Adorno. *Dialectic of Enlightenment*. Translated by Edmund Jephcott. Stanford: Stanford University Press, 2002.

Jonas, Hans. *The Imperative of Responsibility: In Search of an Ethics for the Technological Age*. Translated by Hans Jonas and David Herr. Chicago: University of Chicago Press, 1985.

Kant, Immanuel. *Critique of the Power of Judgment*. Edited by Paul Guyer. Translated by Paul Guyer and Eric Matthews. Cambridge: Cambridge University Press, 2000.

– "On a Newly Arisen Superior Tone in Philosophy." In *Raising the Tone of Philosophy: Late Essays by Immanuel Kant, Transformative Critique by Jacques Derrida*, edited by Peter Fenves, 51–82. Baltimore: Johns Hopkins University Press, 1993.

– *Political Writings*. Edited by Hans Reiss. Translated by H.B. Nisbet. Cambridge: Cambridge University Press, 1991.

– *Religion within the Bounds of Bare Reason*. Translated by Werner S. Pluhar. Indianapolis: Hackett, 2009.

Kayser, Wolfgang. *The Grotesque in Art and Literature*. Translated by Ulrich Weisstein. New York: Columbia University Press, 1981.

Kierkegaard, Søren. *On Authority and Revelation: The Book on Adler, or a Cycle of Ethico-Religious Essays*. Translated by Walter Lowrie. Princeton: Princeton University Press, 1955.

Kivy, Peter. *The Possessor and the Possessed: Handel, Mozart, Beethoven, and the Idea of Musical Genius*. New Haven: Yale University Press, 2001.

Klossowski, Pierre. *Sade My Neighbor*. Translated by Alphonso Lingis. Evanston: Northwestern University Press, 1991.

Krafft-Ebing, Richard von. *Psychopathia Sexualis, with Especial Reference to the Antipathic Sexual Instinct: A Medico-Forensic Study*. Translated by Franklin S. Klaf. New York: Arcade, 1998.

LaCapra, Dominick. *History, Literature, Critical Theory*. Ithaca: Cornell University Press, 2013.

Le Rider, Jacques. "Nietzsche et Baudelaire." *Littérature* 86 (1992): 85–101.

Leask, Nigel. "Toward a Universal Aesthetic: De Quincey on Murder as Carnival and Tragedy." In *Questioning Romanticism*, edited by John Beer, 92–120. Baltimore: Johns Hopkins University Press, 1995.

Lentricchia, Frank, and Jody McAuliffe. *Crimes of Art and Terror*. Chicago: University of Chicago Press, 2003.

Lerchner, Thorsten. "Die Welt als Vorstellung: Arthur Schopenhauer und der theatralische Blick aufs Dasein." *Schopenhauer-Jahrbuch* 94 (2013): 53–75.

Lewis, C.S. *The Great Divorce*. New York: HarperOne, 2001.

– *Mere Christianity*. London: Fount, 1987.

– *A Preface to Paradise Lost*. Oxford: Oxford University Press, 1977.

– *The Screwtape Letters & Screwtape Proposes a Toast.* New York: Macmillan, 1962.

Lindop, Grevel. *The Opium Eater: A Life of Thomas De Quincey.* London: Dent, 1981.

Lombroso, Cesare. *Criminal Man.* Translated by Mary Gibson and Nicole Hahn Rafter. Durham: Duke University Press, 2006.

Lucretius. *De Rerum Natura: The Nature of Things.* Translated by David R. Slavitt. Berkeley: University of California Press, 2008.

Maistre, Joseph de. *Considerations on France.* Edited and translated by Richard A. Lebrun. Cambridge: Cambridge University Press, 1994.

McMahon, Darrin M. *Divine Fury: A History of Genius.* New York: Basic Books, 2013.

McMorran, Will. "Introducing the Marquis de Sade." *Forum for Modern Language Studies* 51.2 (2015): 133–51.

Megill, Allan. *Prophets of Extremity: Nietzsche, Heidegger, Foucault, Derrida.* Berkeley: University of California Press, 1985.

Meltzer, Françoise. *Seeing Double: Baudelaire's Modernity.* Chicago: University of Chicago Press, 2011.

Menninghaus, Winfried. *Disgust: The Theory and History of a Strong Sensation.* Translated by Howard Eiland and Joel Golb. Albany: State University of New York Press, 2003.

Milgram, Stanley. *Obedience to Authority: An Experimental View.* New York: Harper Perennial Modern Thought, 2009.

Mill, John Stuart. *"On Liberty" and Other Writings.* Oxford: Oxford University Press.

Milton, John. *Complete Poems and Major Prose.* Edited by Merritt Y. Hughes. Indianapolis: Hackett, 2003.

Mitter, Partha. *Much Maligned Monsters: History of European Reactions to Indian Art.* Oxford: Oxford University Press, 1977.

Mommsen, Hans. *From Weimar to Auschwitz.* Translated by Philip O'Connor. Princeton: Princeton University Press, 1991.

Neiman, Susan. *Evil in Modern Thought: An Alternative History of Philosophy.* Princeton: Princeton University Press, 2002.

Neuber, Simone. "Morally Corrupt Aesthetic Pleasure?" *Journal of Aesthetic Education* 48.1 (2014): 90–107.

Nicholls, Angus. *Goethe's Concept of the Daemonic: After the Ancients.* Rochester: Camden House, 2006.

Nietzsche, Friedrich. *The Antichrist.* In *The Portable Nietzsche*, edited and translated by Walter Kaufmann, 565–656. New York: Penguin Books, 1976.

– *Beyond Good and Evil.* In *Basic Writings of Nietzsche*, edited and translated by Walter Kaufmann, 179–435. New York: Modern Library, 2000.

– *The Birth of Tragedy.* In *Basic Writings of Nietzsche*, edited and translated by Walter Kaufmann, 1–144. New York: Modern Library, 2000.

– *Daybreak: Thoughts on the Prejudices of Morality*. Edited by Maudemarie Clark and Brian Leiter. Translated by R.J. Hollingdale. Cambridge: Cambridge University Press, 1997.

– *Ecce Homo*. In *Basic Writings of Nietzsche*, edited and translated by Walter Kaufmann, 655–791. New York: Modern Library, 2000.

– *The Gay Science*. Translated by Walter Kaufmann. New York: Random House, 1974.

– *Human, All Too Human*. Translated by R.J. Hollingdale. Cambridge: Cambridge University Press, 1996.

– *Nietzsche contra Wagner*. In *The Portable Nietzsche*, edited and translated by Walter Kaufmann, 661–83. New York: Penguin Books, 1976.

– *On the Genealogy of Morals*. In *Basic Writings of Nietzsche*, edited and translated by Walter Kaufmann, 437–599. New York: Modern Library, 2000.

– *Selected Letters of Friedrich Nietzsche*. Edited and translated by Christopher Middleton. Chicago: University of Chicago Press, 1969.

– *Thus Spoke Zarathustra*. In *The Portable Nietzsche*, edited and translated by Walter Kaufmann, 103–439. New York: Penguin Books, 1976.

– *Twilight of the Idols*. In *The Portable Nietzsche*, edited and translated by Walter Kaufmann, 463–563. New York: Penguin Books, 1976.

– *Werke. Kritische Gesamtausgabe*. Edited by Mazzino Montinari and Giorgio Colli. Berlin: de Gruyter, 1967–.

Nisbet, H.B. "*Das Dämonische*: On the Logic of Goethe's Demonology." *Forum for Modern Language Studies* 7.3 (1971): 259–81.

Parfit, Derek. *On What Matters*. Vol. 1. Oxford: Oxford University Press, 2013.

Paulson, Ronald. "Burke's Sublime and the Representation of Revolution." In *Culture and Politics from Puritanism to the Enlightenment*, edited by Perez Zagorin, 241–69. Berkeley: University of California Press, 1980.

Rollins, Yvonne Bargues. *Baudelaire et le Grotesque*. Washington, DC: University Press of America, 1978.

Rosenkranz, Karl. *Aesthetics of Ugliness*. Edited and translated by Andrei Pop and Mechtild Widrich. New York: Bloomsbury.

Rousseau, Jean-Jacques. *Confessions*. Translated by Angela Scholar. Oxford: Oxford University Press, 2000.

– *Discourse on the Origin of Inequality*. Translated by Donald A. Cress. Indianapolis: Hackett, 1992.

– *Politics and the Arts: Letter to M. d'Alembert on the Theatre*. Translated by Allan Bloom. Ithaca: Cornell University Press, 1968.

Sade, Marquis de. *The 120 Days of Sodom*. Translated by Will McMorran and Thomas Wynn. New York: Penguin, 2016.

– *Juliette*. Translated by Austryn Wainhouse. New York: Grove, 1968.

– *Philosophy in the Boudoir*. Translated by Joachim Neugroschel. New York: Penguin, 2006.

– *Crimes of Love*. Translated by David Coward. Oxford: Oxford University Press, 2008.

Sallis, John. *Crossings: Nietzsche and the Space of Tragedy*. Chicago: University of Chicago Press, 1991.

Sartre, Jean-Paul. *Saint Genet: Actor and Martyr*. Translated by Bernard Frechtman. London: W.H. Allen, 1964.

Schlegel, Friedrich. *Friedrich Schlegel's "Lucinde" and the Fragments*. Translated by Peter Firchow. Minneapolis: University of Minnesota Press, 1971.

Schmidt, Jochen. *Geschichte des Genie-Gedankens in der deutschen Literatur, Philosophie und Politik, 1750–1945*. Vol. 1: *Von der Aufklärung bis zum Idealismus*. Darmstadt: Wissenschaftliche Buchgesellschaft, 1985.

Schopenhauer, Arthur. *Essays and Aphorisms*. Translated by R.J. Hollingdale. New York: Penguin, 1970.

– *Parerga and Paralipomena*. Translated by E.F.J. Payne. Oxford: Oxford University Press, 2013.

– *The Two Fundamental Problems of Ethics*. Translated by David E. Cartwright and Edward E. Erdmann. Oxford: Oxford University Press, 2010.

– *The World as Will and Representation*. Translated by E.F.J. Payne. New York: Dover, 1969.

Scrivener, Michael Henry. *Radical Shelley: The Philosophical Anarchism and Utopian Thought of Percy Bysshe Shelley*. Princeton: Princeton University Press, 1982.

Shaftesbury, the third Earl; Anthony Ashley Cooper. *Characteristics of Men, Manners, Opinions, Times*. Cambridge: Cambridge University Press, 1999.

Sheehan, Paul. *Modernism and the Aesthetics of Violence*. Cambridge: Cambridge University Press, 2013.

Shelley, Percy Bysshe. *A Defence of Poetry*. In *Shelley's Prose*.

– "Essay on the Devil and Devils." In *Shelley's Prose*.

– "A Refutation of Deism." In *Shelley's Prose*.

– *Shelley's Prose, or The Trumpet of a Prophecy*. Edited by David Lee Clark. Albuquerque: University of New Mexico Press, 1954.

Shklar, Judith N. *Ordinary Vices*. Cambridge, MA: Belknap, 1984.

Southey, Robert. *The Poetical Works of Robert Southey*. London: Longman, Brown, Green, and Longmans, 1845.

The Spectator. Vol. 3. Edited by Donald F. Bond. Oxford: Oxford University Press, 1965.

Stangneth, Bettina. *Eichmann before Jerusalem: The Unexamined Life of a Mass Murderer*. Translated by Ruth Martin. New York: Knopf, 2014.

Stock, R.D. *The Holy and the Daemonic from Thomas Browne to William Blake*. Princeton: Princeton University Press, 1982.

Stockhausen, Karlheinz. "'Huuuh!' Das Pressegespräch am 16. September 2001 im Senatszimmer des Hotel Atlantic in Hamburg." *MusikTexte* 91 (2001): 69–77.

Stoker, Bram. *Dracula*. Oxford: Oxford University Press, 1996.

Svendsen, Lars. *A Philosophy of Evil*. Translated by Kerri A. Pierce. London: Dalkey Archive Press, 2010.

Swayne, Virginia E. *Grotesque Figures: Baudelaire, Rousseau, and the Aesthetics of Modernity*. Baltimore: Johns Hopkins University Press, 2004.

Tambling, Jeremy. *Blake's Night Thoughts*. New York: Palgrave Macmillan, 2005.

Taylor, Charles. *A Secular Age*. Cambridge, MA: Belknap, 2007.

– *Sources of the Self*. Cambridge, MA: Harvard University Press, 1989.

Tertullian. "The Shows, or De Spectaculis." In *Ante-Nicene Fathers: The Writings of the Fathers down to A.D. 325*, vol. 3, edited by Alexander Roberts and James Donaldson, 79–91. Peabody: Hendrickson, 1994.

Voltaire. *Letters on England*. Translated by Leonard Tancock. London: Penguin, 1980.

– *Philosophical Dictionary*. Paris: DuMont, 1901.

Wagner, Richard. *"The Art-Work of the Future" and Other Works*. Translated by William Ashton Ellis. Lincoln: University of Nebraska Press, 1993.

Waldock, A.J.A. *"Paradise Lost" and Its Critics*. Cambridge: Cambridge University Press, 1961.

Weber, Christian. "Goethes *Prometheus*: Kritik der poetischen Einbildungskraft." *Goethe Yearbook* 16 (2009): 101–33.

Wellbery, David E. *The Specular Moment: Goethe's Early Lyric and the Beginnings of Romanticism*. Stanford: Stanford University Press, 1996.

White, Stephen K. *Edmund Burke: Modernity, Politics, and Aesthetics*. Oxford: Rowman & Littlefield, 2002.

Young-Bruehl, Elisabeth. *Hannah Arendt: For Love of the World*. New Haven: Yale University Press, 2004.

Young, Edward. *Conjectures on Original Composition*. London: Longmans, Green & Co., 1918.

Young, Julian. "Richard Wagner and the Birth of *The Birth of Tragedy*." *International Journal of Philosophical Studies* 16.2 (2008): 217–45.

Žižek, Slavoj. "Introduction." In Maximilien Robespierre, *Virtue and Terror*, edited by Jean Ducange, translated by John Howe, vii–xxxix. New York: Verso, 2007.

– *Violence: Six Sideways Reflections*. New York: Picador, 2008.

Index